Goldwork Embroidery

Techniques and Projects

GOLDWORK EMBROIDERY

Techniques and Projects

Lizzy Pye

THE CROWOOD PRESS

First published in 2020 by
The Crowood Press Ltd
Ramsbury, Marlborough
Wiltshire SN8 2HR

enquiries@crowood.com

www.crowood.com

This impression 2023

British Library Cataloguing-in-Publication Data
A catalogue record for this book is available from the British Library.

ISBN 978 1 78500 647 0

Embroiderers' acknowledgements
The author and publishers would like to thank the following embroiderers for permission to use their work as the opening images to the following chapters – Chapter 2: Becky Quine; Chapter 4: Helen Richman; Chapter 7: Death by Chocolate by Jo Heyde; Chapter 8: Jay Feather by Helen Richman; Chapter 9: Waterfall by Becky Quine.

Graphic design and layout by Derek Doyle & Associates, Shaw Heath.
Printed and bound in India by Thomson Press India Ltd.

Contents

Introduction

Goldwork is a fascinating type of embroidery which has captivated audiences for more than 2,000 years. It can be any work in which gold is stitched to cloth, and has varied as much through history as it has across the world.

Stitchwork in metal threads has always denoted wealth and power. By the nature of the work it must be valuable, not only for the physical content but also because of the lengthy hours of labour.

This book does not set out to recall the entire history of the work, but in order to engage with traditional techniques we must begin by touching on its origins.

The earliest gold threads were pure gold, flattened and cut into strips. It became common to wrap gold or gilded silver around a core of silk thread, animal gut or paper. This is what is commonly called 'Japanese thread'. The same techniques are still in use, but the gold content is far smaller. The plated metal is typically wrapped around a cotton core in modern threads, to make all sorts of different types of thread such as smooth passing and rococco.

When wire drawing developed, it became possible to coat a fine silver wire with gold, which could then be formed into many of the purl wires we still use today. Initially this would have been a very slow process in which a metal bar was drawn through progressively smaller holes until the desired diameter was reached. Modern machinery allows the metal to be drawn through many holes in one operation.

To thoroughly research goldwork, one must look to all corners of the Earth, from the first production of 'Japanese' thread in China, through the glorious purl embroideries of India, to the ecclesiastical splendour of Britain. So many hands have touched this technique that one could not hope to learn it all.

Begin in the East with the ceremonial garb and well known rank badges of Imperial China. In Chinese goldwork, the dominant technique is the couching of bright, metal-wrapped thread known today as 'Japanese thread'. Swirling waves of gold and stunning backgrounds complement fine silk embroidery featuring cranes, tigers, and many more symbols.

Antique Japanese threads in silver and gold, stored in paper twists.

Opposite: Chinese rank badge with a crane design. The bird is couched with Japanese thread in silver and gold – the silver with matching thread to blend in, and the gold with the traditional red thread which brings out the warmth in the metal. The background is worked mainly in couched silver Japanese thread – various different colours of silk thread are used for the couching to enhance the design. The crane has been worked separately and applied – it may be a later addition.

Indian purse, eighteenth to nineteenth century, from the author's collection. Most of the metal looks silver now, but some parts were originally gold. Fine metal threads are strapped over string padding and the shapes outlined with a wavy thread similar to check thread. The central shapes are stitched with cutwork in a combination of purl wires.

Travelling north, as did the gold threads themselves, it is worth looking at traditional Russian goldwork. Pieces of high quality were produced from the moment that Christianity was accepted in the country, and likely before that. In this distinctive style, the gold threads and wires were often combined with pearls, giving a pleasing contrast and added richness to the work.

If one begins to look west, the goldwork of India and the surrounding regions comes to the fore. In contrast to Chinese work, the gold embroidery of India is almost exclusively worked with purl wires, with little or no couching. There are many forms of goldwork in this part of the world, the most famous of which is Zardosi embroidery. There is a focus on rich, dense textures with the inclusion of looped purls and spangles, and the combination of metal thread with bright-coloured silk embroidery and even beetle wings.

Throughout the Middle East beautiful goldwork was stitched for religious artefacts and other ceremonial purposes.

Further west in Europe early goldwork was typically seen on articles of a religious nature, with pieces for the Christian Church worked mainly in couched threads. The technique Or Nué, shaded with silks over a ground of metal threads, was worked throughout Europe but most notably in Italy.

One of the most famous types of embroidery is Opus Anglicanum, which translates simply as 'English Work'. This embroidery featured beautiful silkwork, usually religious figures, with a striking background of gold embroidered with the underside couching technique. This work was extremely expensive, yet it was exported in great quantity to other parts of the world, especially the Vatican.

Part of an ecclesiastical sampler from the Royal School of Needlework's embroidery collection. It features traditional couched Japanese thread with bright blue silkwork.

In Britain, much of the early embroidery for the Catholic Church was sadly destroyed by decree of King Henry VIII in the sixteenth century. However, this could be said to have kick started goldwork's popularity in secular society. Goldwork took a prominent place in fashion from then until the late nineteenth century, with stunning pieces luckily preserved in museums all over the world. The couched threads of earlier times were joined by a gorgeous variety of purl wires allowing for highly raised work for military use, and all kinds of intricate details in fashion.

In the twentieth century goldwork was mostly reserved for the military, and ceremonies such as royal coronations. However, it can be seen to great effect on the gowns of designers such as Schiaparelli and Dior. Designers still favour gold for their finest work, and looking back down its fascinating history can inform and inspire our embroidery today.

Coronation gold sampler on silk velvet, worked by the author. The motifs in this design are those chosen by Queen Elizabeth II for the Robe of State for her coronation on 2 June 1953. Laurel leaves, olives and wheat ears symbolize victory, peace and prosperity.

CHAPTER 1

MATERIALS AND EQUIPMENT

METAL THREADS

Metal threads, including metal-wrapped threads, purl wires and spangles.

The most important materials for goldwork are of course the metal threads. As you can see from the examples in this book, not all goldwork must be gold. There are so many threads to choose from, and once you start to stitch you will soon find your own 'go to' threads.

In goldwork there are two main types of thread: metal-wrapped threads, which are secured by stitching over them with a sewing thread; and purl wires, which are hollow and are usually stitched through in a similar way to beads. There are also plenty of additional materials to consider, such as spangles, kid leather and plate.

Most of the threads are available in a range of weights or gauges so that you can choose according to the needs of your design. The finest threads are most suitable for detailed, intricate designs. The larger sizes make more of a statement and are good for bolder designs. A good variety of threads are available in a range of colours.

When choosing gold threads, you will need to think about the type of techniques you wish to include in your project, how shiny or glittery you want it to be, and sometimes your budget.

The price of metal threads varies by weight, so heavy things such as broad plate and spangles tend to be rather pricey, whereas Japanese thread and smooth passing are on the lower end of the scale.

Gold or Gilt?

Historically gold threads had a very high gold content, but nowadays the story is different. In fact, the highest quality gold thread is only 2 per cent gold and the more commonly used version is 'gilt', which contains about 0.5 per cent gold. Silver is available in 90 per cent silver or silver plate. In general, the higher the content, the warmer the tone of the colour will be, which makes for a very pleasing finish; however, the price difference is considerable. For most projects gilt and silver plate work perfectly well, unless a piece demands an exceedingly high quality or the threads must match those of a historical piece.

METAL-WRAPPED THREADS

Imitation 'Jap' (Japanese Thread)
The 'imitation' here is the plate. Cotton thread is wrapped with a wide strip of metal-coloured synthetic plate. It is very shiny, and can be vulnerable to damage.

Smooth Passing
This thread has a cotton core, but unlike Japanese thread, the metallic strip with which it is wrapped is finer, producing a sturdier and more versatile thread.

Check Thread
Similar to passing thread, check thread has a distinctive zigzag but is small enough to sit well against smooth threads in combinations.

Rococco
Rococco has a defined zigzag wave, making it a useful decorative thread.

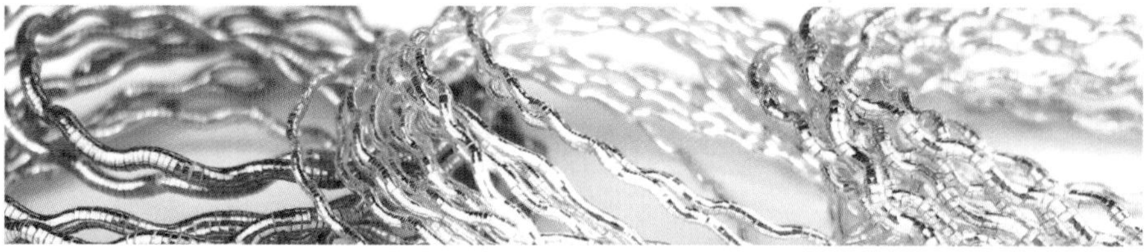

Twist
Usually three strands of metal-wrapped threads twisted together to create a decorative texture.

Elizabethan Twist
A twist of super-fine strands of thread each wrapped with metal; this thread is useful for small details.

Millary
A combination of metal-wrapped thread with a coil of firm wire makes for a very decorative thread.

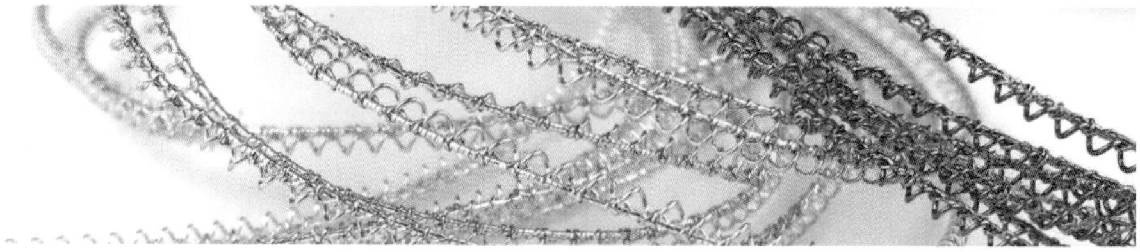

PURL WIRES

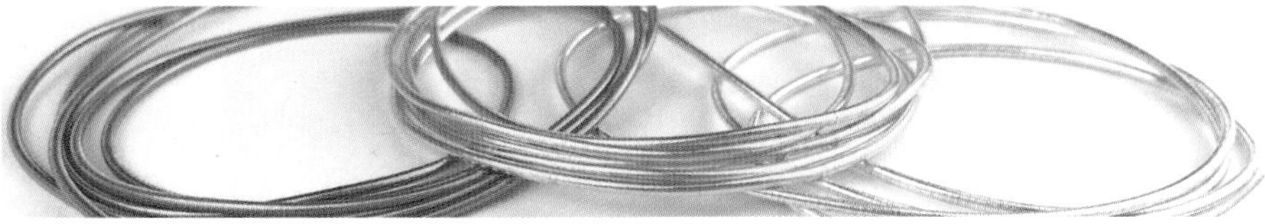

Smooth Purl

A smooth, shiny, super-fine wire coiled into a cylinder. The coiled wire is cut into short lengths that are stitched through like beads.

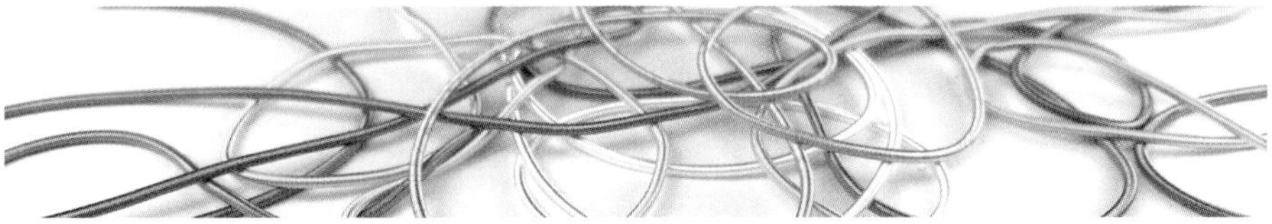

Rough Purl

A smooth but matte-surfaced super-fine wire coiled into a cylinder, which is cut and stitched like smooth purl.

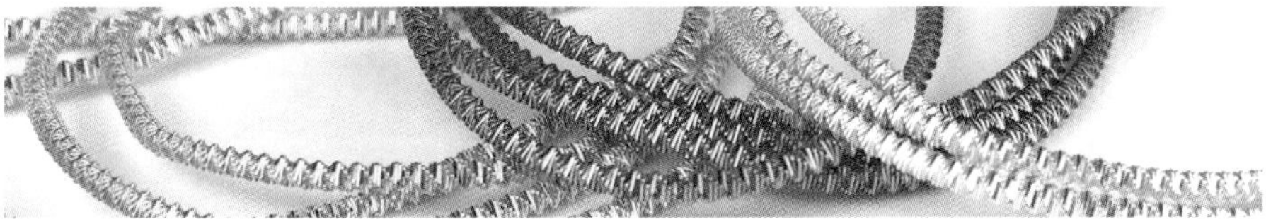

Bright Check

A bright, shiny, super-fine wire shaped into a faceted coil, which is cut and stitched like smooth and rough purl.

Wire (Dull) Check

A matte-surfaced super-fine wire shaped into a faceted coil. It is used like bright check.

Pearl Purl

A round-profiled wire in a tight coil. This wire must be 'relaxed' to allow a thread to pass between coils.

Lizerine

A square-profiled wire in a tight coil. Like pearl purl, it must be 'relaxed'.

MISCELLANEOUS

Spangles

These sequin lookalikes are made of plated metal, curled into a circle and then pressed flat.

Plate

Plate is a shiny, flat strip of metal; whipped plate is wrapped with a very fine wire.

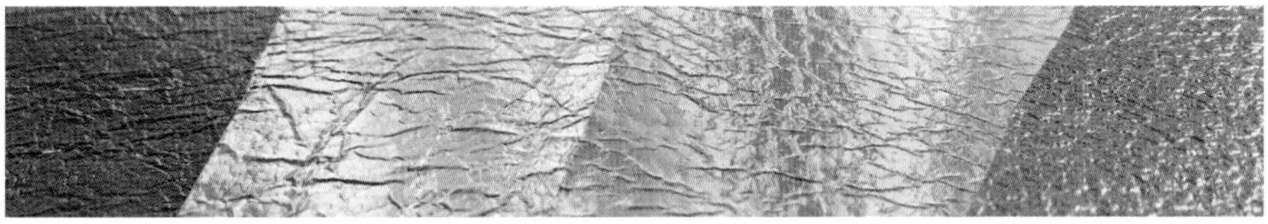

Kid Leather

Fine leather coated with a metallic foil.

PADDING MATERIALS

Felt

Choose a good quality felt, preferably with a high natural fibre content (usually wool or cotton). Felt is available in many colours to match the metal threads.

Extra Thick Felt

Traditionally 'carpet felt' is used to create highly padded shapes. Good carpet felt is hard to get hold of these days, so a very dense thick wool felt is an ideal (and much more pleasant) substitute.

'Soft String'

Soft string is a cotton thread/yarn that will compress down well when stitched. There are a few brands of tapestry cotton available in a wide range of colours to match the metal threads.

'Hard String'

Parcel string is used for padding to create basket-weave patterns. It can be dyed or painted to match the metal threads if required.

Interfacing

Firm interfacing of the thickness usually used for curtain pelmets or firm waistbands is suitable for padding very defined shapes. It can be painted to match the metal threads if necessary.

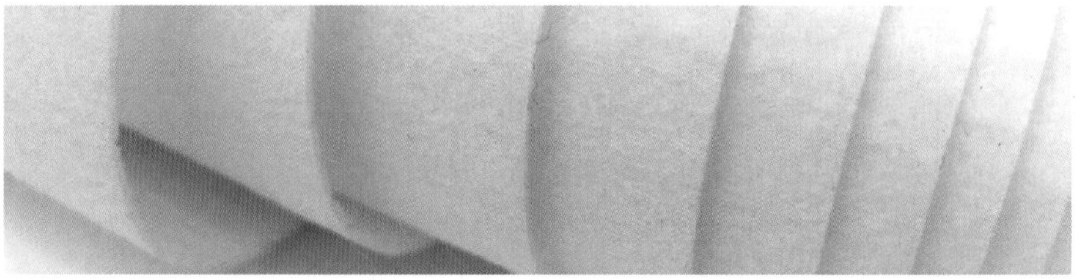

Card

Thick paper or card may be used as a substitute for interfacing. It is more readily available, but it can suffer in damp environments.

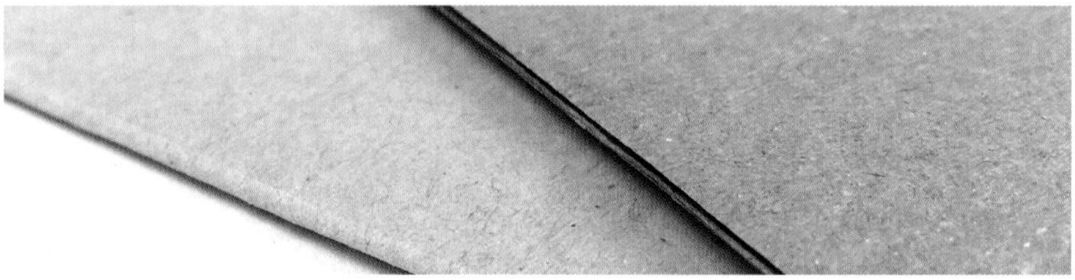

SEWING THREADS

Machine Threads

Machine sewing threads are used to secure the metal threads and wires. A 100 per cent polyester thread is best because there is a little give in the thread, which makes it more resilient to the abrasive metals.

Stranded Cotton

Stranded cotton is useful to add some colour to a design. It may be used to secure metal threads or for decorative stitching.

Silk

Silk is available in lots of different thread types, from stranded to floss. It may be used in the same way as stranded cotton.

Synthetics

Man-made fibres, such as rayon or viscose, are more readily available than silk. They usually have a higher shine than real silk. Take care as they can be very slippery and springy when stitched.

OTHER MATERIALS

Beads and Charms

Beads can be a lovely addition to goldwork embroidery. Try a variety of colours, shapes and sizes.

Sequins

Sequins are stitched in the same way as spangles, and can add some extra colour and shine to a design.

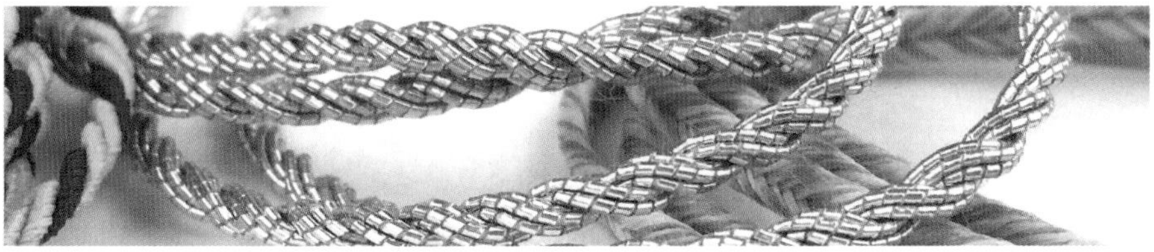

Braids and Cords

Gold decorative trims are traditionally combined with military goldwork, but colours are also useful for a more modern interpretation.

FABRICS

There is no reason that any particular fabric cannot be used for goldwork, so don't be afraid to try goldwork on anything in your fabric stash. However, there are some combinations that are known to be successful.

The traditional fabrics are listed here with some tips that will help you to decide how to use your fabric, and which techniques are most appropriate.

Velvet

Usually silk or cotton velvet (synthetic can be rather springy, which makes it more difficult to work with and viscose degrades quickly). Velvet is usually the ground fabric for ceremonial garments such as the coronation robes of the British monarchy. The deep pile texture adds to the richness of the fabric and makes the metal threads stand out beautifully.

Silk

A heavy satin, dupion silk or taffeta may be used to give a gorgeous lustre that is very effective with goldwork. These fabrics are available in a wide variety of colours and finishes, which makes it easy to choose a suitable colour.

Linen

Fine textured, closely woven linen is the perfect ground for goldwork because it is naturally sturdy. Linen is one of the traditional fabrics for ecclesiastical embroidery, which has always included a lot of heavy stitchwork.

Damask

Usually made from silk or cotton, damask is another fabric traditionally used for ecclesiastical work. The fabric is one colour, but has a woven pattern that makes for an interesting ground for goldwork and silk embroidery.

You may have noticed that these fabrics are all rather unusual and/or expensive; this is because goldwork was traditionally either an investment, or quite deliberately stitched to show off wealth and power.

Nowadays the gold itself is not nearly so pricey, and many embroiderers are stitching for pleasure, so we may broaden the range of fabrics to include some more everyday examples.

When you first try goldwork you may wish to practise on some simple calico or quilter's cotton. It is a good idea to use a double layer of these for goldwork, simply to hold the weight of the metal threads and to avoid causing any distortion as you stitch.

Many fabrics that you may wish to use will need some extra substance to help support the metal. For any fabric except sheer fabrics, the best way to add this is to back the fabric with medium-weight calico, plain cotton or linen. This is particularly important for any fabric with an open weave or felted texture to make sure there is enough strength to support every stitch evenly throughout the design.

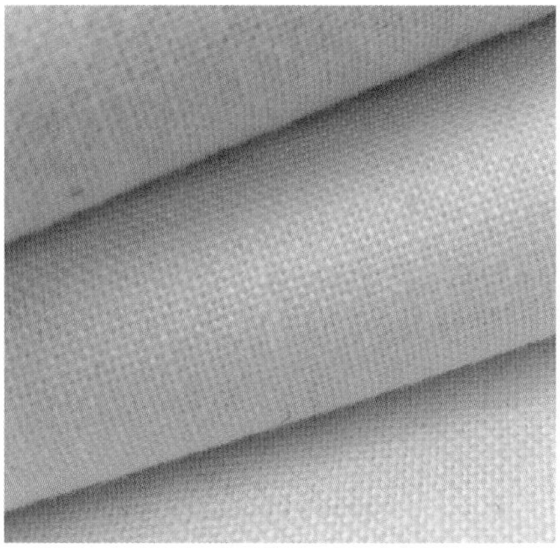

When choosing fabric, consider the texture and how this will interact with the gold; try to choose fabric that has an all-over texture and preferably a smooth finish, rather than intermittent features such as slubs in silk, which could be difficult to stitch through and may push the gold threads out of line. As you gain confidence you may wish to bend this rule.

Consider the colour: are you looking for a high contrast with the metal, or do you want a subtler effect? For high drama you might choose a strong red, navy or black; for a subtle look, you may wish to try a soft pink with gold, or light blue with silver.

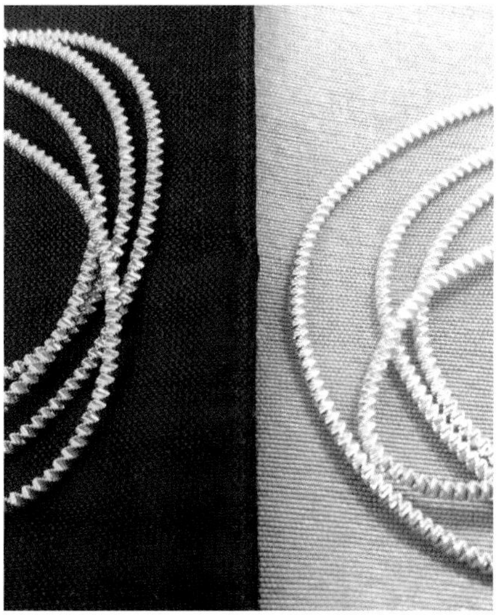

Some fabrics are woven in such a way that they shimmer with two colours when draped (many taffetas, velvets and dupion silks are woven this way – it is known as 'shot'); these can be stunning for garments or accessories, but the qualities will likely be lost in a framed embroidery, and they can highlight flaws such as holes from finishing gold threads.

Sheer fabrics such as organza with a firm texture are lovely for goldwork, but you do have to be more careful when taking couched threads through to the back as you can easily make visible holes or tear the fabric. When working on sheer fabric it is often best to stitch straight to the fabric with no padding. Very fine, soft fabrics such as chiffon are not really suitable to stitch goldwork on, but can form lovely additional details.

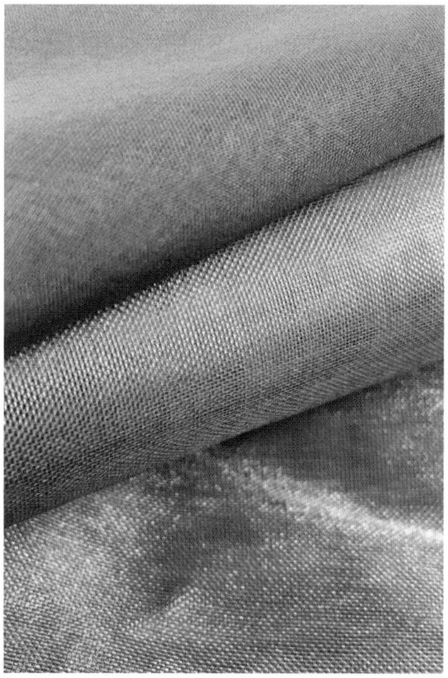

If you doubt the strength of your chosen fabric, choose techniques that will mean you pass less gold through the fabric. Cutwork, chipping and couched pearl purl are all good for less sturdy fabrics.

In summary, there is no real right or wrong choice of fabric for goldwork. However, it is important to consider your project carefully both in terms of your comfort and ease whilst stitching, and the practicality of the piece once complete. The best idea is always to practise on as wide a variety of fabrics as you can, to gain experience of the play between fabric and threads.

FRAMES

Choosing a frame is very important, because goldwork is best stitched with the fabric at high tension. For small projects a good ring or hoop frame will be sufficient, but for anything larger than 20cm (8in) a slate or roller frame is preferable. This allows you to keep a large area of fabric stretched all at once, and with a much greater and more even tension than can be achieved with a hoop. With a slate or roller frame you will also need webbing tape and parcel string.

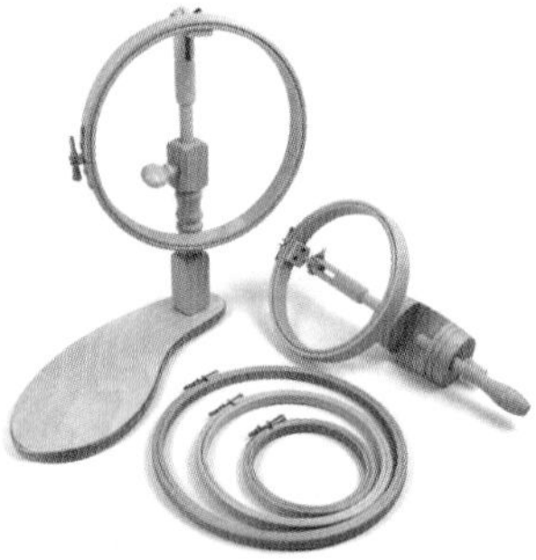

Hoop frames (various sizes with seat and clamp attachments).

Slate frame, roller frame, trestle supports, webbing tape, string, bracing (spring) needle and bodkins.

NEEDLES

When undertaking any embroidery project, it is important to choose the correct needles for each task. Generally, needles should be large enough to allow the thread to pass through comfortably, but small enough not to leave a large hole in the fabric.

Goldwork usually demands a selection of fine embroidery needles, and one or two large sharp needles to allow you to pass the thick metal threads through to the back of your work. If you use a slate frame you will also need a very large bodkin or 'bracing needle'.

EMBROIDERY NEEDLES

Embroidery needles have a sharp point and a narrow shaft. The long eye allows reasonably easy threading. Use the smallest size that you can comfortably work with: the finer the needle, the more accurate your stitches will be.

9
10
12

SHARPS

Sharps are usually slightly finer than their equivalent size in embroidery. They have a narrow shaft and a small eye. Use these needles for stitching where the thread must pass through the gold with a doubled thread.

10
11
12

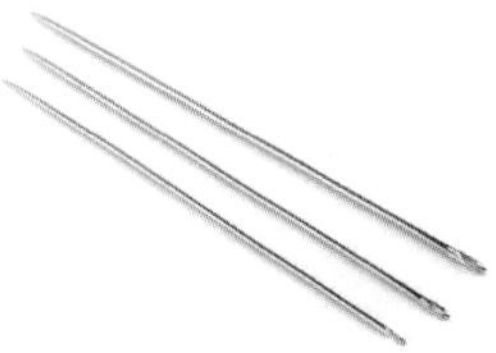

CHENILLE NEEDLES

Chenille needles are sturdy needles with a long, wide eye and a sharp point. Use them to pass thick metal threads to the back of the embroidery: this is known as 'plunging'. Choose the size according to the thickness of the metal thread: the needle must make a large enough hole for the thread to pass through it easily.

18
20
22

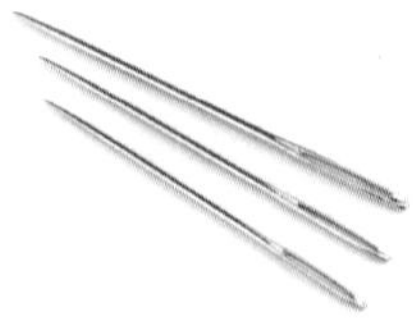

TAPESTRY NEEDLES

Tapestry needles are sturdy needles with a long, wide eye and a blunt tip. These needles are not used very much in traditional goldwork techniques, but they can be very useful for weaving techniques.

20
22
24

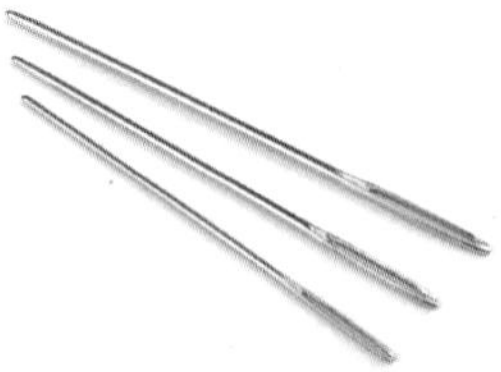

CURVED NEEDLES

Curved needles are just as their name indicates: needles with a curved shaft. They come in various sizes and different curves. For goldwork you will need a fine needle with a sharp point.

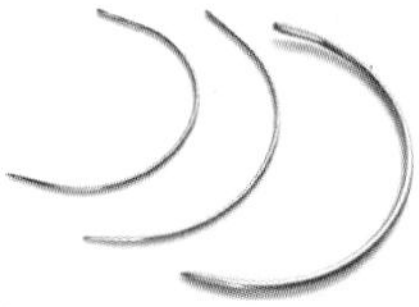

TOOLS

SCISSORS

For goldwork you will need at least two pairs of scissors.

The first pair should be good quality embroidery scissors exclusively for cutting your sewing threads. I also keep a pair of curved scissors handy for any trimming of threads in awkward corners.

The second pair should be a good quality pair of straight embroidery scissors exclusively for cutting the metal threads. You can get 'goldwork scissors' which have a serrated blade; these can be excellent, but make sure that they have a fine tip and narrow blades. Any embroidery scissors with these qualities will be perfectly good for goldwork.

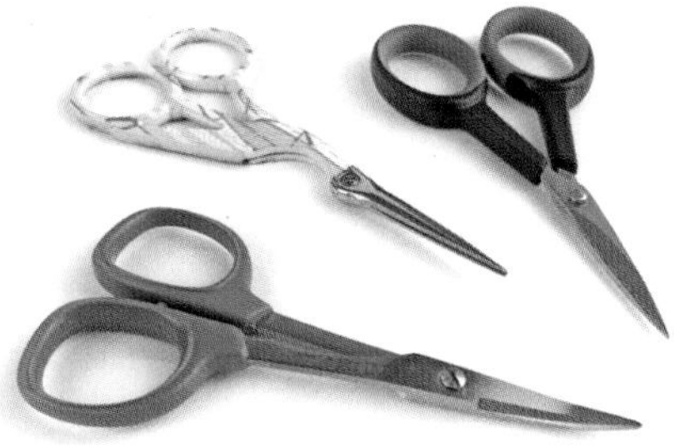

Scissors for gold should have narrow blades (left and right), whereas scissors for thread may be wider (centre).

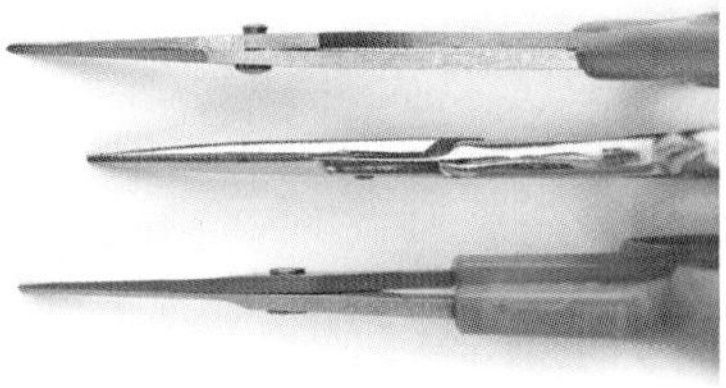

Goldwork scissors should have narrow blades when viewed from the side.

Mellor

The mellor is a little known tool that makes goldwork embroidery so much easier. The flat end can be used to manoeuvre threads into position without having to handle them too much. The pointed end can be used to hold your stitching threads while you guide the stitches into place, meaning much more accurate stitches and less damage to the delicate metals. This tool is also known as a mellore.

Thimble and Needle Grabbers

For obvious reasons, when you are using very fine or very sharp needles, a thimble is a sensible addition to your toolkit. A leather thimble can be handy so that you can still feel what you are doing. Needle grabbers are textured rubber discs that are indispensable when tying back threads with a curved needle on taut fabric.

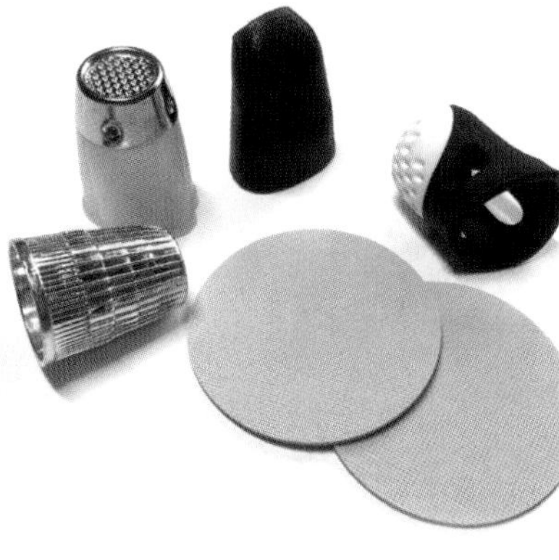

Stiletto

A stiletto is a tapered length of wood or metal that may be used to create holes to pass very thick threads through to the back of the work.

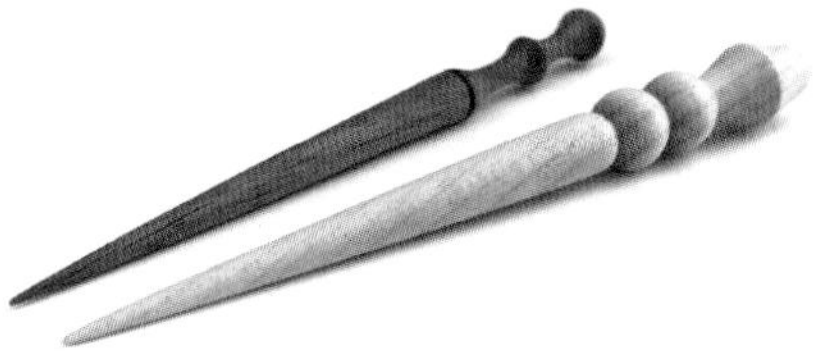

Beeswax

Beeswax protects the sewing threads from being damaged by the metals.

Tweezers

Tweezers are very useful, particularly if you should need to unpick anything. The metal threads should be handled in your fingers as little as possible to prevent tarnishing, so having a pair of fine-tipped tweezers is essential.

SEWING KIT

It is always good to have a well-stocked sewing kit, including the following:

- Tape measure
- Glass-headed pins
- Screwdriver
- Prick and pounce kit
- Baby hairbrush
- Extra strong (button) thread
- Fabric scissors
- Pinking shears
- Paper scissors

Sewing kit with all the useful bits and bobs you need to get up and running with an embroidery project.

OTHER EQUIPMENT

TISSUE PAPER

Acid-free tissue may be placed over your embroidery to keep it clean and safe when you are not stitching. If you can't find acid-free tissue, use an old sheet or pillowcase.

LAMPS

Good light is so important while you are stitching. Help prevent eyestrain by investing in a good daylight or white LED lamp. Bear in mind that standard bulbs can get quite hot, whereas LED bulbs stay cool.

Tissue paper, lamp, magnifier, beading mat, velvet board, and an example of goldwork.

MAGNIFIERS

A magnifier is a fantastic way to deal with intricate details; there are many types, including ones that clip to a table. Some even come with a built-in lamp.

VELVET BOARD/BEADING MAT

Plush-covered boards are brilliant for stopping chips of metal thread flying all over the place. Cut and store the metal threads on these surfaces while stitching.

Gather your preferred design equipment before embarking on a design session so that you don't have to go hunting for something and interrupt your thought process.

DESIGN EQUIPMENT

PAPER

Any paper will do, whether it is an artists' sketchbook or simple copier paper. For an initial sketch, white paper works perfectly well, but to really see what your design will look like when stitched, a colour similar to your fabric is ideal.

TRACING PAPER

You can use tracing paper to trace designs from all sorts of sources; these images can then be pieced together to make your own new design. Tracing paper may also be used to transfer your design to fabric.

PENCILS

A basic HB or propelling pencil is enough, but it can also be useful to have a selection of other grades such as 2B and 4B. These can help you in creating shaded drawings.

ERASER

A good quality eraser saves a lot of time and effort when working through your design. A separate eraser is usually best.

COLOURED PENCILS

Coloured pencils can be used to get a good idea of what your final piece will look like. You can also use coloured pencils to trace designs on to fabric.

PAINTS

Even if you are not a confident painter, it is well worth having a go at creating a design with paints. Paint is also the traditional medium for transferring designs.

ADHESIVE TAPE

If you make changes to a design, an adhesive tape that can be repositioned easily is very useful.

Chapter 2

Design

Creating and planning a design is a very important and exciting stage of your goldwork project. Try not to give in to the temptation to make it up as you go along, at least not when you first start to design your own embroidery. It is always possible to revise a plan while you work, but having a framework will allow you to stitch at your best and to make sure you have enough materials for the project.

This chapter will guide you through the various considerations of designing for goldwork, enabling you to make decisions about the design itself and the placement of techniques.

Choosing a Subject

The best way to choose a subject or theme for your project is to go with your gut instinct – something you love. More often than not, you are stitching for a purpose: a gift for a loved one, a project for your local community, or perhaps something for your home. Therefore, you may wish to consider what other people will appreciate and what will suit the purpose. For example, if you are embarking on a project for a gift you may wish to depict one of the recipient's favourite things.

You can gather ideas from anywhere – in fact you have been gathering ideas all your life without realizing it. It is what you do with your inspiration that will turn it into a beautiful piece of goldwork embroidery.

If you struggle to come up with something, try looking to the past. Goldwork has traditionally been used for all sorts of things, but one recurring theme is floral motifs. Look at scrolling stems with lovely flowers attached – and try incorporating birds and bugs.

The projects at the back of this book will get you started with the techniques, but once you have had a little practice you can really translate anything into goldwork. All sorts of themes lend themselves to goldwork, from sea monsters to family crests and skulls to monograms.

Source image collection – photographs, drawings and paintings.

Use tracing paper to create separate elements of a design, and move them around to create a pleasing composition.

DEVELOPING A DESIGN

Once you have settled on a theme or subject you will need to put your ideas on to paper. You can begin this process in many ways, depending on your own skills and confidence.

If you have a clear image in your head, you may wish to commit this to paper straightaway, but the chances are you have formed a vague idea that could do with some refinement. Therefore, the first thing to do is to research your subject. Look at books, magazines, the internet, your own photos or artwork, galleries, anywhere you can gather a collection of relevant images.

Once you have gathered your thoughts, it is time to start drawing. This might mean that you simply grab a pencil and paper and get started. However, if you have no idea where to begin, try copying images on to tracing paper first. You can copy more than one image this way, and then begin to add images together.

Once you have a rough design worked out you will need to start thinking of it in terms of stitching. This doesn't mean you have to consider every stitch right now, but you should begin to think of the image in gold, rather than as pencil lines.

STYLIZING SHAPES

Some subjects in the world around us translate perfectly first time, but sometimes we need (or want) to make a design a bit more stylized. There are some simple ways to go about this; it is usually a matter of simplifying lines and emphasizing what is already there.

The following example shows how you can stylize a simple floral spray. In reality the flowers may be placed on a crooked stem with barbs and broken elements. It may be more pleasing for the stem to flow smoothly, perhaps with defined thorns and curling tendrils.

Once you are happy with your design, make a copy of it on to a single sheet of tracing paper. Make sure that the lines are as smooth and clear as possible. This final copy will be used to transfer on to your fabric. If you are technologically minded, try using a vector drawing program on a computer.

1 Lay a piece of tracing paper over your initial sketch and create a new stem with a single sweep of your pencil.

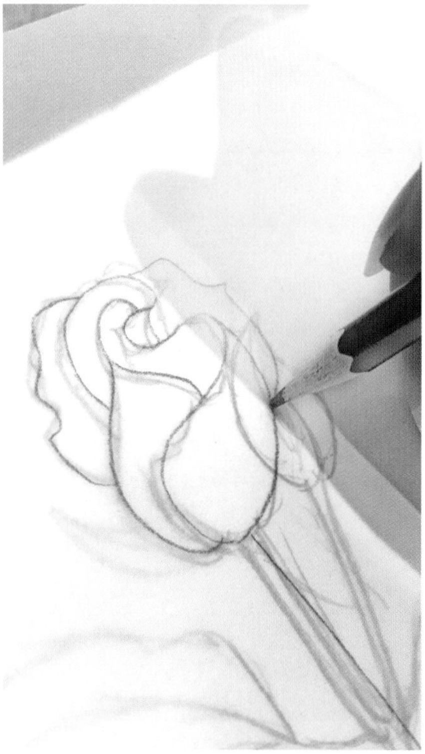

2 Draw the petal shapes, but with each line emphasize the smooth curves and sharp points; exaggerate any overlapping parts.

3 Leave out any tiny elements that may be confusing, but accentuate important details such as stamens.

STITCH DENSITY

Designs usually work best with a good balance of densely worked stitching and more delicate open areas, so you will need to consider how much open space you may wish to have within your design. Conversely, some designs benefit from being extremely heavily worked, so use your judgement here.

There are usually obvious areas to leave blank – voids between parts of the design, for example – but you may wish to consider leaving some areas with more open stitches, too. Scattered spangles or chips can give an attractive contrast to more densely stitched couching or cutwork.

Consider how the colour of your background fabric may impact on the design. A high contrast will mean that more open stitches show up strongly, whereas a subtler background will make them less obvious.

Think about the style of your design. Certain styles demand heavily stitched areas with expanses of blank background, whereas others benefit from more evenly distributed open space.

This embroidery stitched by the author makes use of delicate stitchwork in open areas within the design to utilize the background fabric.

This is a very densely worked embroidery by Becky Quine which leaves nothing blank, creating beautiful contrast with the background.

STITCH DIRECTION

The direction in which your threads are laid can make a big difference to the overall look of the piece. Each direction should enhance the flow of the embroidery, rather than distract from it.

The most obvious place where direction makes a difference is within an area of couched threads. There are many options to choose from: starting in the middle with a line through the shape such as the vein of a leaf; starting on the outer line and spiralling in towards the centre; or choosing a swirling line within the shape and then filling the gaps. All can be equally effective in different areas.

The directional lines of couching should work in harmony with the padding of each area to encourage light to play across the surface of the embroidery in a pleasing way.

The directional lines in this piece by Becky Quine lead the eye along a river of icy blue and silver.

Cutwork is the other obvious place where the chosen stitch direction can have a huge impact.

The traditional directions are either a 45-degree angle to the shape (known as 'slanted'), or at a right angle to the shape (known as 'straight'). In most cases, one of these will be a good starting point: for example, straight lines in geometric designs often look very effective with straight cutwork, whereas curves benefit from slanted cutwork. In some cases it may be useful to take an even more slanted angle – for example, to emphasize the pointed tip of a leaf. Sometimes cutwork will need to change as it flows along a curve.

You may find it useful to mark the direction lines on a copy of the design: with a pencil, draw the direction of the couching threads and the angles of cutwork. It is easier to try this out with pencil, rather than dive in without a plan and risk having to unpick your stitching later.

Cutwork at different angles – note the difference in overall appearance between slanted and straight cutwork.

PADDING

In some cases, goldwork may be stitched entirely without padding – for example, if you are working on a very fine or sheer fabric and don't want to add too much weight. Usually, however, at least some padding is required to stitch goldwork to its full potential.

There are many padding techniques, each with its own purpose. At this stage, it is not necessary to go into detail of the type of padding to be used, merely to consider the height required.

Generally, the areas with most padding are the centres of attention (particularly if they are also stitched with a very shiny technique). High padding can give a sculpted look to a design, which can be very effective; but even low levels of padding can add depth and interest.

Adding relief to a design in the form of padding gives an extra dimension to the metal threads, allowing them to flow in interesting ways across the shapes, and reflecting the light in different directions.

Mark on your design the areas you wish to highlight with padding – label them with something you can easily identify, for example from 'very high' to 'flat'.

Planning your padding at this early stage allows you to create a better vision of the overall design. It may also highlight any tricky areas early on, saving you trouble at a later stage in the project.

Padding diagrams: first labelled 'very high' to 'flat', then labelled with the exact padding to be used.

TEXTURE AND SHINE

When you plan goldwork embroidery, one of the main things to consider is the texture of the gold threads. By their nature all metal threads are shiny to some extent, but the amount of light they reflect is affected by their texture.

Some materials are very smooth, which means they reflect a lot of light in one direction, such as Japanese thread and kid leather. Others have a rough surface and so reflect less light, such as rough purl and wire check. In between, there are materials that have shiny surfaces but reflect light in many different directions, such as twist and bright check.

The way you place different levels of light reflection within your design can have a big impact on the overall look. In general, the shiniest areas will draw the most attention, so these should be placed in focal points. Conversely the areas with rough-surfaced threads will get the least attention.

The images of stitched threads here will help you choose which threads to use in which area, but remember that this is not the only factor to consider. The shininess of the threads is altered by the direction in which they are worked, particularly when they are couched. The height of the padding will also have an impact on the shine – high padding will create both a highlight and a shadow.

Consider using threads in combination within one area to achieve interesting textures. Shading can be achieved within an area of couching by using textured threads on one side and smooth on the other, blending them through the middle section. The same applies to cutwork or chipping, with which you can blend from matte to shiny to suit the shape.

Most shiny

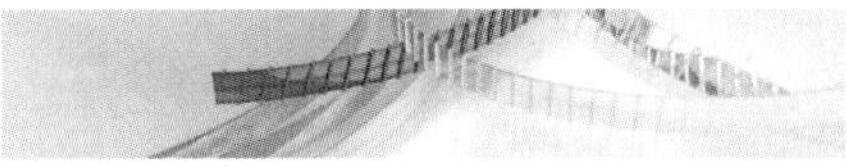
Plate

Spangles

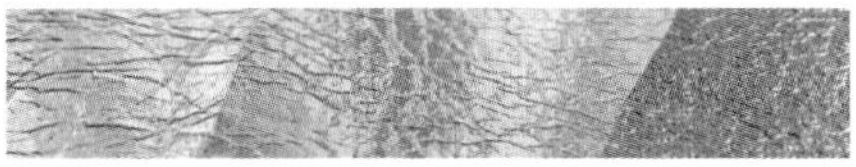
Kid leather

Japanese thread/imitation 'Jap'

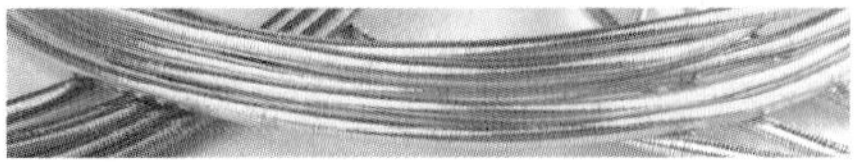
Smooth purl

Smooth passing

Lizerine

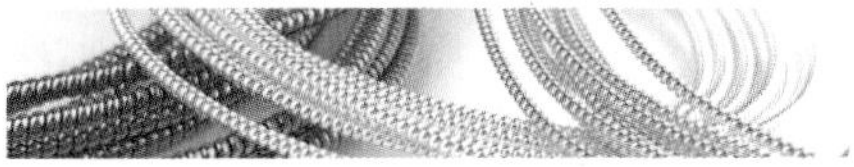
Pearl purl

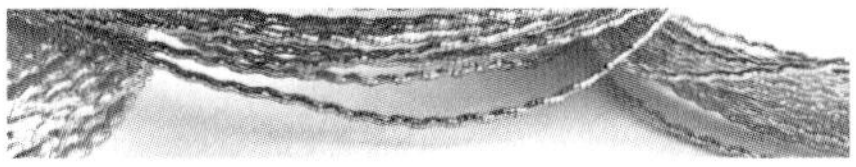
Check thread

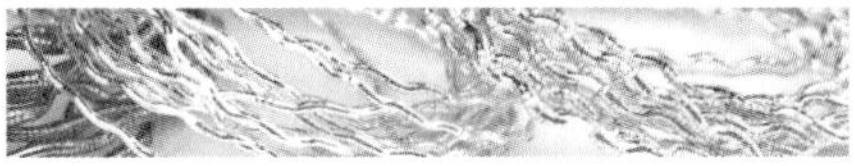
Rococco

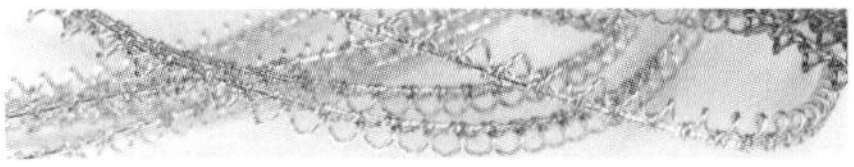
Millary

Bright check

Elizabethan twist

Twist

Rough purl

Wire check

Least shiny

ILLUSTRATING DESIGNS

Creating a fully illustrated image of your design may seem like a waste of time, but it can be a very good way to clarify your design in your mind, and may draw your attention to issues you had not noticed before – it is much better to spend time on the design stage rather than unpick your careful stitchwork.

Don't worry if you aren't a natural or practised artist – think of this as a technical aid to stitching rather than a work of art (after all, nobody else needs to see it).

The following instructions demonstrate exactly how you can illustrate your design to get an accurate view of it before you put needle to fabric. It shows how to colour for gold threads, but the same method applies for any metal.

For the colouring, use coloured pencils, pens or paints, whichever you are most comfortable with. The illustrations here use coloured pencils.

Start with a copy of your outline design. If you can, use paper coloured the same as your fabric, particularly if the fabric will be dark. You can use white acrylic paint or Tippex underneath the gold areas if the colour doesn't show. Otherwise, work on white and colour the background later.

1 Begin by filling in with a medium gold tone all over the areas that will be stitched.

2 Imagine that the light is falling on your design from one direction (in this case from the top right-hand side). Use a darker shade to add shadows wherever they would naturally fall – think about where the padding will be.

3 Next, use a lighter tone or white to add highlights wherever they would occur – the areas facing the light. If you are using pencils, a pen or paint may be handy at this point.

4 With a slightly darker shade, mark in the way the stitches will fall (for example, lines along a shape for couching; lines across a shape at 45 degrees for cutwork).

5 Work over the design adding extra details and smoothing the blend between shades to complete the illustration.

Try, Try Again

Try this process more than once with each design; you may be surprised how many different variations you can achieve with a single idea.

When you have multiple elements to work with it can be useful to go through this process with each element on a separate sheet of tracing paper so that you can combine them in different ways.

CHAPTER 3

GETTING STARTED

ORDER OF WORK

Before you start your goldwork, it is important to have a plan. Sometimes you will change this slightly as you go along, but having the initial order of work is a really good idea.

BASIC PRINCIPLE

The dominant lines of a design should be stitched last, so that they are a perfect shape and slightly overlap other elements. The other parts are stitched up to these lines, leaving enough space for the more dominant line. For example, if you are stitching an animal you would stitch the legs behind the body first, then the body, then the legs in front.

STITCHING ORDER

This incorporates all possible techniques; if you are using only a selection, keep the same order. If you are applying large pieces of fabric that will have padding over the top, apply these first on a slack frame.

Padding
Felt goes first, one layer at a time. This is followed by soft string, and then hard string. It is important to complete the padding before anything else because the materials can create fluff that gets trapped in the gold and other stitching.

Applied Fabrics and Stitching
Any fabrics to be applied over padding should go first; then kid leather. Any surface stitches should be finished next.

Couching
First, couch the threads (for example, Japanese thread or rococco). It is important to get these finished off before stitching any of the more delicate work to avoid damaging the fragile threads. Then stitch the wires (for example, pearl purl).

Delicate Work
Chipping comes next because it is less delicate once stitched down. If you are using beads, they can be applied at the same time as chips. Plate is susceptible to dents and scratches, so it is a good idea to stitch it near the end of the project. Follow that up with spangles, and then cutwork, which is the most fragile.

Remember that gold threads can be quite vulnerable while you are working, but they are much more resilient once they are securely attached to the fabric.

Conflicting Rules

What if the dominant line is couching or pearl purl? When should you stitch it? The answer varies depending on how fragile the gold involved might be. If the dominant line is couching, it may need to be stitched earlier on, because the process of plunging the couched threads can be very damaging to other stitching such as cutwork.

If the dominant line is pearl purl, it is fine to stitch this later because it is less likely to cause damage.

Whichever techniques you choose, make sure to stitch up to the line very carefully with the other techniques, leaving enough space for the next part to sit properly on the fabric or padding with a neat edge.

FRAMING UP

SLATE FRAME

The following illustrations show the method for setting up a slate frame. Remember that although a slate frame holds the tension well, it will need to be tightened repeatedly throughout the stitching process. When tightening, make sure to keep an eye on the grain of the fabric so that it stays straight.

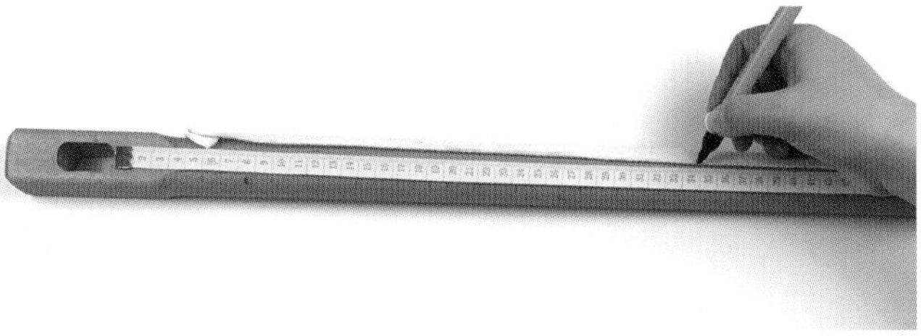

1 Mark the centre of each bar of the slate frame. Measure from the hole in the wood, not the webbing itself (this gives the most accurate measurement).

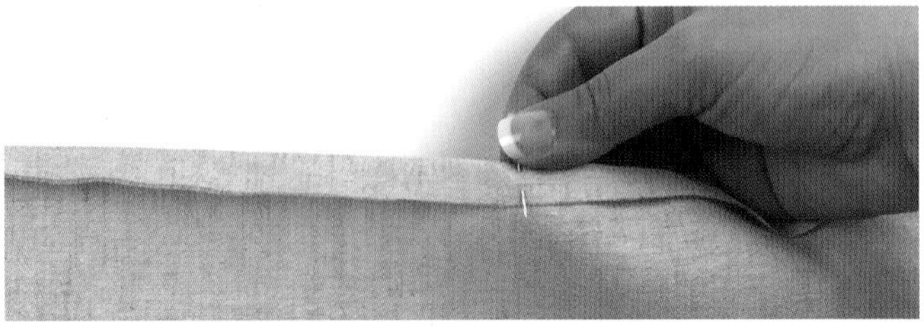

2 Straighten the edges of the fabric by pulling away any stray fibres that remain after cutting. Fold under 10mm (3/8in) at the top and bottom edges of the fabric, and find the centre of both ends. Mark with a pin.

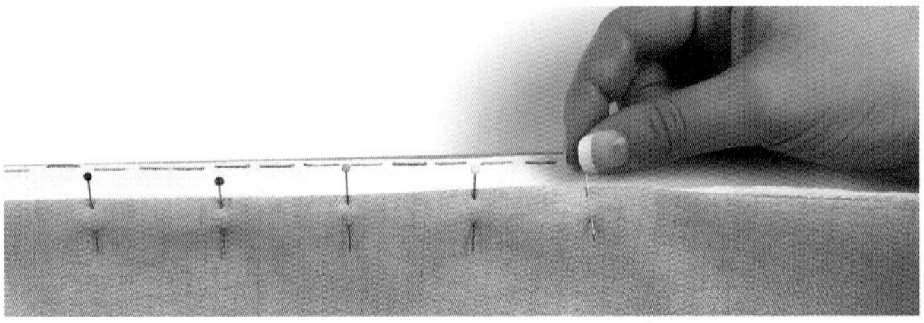

3 Match up the centres to the marks on the bars of the frame, and pin in place with the pins at 90 degrees to the edge. Pin from the centre all the way along.

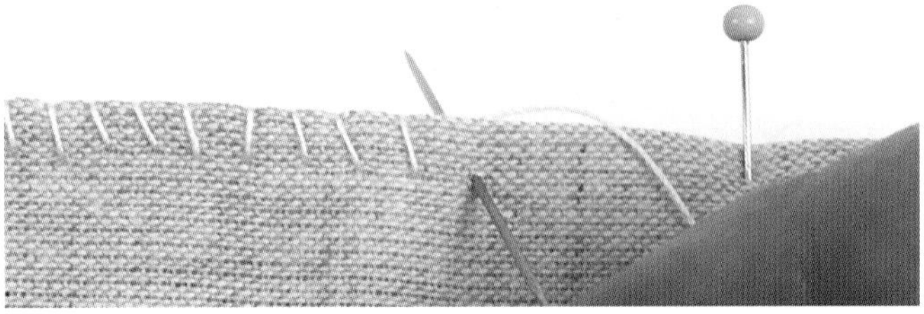

4 Use extra strong thread to overcast the fabric to the webbing tape. Pass the needle straight through both layers to make stitches about 5mm (3/16in) long and 5mm (3/16in) apart all the way along. Start in the centre with a knot, or by stitching three times in one place.

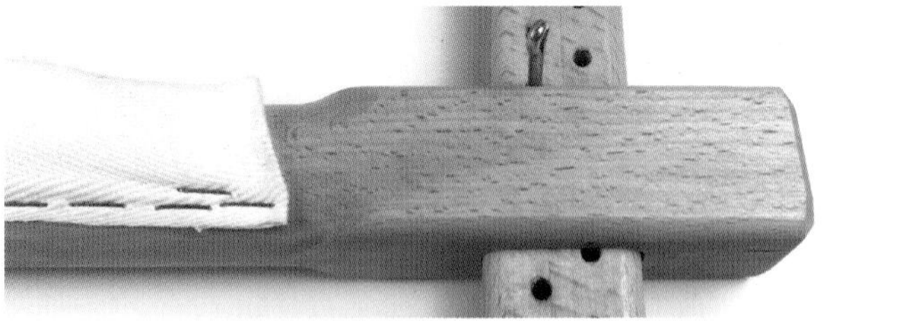

5 Place the arms into the holes in the bars and secure with split pins. The frame doesn't need to be tight at this stage, just stable.

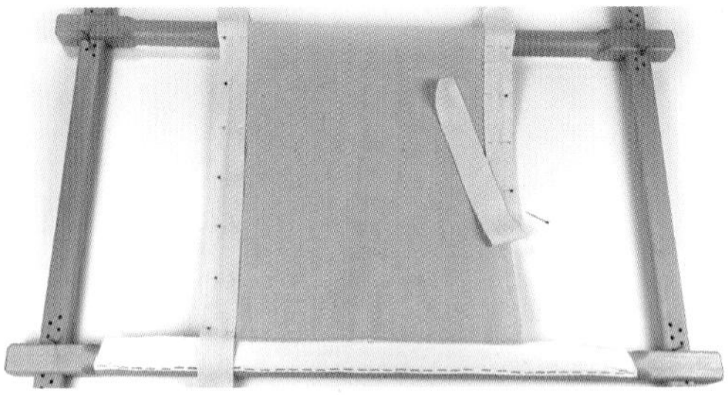

6 Cut a length of webbing tape and pin it along the sides of the fabric, with the pins at 90 degrees to the edge. The edge of the fabric should sit along the third band of the webbing tape.

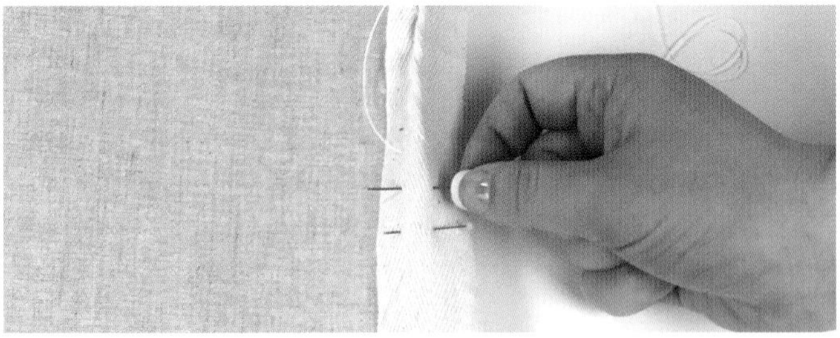

7 Starting at one end, stitch the webbing tape in place. Begin with an overcast stitch at right angles to the webbing. Make the next stitch about 15mm (5/8in) down the webbing, and so on. Finish by overcasting at the other end. Pull very tight as you stitch to create a ridge.

8 Begin to tighten the frame by moving the split pins further apart (keep them the same on each side, like a mirror image).

9 With a very large bodkin or 'bracing needle', take parcel string down through the webbing at 25mm (1in) intervals along each side and wrapping it around the side bars. Take the string straight from the ball.

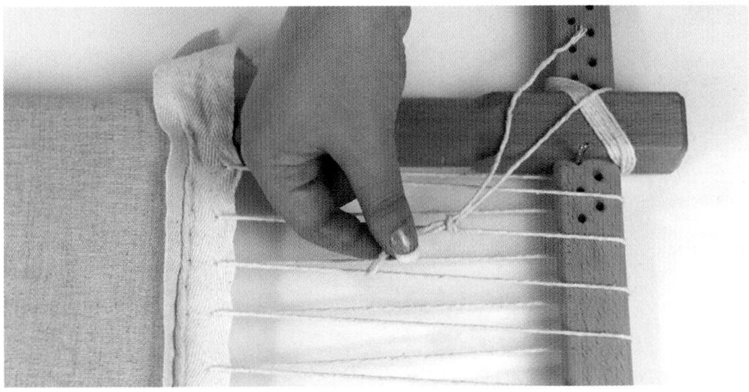

10 Tighten the frame by pulling the string. Bind the excess string around the corner and tie with a slip knot, then pull all the way along to tighten. It is best to pull gently on each side and repeat, then fasten with binding and a slip knot. Repeat at least twice on each side.

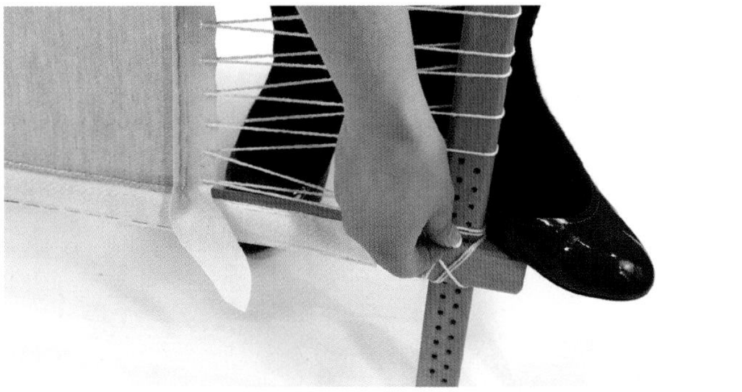

11 Complete the process by stretching once more from top to bottom. Use your foot to press down on the bar, and move the split pin one hole at a time on alternate sides until it won't go any further. Make sure both sides are set the same so the frame remains straight.

Conflicting Rules

- Slate frames are brilliant for large projects; they are perfect for the advanced projects later in this book.
- They are quite heavy, and you must have some way of supporting them (i.e. a trestle support).
- Slate frames can be made in any size for any project.
- Large frames may take up a lot of room while working and in storage.
- A slate frame will leave no mark or distortion on the fabric so there is no need to remove projects from the frame until they are complete, great for long-term embroideries.
- Much better tension can be achieved with a slate frame rather than a hoop frame or roller frame.
- More than one person can stitch at a slate frame at one time, meaning you can share large projects with other embroiderers.
- Slate frames can allow for a better sitting position, depending on the trestle supports. This can be better for your posture.

Roller frames are somewhere between hoop and slate frames: they are larger than hoops so stretch more evenly without hoop marks, but they are not as strong or versatile as slate frames for large projects. Framing up a roller frame is much the same as for a slate frame, but refer to the manufacturer's guide for tensioning instructions.

HOOP FRAME

Hoop frames are the simplest to set up and are easy to carry around once ready. Before you start, make sure that the hoops sit snugly together, rather than loose. This will allow the frame to grip the fabric immediately, which means the fabric is straight from the outset. Not having to tighten the hoop too much or tweak the fabric means that it should stay both straighter and tighter throughout the project. That said, it is important to tighten the fabric from time to time, as the pressure of stitching will loosen it throughout the project.

1 Place the larger of the two hoops upside down on a flat surface (so that when you turn it over, the screw mechanism is on the side that is most comfortable to turn).

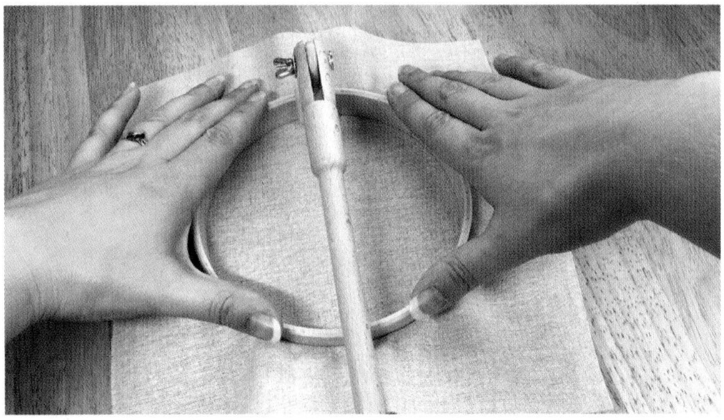

2 Place the fabric upside down, centred over the hoop. Position the small hoop on top of the larger one and press it down firmly to secure the fabric. It should take some effort – if it doesn't, the hoops probably weren't quite tight enough in the first place.

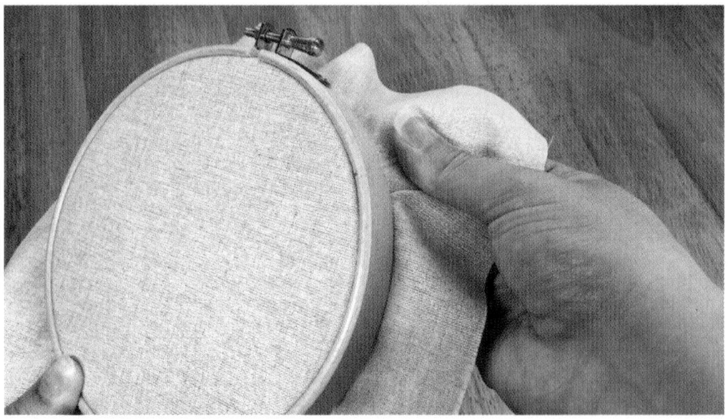

3 Turn the hoop right side up and tweak the fabric between finger and thumb if necessary. Tighten the screw (if you have to do this a lot, you are starting with the hoops too loose, so go back to the start for a better result).

When stitching on a hoop frame, keep as much of the project covered with tissue as possible while working.

Hoop Frame Pros and Cons

- Hoop frames are fantastic for small projects; in fact, they are perfect for the smaller projects later in this book.
- They are easily portable, lightweight, and don't take up a lot of room.
- Hoops can be good for really large projects where a slate frame is not big enough.
- The hoops can leave a mark of distortion, particularly on some fabrics. Make sure the frame is big enough for the mark not to be an issue, or that you bind the hoop with a strip of cotton tape before use, and remove the work from the frame as often as possible.
- If you are using a delicate fabric with a hoop frame and both layers are big enough to fit the hoop comfortably, you may treat them as one fabric, or machine sew a zigzag around the edge to hold them together.
- There are various types of hoop frame supports suited to different environments (seat frames for the sofa, clamp frames for a desk, floor standing supports).

DELICATE FABRICS

With a delicate fabric, you will need to apply it to a support fabric.

If the delicate fabric is too small for the hoop, or if you are using a slate frame, you will need to frame up the support fabric first, and then apply the delicate fabric by hand.

The principle is the same whether you are using a hoop or a slate frame: make sure that the support fabric is slightly slack in the frame before you begin.

Straighten the edges of the delicate fabric and place it on the support fabric, lining up the grain of the two fabrics.

1 Halfway along the top edge, place a pin facing outwards to start with, then flip the pin back on itself so that it faces the middle.

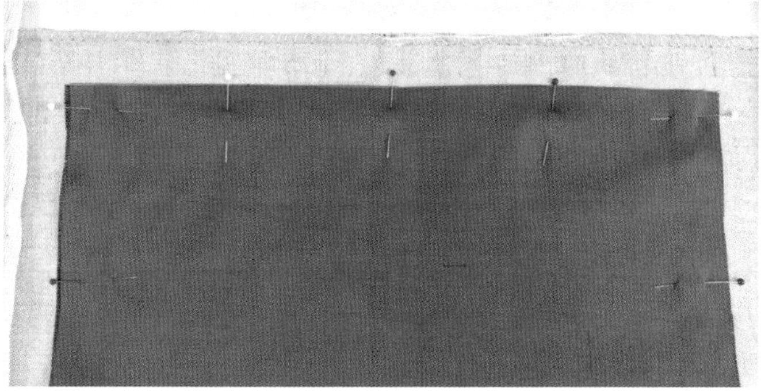

2 Repeat with a pin halfway along the bottom edge, and then the sides. Place a few more pins on each side. Flipping the pin in this way means that the delicate fabric is slightly stretched on to the support fabric.

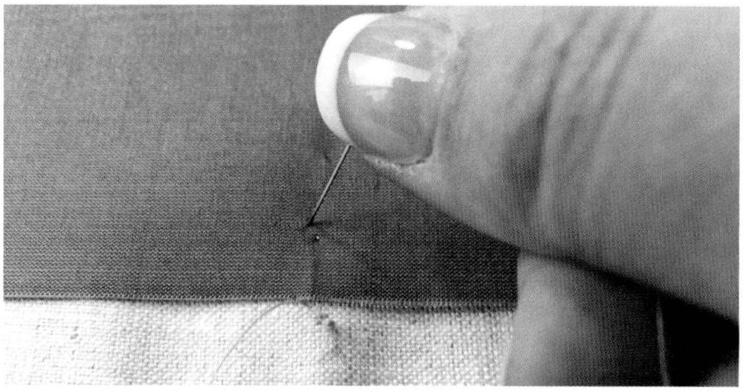

3 Halfway along one side, use machine thread to come up in the support fabric (just outside the edge of the delicate fabric). Make a stitch about 5mm (3/16in) long into the delicate fabric at 90 degrees.

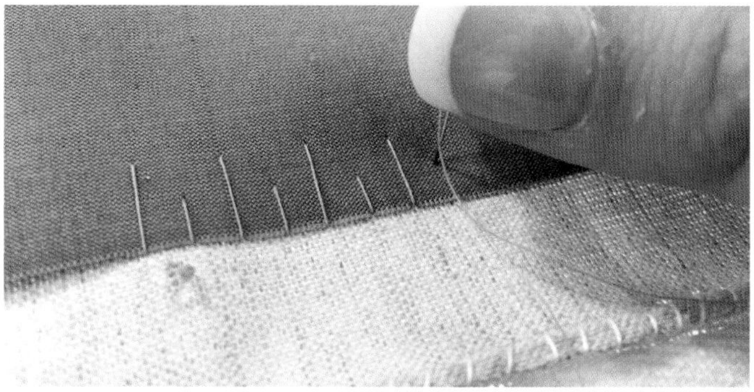

4 Move along about 5mm (3/16in) and make another stitch: this time it should be about 10mm (3/8in) long. Repeat all along the side of the fabric, alternating the two lengths.

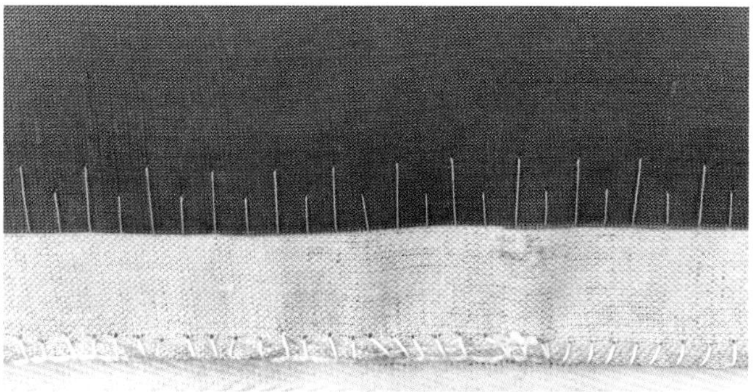

5 Go back to the middle and work to the other end, then repeat for each side of the fabric in turn. Remove the pins, tighten the frame, and you are ready to go.

TRANSFERRING DESIGNS

PRICK AND POUNCE

This method is suited to any type of design and any type of fabric, but it can be the most time-consuming. It is especially useful for dark or thick fabrics, through which it is not possible to trace a design even with a lightbox.

This is the most traditional method – the one used historically for all kinds of embroidery.

Before you can prick and pounce your design, you must have a good copy on tracing paper. Use a size 12 embroidery needle for the pricking.

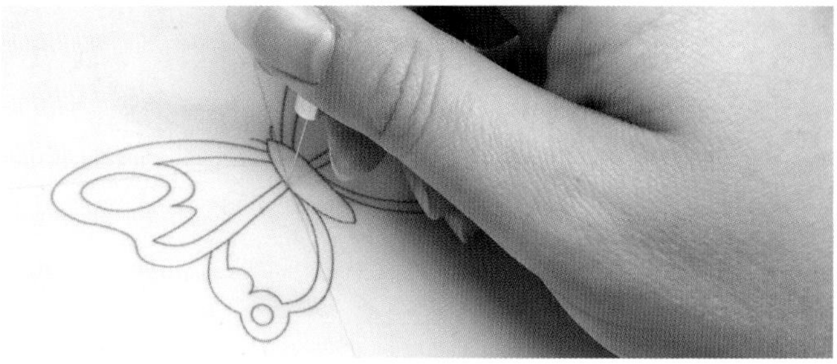

1 Place your tracing paper design on top of some folded fabric or a padded board. Use your pricker to guide the needle straight down through the paper and out again. Make holes on all the design lines, about 2mm apart (a little further apart on long smooth lines, closer on tight curves or complicated areas). If you make a mistake, use tape to mend the area and try again.

2 Place the paper over your stretched fabric, lining up the straight grain. Pin in place with as few pins as you need to hold it securely.

3 Use a pounce pad to collect some pounce powder (use the colour that contrasts best with the fabric). Starting in the middle, work in small circular motions. Don't use any pressure, just sweep over the design.

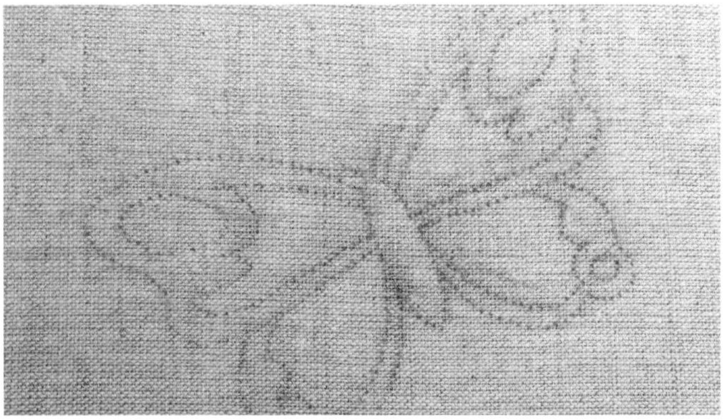

4 Gently remove the pins without disturbing the paper, and then lift off the paper. Blow off any excess powder to leave just little dots.

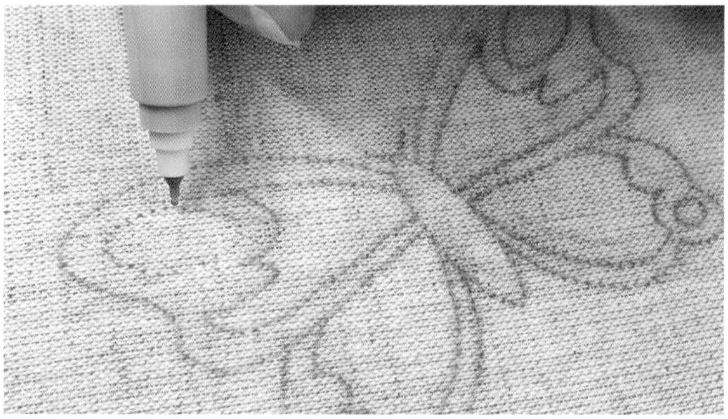

5 Either paint or draw over the lines, connecting the dots. Be careful to wash your brush or wipe off your pen/pencil as they may collect powder and leave blobs on your line. Once dry, use a soft brush (such as a baby hairbrush) to gently brush off the excess pounce powder.

Painting and Drawing

Painting is the very best way to transfer designs – you can mix the exact colour you want and it will not penetrate the fabric and cause a reaction. Watercolour, acrylic and fabric paints are all suitable. Make sure that if you use fabric paint you iron it to set the colour before stitching.

Mix up some paint to the consistency of double cream. This will sit nicely on the surface of the fabric without bleeding, but will also flow well from the brush. Use a very small paintbrush (000 is a good size) to cover small lengths of line at a time. Wash and dry the brush frequently as you paint.

Drawing is a good substitute for painting, particularly for small designs. It can be quicker, and many people feel more comfortable with a pen or pencil than a brush.

If you are using pencil, keep it very sharp as you draw. Be careful to avoid dragging the fabric as you go.

If you use a pen, test it for colourfastness before you draw. Some pens can be set with heat from an iron.

Whichever method you go for, choose a colour that nearly matches either the fabric or the metal threads, but is different enough that you can see it clearly.

TRACING

Tracing a design is by far the quickest method of transferring it, but is only possible for fabrics that can be seen through with a lightbox. This usually means that light colours and relatively fine fabrics are most suitable.

Tracing should be done before framing up with a hoop, or after framing up with a slate frame (which means that you need to consider both layers if you are using a delicate fabric with a support).

1 Place your design on a lightbox and secure it with tape. Either tape your loose fabric or position your slate frame over the top.

2 Carefully trace over the design lines with pencil, pen or paint.

STITCHING ENVIRONMENT

It is not possible to stress enough the importance of good light to an embroidery project. With good light, you can make more accurate stitches; you can pick up on mistakes and discrepancies in the threads; you will help prevent eyestrain and tiredness. All these things contribute to good stitching.

You may also find it valuable to use a magnifier, even if it is just for certain techniques. It is difficult to keep stitches invisible on pearl purl, for example, so a magnifying lens may help you to see the tiny stitches.

It is also important to keep your work clean and tidy as much as possible. Metal threads are more susceptible to environmental changes than other fibres, so it is best to pack away your threads and work when you leave it for a while.

Keep everything packaged in individual pieces of acid-free tissue or glassine bags to protect it while you work. Metal threads do not like plastic, so try to avoid storing them in plastic bags – however, a large plastic box to keep all your threads together in their individual packages can be very useful – just remember to label everything.

When you sit at your frame, keep as much of your work covered with acid-free tissue as possible, revealing only enough for you to see what you are doing. This way you can avoid bleaching by the sun, wax marks from the beeswax on your threads, and general grubbiness from rubbing the fabric or collected dust.

Once you have started stitching the metal threads, it is useful to create a little frame of bubble wrap or tissue to keep other things away from their surface. Simply roll up some bubble wrap into a tube, and fold and tape it into shape. Make sure it is big enough to surround all the stitching. Place this over the work before wrapping it with tissue for storage. This is a very good way to prevent the metal threads being squashed or poked and damaged.

Embroidery protected with a bubble-wrap frame, with acid-free tissue, and metal threads protected in glassine bags.

The author, stitching in her studio. Lights are set up to illuminate the area and prevent eyestrain. The stitching is protected with tissue paper, and all the tools required are near at hand.

Metal threads stored in glassine bags and wrapped in acid-free tissue to protect them from environmental damage.

HOW MUCH GOLD DO I NEED?

How much gold you will need is a tricky question, and there is no doubt that experience helps. Expect to 'waste' more on your first projects as you practise the techniques and get used to working with the metal threads. When you purchase gold, keep this in mind so that you always have enough to finish a project – gold threads are much like knitting yarns, they come in batches, which may not be an exact match one to the next.

The main techniques are listed here; the others can be worked out in similar ways.

COUCHING METAL-WRAPPED THREADS

Measure the longest single length of thread required (this depends on the direction line of the couching), and add 10cm (4in) of excess. Then measure the widest part and figure out how many times the metal thread will fit in that width. Multiply one by the other to calculate the length needed.

For example, if the shape is 10cm (20cm/8in including the excess) long by 10mm wide, and the thread is 1mm wide, the thread will fit ten times into the width, so 10 × 20 = 200cm (79in). You should buy at least 2m (6.5ft) of thread.

PEARL PURL

For this wire, no excess is needed because it is added when the wire is stretched – so you need only measure the exact length needed, and buy a little extra in case it gets damaged.

CHIPPING

Measure the widest part of the shape, and figure out how many times the metal purl will fit into that width. Measure the longest part of the shape. Multiply one by the other and add 20 per cent to calculate the length needed.

For example, if the shape is 10cm (4in) long by 15mm wide and the purl is 1.5mm wide, the purl will fit ten times into the width, so 10 × 10 = 100cm (40in), plus 20 per cent equals 120cm (47in). You should buy at least 1.2m (4ft) of purl.

CUTWORK

Measure the length of the shape and divide that by the width of the purl. Measure the widest part of the shape (that is, the longest 'chip'), and multiply one by the other and add 20 per cent for wastage.

For example, if the shape is 15cm (6in) long by 10mm wide and the purl is 1.5mm wide, 10 × 10 = 100cm (40in), plus 20 per cent equals 120cm (47in). You should buy at least 1.2m (4ft) of purl.

PREPARING SEWING THREADS

It is important always to use short lengths of thread for embroidery, particularly goldwork, because the metal threads are abrasive and can tear through the sewing thread. 25cm (10in) is plenty.

Whenever you use metal threads, you need to protect the sewing thread with a light coating of beeswax (or thread conditioner, though this can be a bit sticky).

Make sure that you keep beeswax in a reasonably warm environment, preferably in a bag so that it doesn't dry out. If it is dry it may become flaky, which can leave unsightly deposits on your embroidery. In any case, when you wax a thread, try to do so away from your embroidery.

1 Place the thread on the surface of the wax and hold it with your thumb. Gently pull the thread through. Repeat this two or three times.

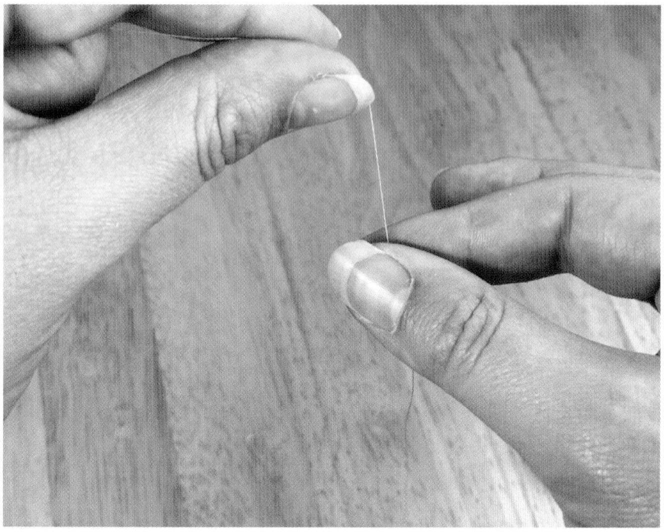

2 Run the waxed thread through your fingers to check if it is sufficiently waxed. It should feel smoother than unwaxed thread, but not sticky. If it does feel sticky, use some scrap fabric to remove some of the wax.

DOUBLE THREADS

For some techniques, such as cutwork, you will need to use a double thread. Cut a double length, pass one end through the eye of the needle and then tie the two ends together.

This means that the bulk of thread through the eye is kept to a minimum, which makes passing it through the gold much easier and prevents damage.

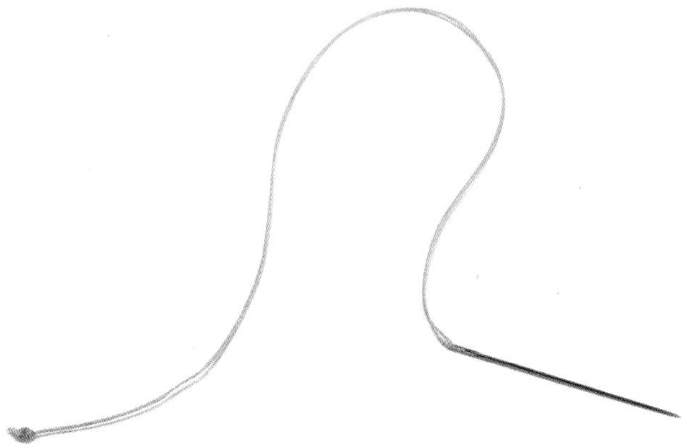

Looping the thread through the needle minimizes bulk so that it can pass easily through purl wires.

STARTING AND FINISHING THREADS

Throughout this book you will find starting and finishing threads referred to as 'casting on and off'.

This method of casting on is called the 'waste knot technique' because you begin with a knot on the top of the fabric (never underneath), which is then removed to leave a couple of small stitches that are secure but invisible.

It is very important not to use knots on the back of the work as these can loosen and pull through to the front, leaving your hard work vulnerable. This method also avoids lumps on the back of the embroidery through which you might have to stitch.

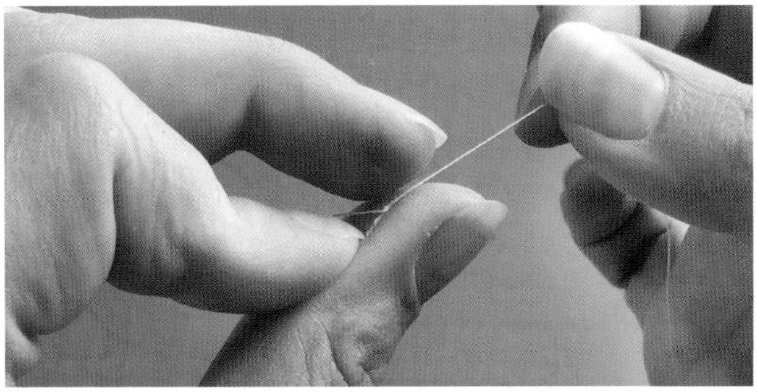

1 First, make a large knot in one end of the thread. A good way to do this is to wrap the thread clockwise round your forefinger, pinch with your thumb, and then roll the thread off your finger, pulling tight with your middle finger. This should result in a nice bundle of thread.

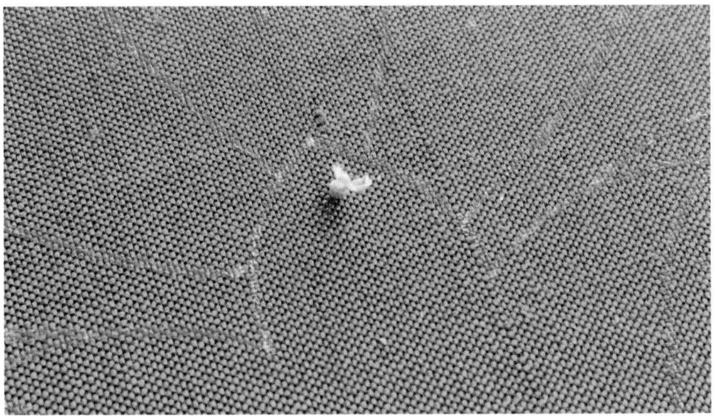

2 Pass the other end of the thread through the eye of the needle. Take the needle down through the fabric, inside the area to be stitched, leaving the knot on the surface.

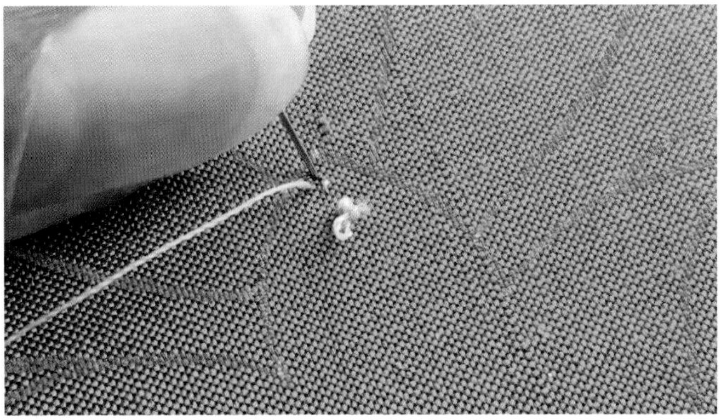

3 Bring the needle up close by and make two small stitches, preferably parallel but not on top of one another. Trim away the knot. To finish the thread later, make two little stitches in the same way. Bring the thread up to the top and cut it off.

STAB STITCHING

When you stitch goldwork on to delicate fabric (or any time you have two layers) it is important to stab stitch the two fabrics together to improve their stability and help prevent puckering.

These securing stitches will be completely covered, but don't be tempted to skip them as they perform an important job. Choose thread to match the background fabric or metal threads as closely as possible, just in case a stitch should peek through.

The stitches should generally be placed just inside the design lines on areas that will be solidly stitched. For a single line of stitching, make sure to place the stitches accurately on the line.

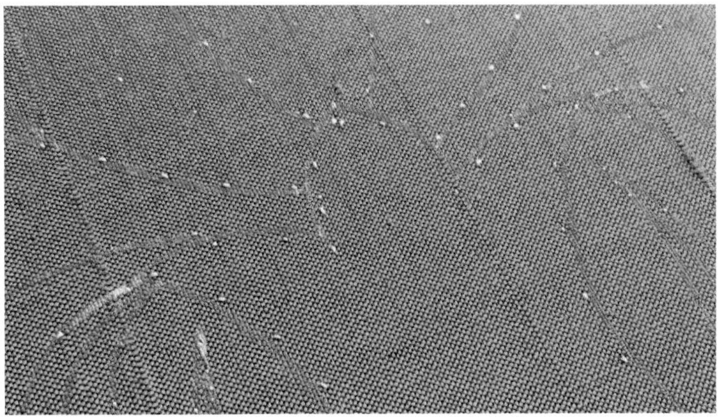

Make tiny stitches, 1mm (1/32in) in length, every 6–10mm (1/4–5/8in) around the design. Remember to stitch inside solid areas and accurately on the line for single stitched lines (for example, tendrils).

CHAPTER 4

PADDING

Padding is always the first thing to be stitched in any goldwork project.

It is important to complete the padding before any gold is stitched, because the padding techniques often shed fibres on to the work, which could easily become trapped in the gold threads.

The order in which padding should be worked is as follows: felt (including extra thick felt), soft string, hard string and then interfacing or card.

Some of the padding techniques can be combined: for example, hard string padding or interfacing may be worked over felt padding for extra relief.

FELT PADDING

Felt padding is incredibly versatile, and luckily it comes in a good range of colours.

The first reason to use felt padding is actually not as padding at all, but to give a colour underneath your goldwork. This gives a more consistent colour to an area because it doesn't allow any of the background fabric to peek through; this is particularly useful with dark fabrics. To achieve this, you simply apply a single layer of felt. The second reason is to give height to your goldwork.

Felt padding should be used whenever the padded area will be stitched with couching, because the felt is soft enough to pass the needle through (unlike string padding).

If more extreme height is required, extra thick felt should be used.

Felt is also sometimes useful underneath cutwork, when only a gentle slope is required. To determine how many layers are needed, consider how high you want the padded elements to appear in relation with one another. It is a good idea to start off with the lowest level and give that one layer, and then work higher from there.

Felt padding with two, three and four layers of felt. Notice the difference in height on the same shape.

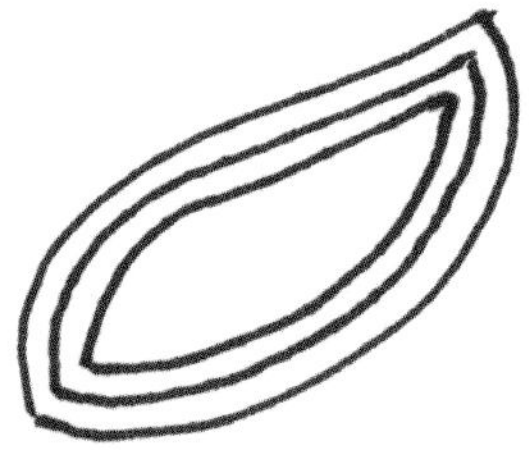

1 First you must draw out the felt outlines. Using your original design, trace just the area to be padded, and then separately trace each layer a little smaller.

2 Transfer your outlines on to the felt. You can either prick and pounce (there is no need to draw, as the pounce will stick), or create paper templates to cut around.

3 Position the smallest piece of felt on the design. Keep it in place with pins if need be. Cast on a single matching machine thread underneath the edge, and bring the needle up just outside the edge of the felt.

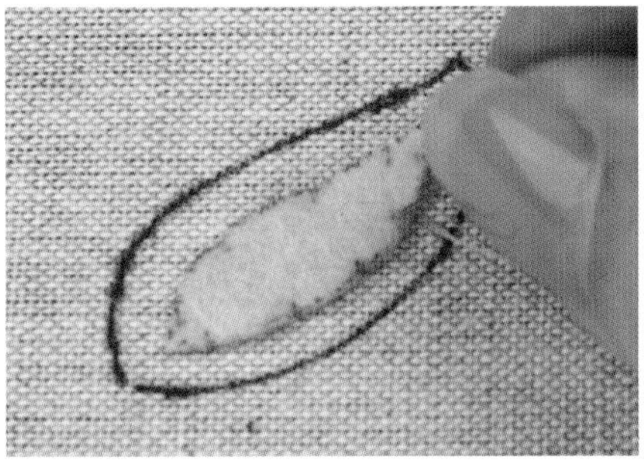

4 Make a stitch about 1.5mm ($^{1}/_{16}$in) into the felt. Move along the outline about 8mm ($^{5}/_{16}$in), bring the needle up just outside the felt again and take it down into the felt. Repeat this all the way around the shape to secure it.

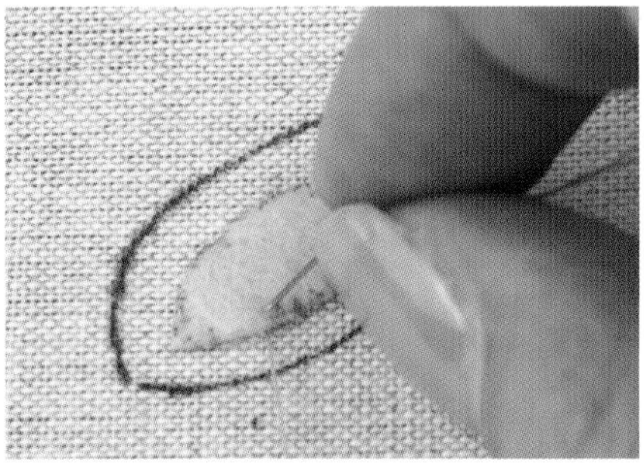

5 Work your way around the felt shape again. This time make the same small stitches, but about 1.5mm ($^{1}/_{16}$in) apart. If the shape has sharp corners, make a slightly longer stitch right on the corner.

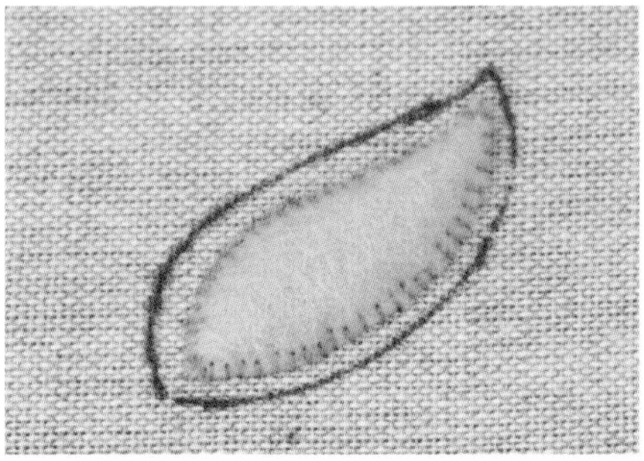

6 Position the second layer on top of the first and secure in the same way. If there are more than three layers, repeat this for each but the top one.

7 For the top layer, stitch in the same way, but make sure that when you bring the needle up it is on the design line on the fabric. Felt has a little stretch to it, so if you need to, you can pull it just a little to meet the outline.

8 Once complete, the felt shape should be smooth and have a neat edge with little or no fluff around the stitches.

Watch out for the 'pie crust' look. If your stitches are too far apart, the edge will look like this and fluff might poke through the gold. Resolve it easily by putting extra stitches in between.

EXTRA THICK FELT PADDING

Extra thick felt should be used for large areas that need to be highly raised.

It is also useful when a shape needs to have a particularly intricate padded form, such as the body of an animal.

Historically it would be used to define the musculature of the creatures on a coat of arms, such as the familiar forms of the lion and unicorn on the coat of arms of the British Royal Family.

BASIC METHOD (SINGLE LAYER)

To pad a simple, slightly domed shape with extra thick felt, first make a paper template of the shape to be padded. Cut the extra thick felt about 1.5mm ($^{1}/_{16}$in) smaller than the outline.

1 Once the shape is cut out, chamfer the edges. Take a pair of embroidery scissors and cut down the edge of the felt at a 45-degree angle. This will give a sloping edge to the shape, allowing the metal threads to sit nicely over the top.

2 Position the felt on the design and pin in place if necessary. Cast on a double waxed thread and make a few long stitches over the felt, taking the needle up and down in the fabric just outside the felt. Make a criss-cross pattern to hold it securely.

3 Once the felt is held in place, work around the edge making long stitches into the felt. Bring the needle up just outside the felt and down about 10mm ($^{3}/_{8}$in) in from the edge. This holds the edge firmly, keeping the shape and preventing fibres escaping.

4 Once the extra thick felt is secured, use the same template to cut a piece of craft felt (make it the exact size of the design this time). Place this on top of the thick felt and stitch it as you would for felt padding.

COMPLEX SHAPES (TWO OR MORE LAYERS)

The method described here is an extension of the basic technique, and is useful for more complex shapes, or areas needing more than one layer of felt.

Make a paper template of the shape to be padded. Cut a piece of extra thick felt about 1.5mm ($^{1}/_{16}$in) smaller than the outline. This will be the largest layer. Chamfer the edge at a 45-degree angle as you would for the basic method.

Make another template a bit smaller than the first (usually about 5mm, or $^{3}/_{16}$in, smaller). Cut out this piece of felt and chamfer the edge as before.

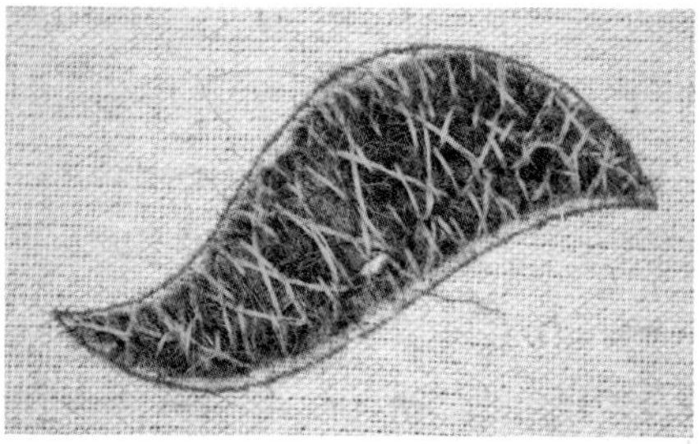

1 Stitch the first layer as you would for the basic method. Then place the second, smaller layer on top. Make criss-crossing stitches over the felt, and then secure the edge with long stitches. This should give a smooth, rather than a stepped shape.

2 To make more complex forms, you can add layers of carpet felt to only part of the shape, such as raising the middle further, or creating the musculature on an animal. The layers should be cut and placed in the same way so that the layers blend together smoothly.

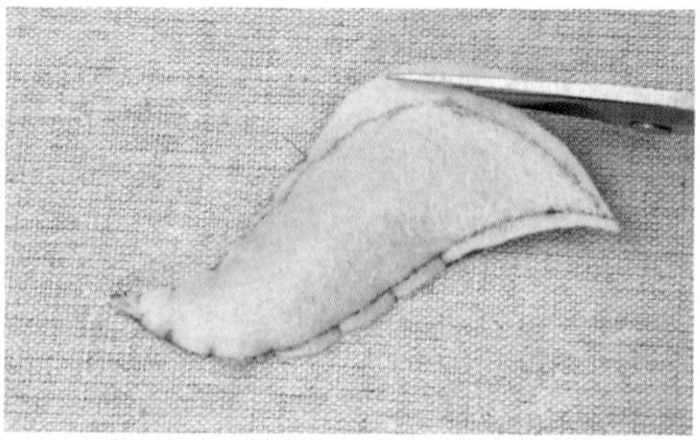

3 When covering a complex shape with craft felt, it can be useful to cut the felt a little bigger than the original template to allow for the height it needs to cover. If necessary, some parts can be trimmed away to allow the form to be covered accurately.

Carpet felt with varying layers on the same shape. Note that the height changes quite dramatically.

'HARD STRING' PADDING

Hard string padding is used to create decorative effects in goldwork. It is most commonly used with couching, but can also be very effective with plate and cutwork. Hard string can be used to create striped areas or basket-weave designs, with straight or curved lines.

Ordinary cotton parcel string is perfect for this technique, and may be dyed to match the metal threads.

There are two methods; choose the one that gives you the best results.

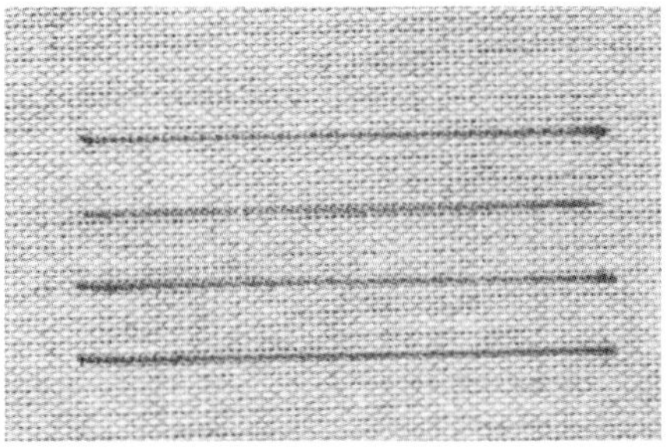

1 Mark the fabric with straight lines across the shape, equally spaced 6mm (1/4in) apart. This assumes your string is about 3mm (1/8in) wide; if it is wider, add a little more space. Wax a good length of string, and cast on a single waxed sewing thread.

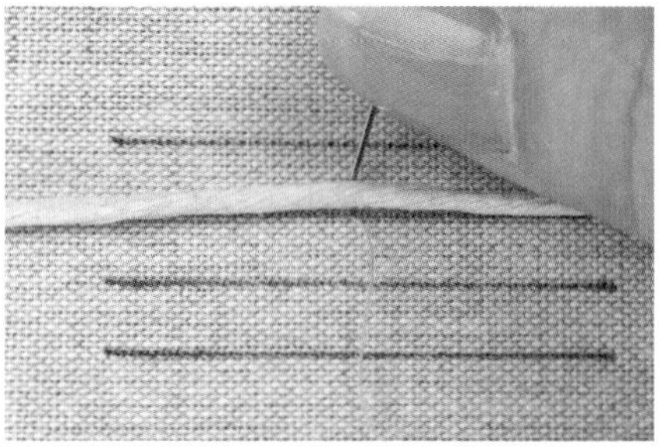

2 Begin your thread in the middle of a line. Lay the string on the line, so that you can just see the line on one side. Bring the needle up on the line, carry the thread over the string, and take the needle down just on the other side so that the string is secured.

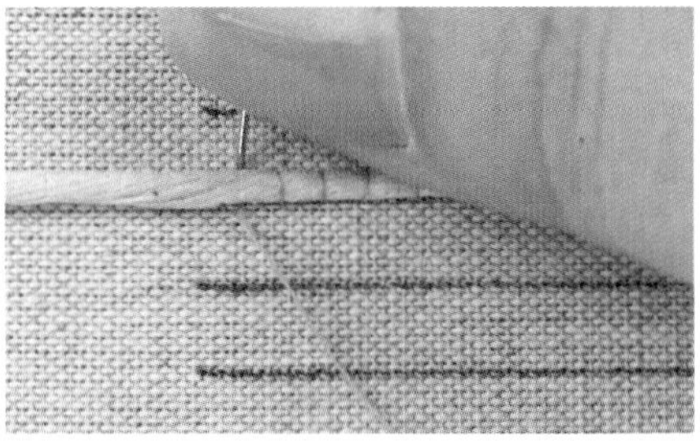

3 Bring the needle up about 3mm (1/8in) along the line and make another stitch. Keep the stitches accurate in size so that the string cannot move around, but is not pinched too tightly. Make sure each stitch is at 90 degrees. Repeat to the end of the line.

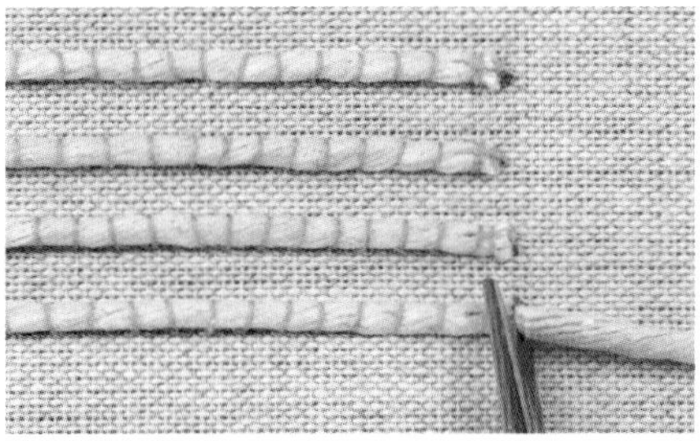

4 At the end of the line, make an extra stitch close to the last one. Trim the string just inside the design line, chamfering it at a 45-degree angle so that it tapers down to the fabric.

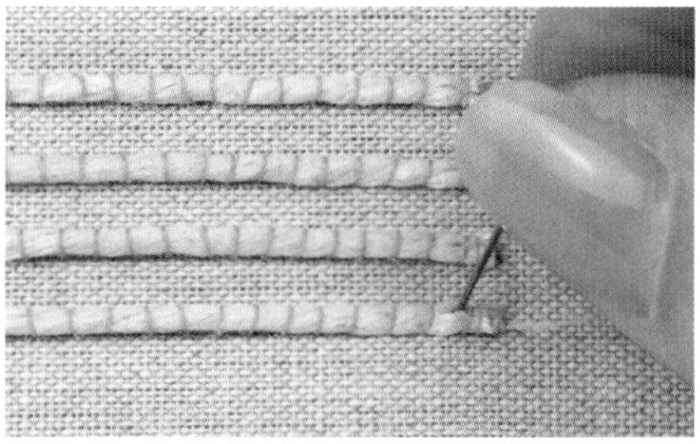

5 Secure the end with a stitch running parallel with the string. Bring the needle up in the fabric and down through the middle of the string. Add extra stitches at 90 degrees to neaten the end if necessary.

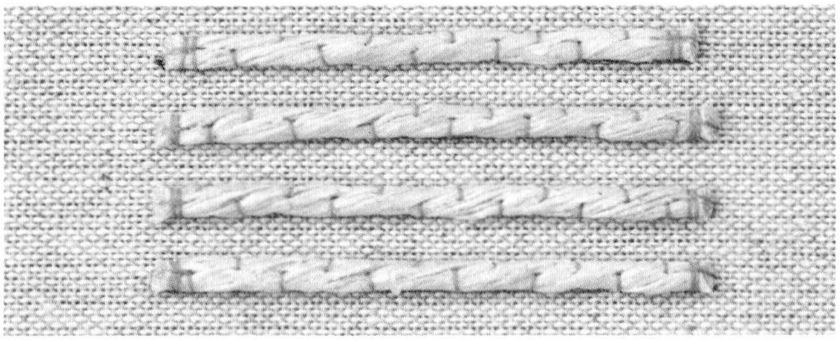

For the second method, with each stitch bring the needle up in the fabric and down into the string, piercing it through the middle. The stitches should alternate from side to side, always coming up through the fabric and down in the string. Finish the ends in the same way as the first method.

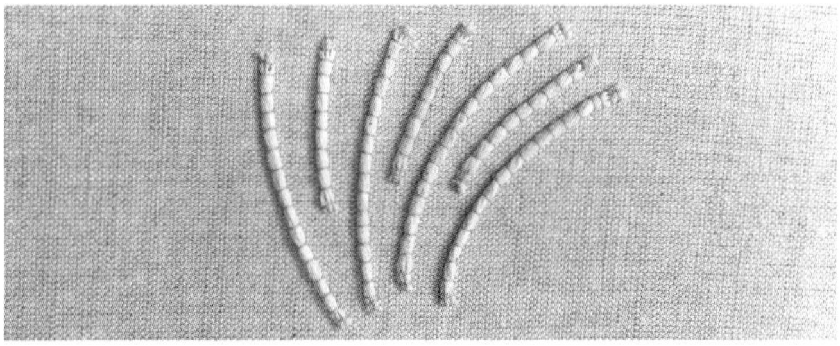

To stitch hard string padding on a curve, the lines must either be kept evenly spaced, or fanned out to fill the space. Sometimes it may be necessary to add extra lines in places, so that the gaps between strings are not too large (the maximum should be about 10mm (3/8in).

'SOFT STRING' PADDING

Soft string padding should be used under areas of cutwork or plate that need to be highly raised. This type of padding lends itself to long, slim shapes.

Various types of thread or string can be used. The most commonly available is tapestry cotton, which is a very soft, thick, pliable cotton thread. Choose a colour to match the metal threads.

First you need to measure the length of the area to be padded from end to end.

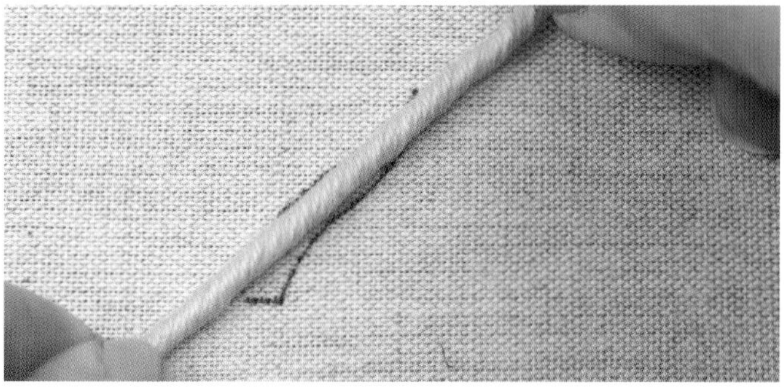

1 Fold the 'string' thread multiple times and twist the resulting bundle together to check if it will fill the shape and give the desired height. This shows accurately what will result after the threads are compacted with stitches. Usually it is best to limit the number of threads needed to around twenty, to keep the padding stable.

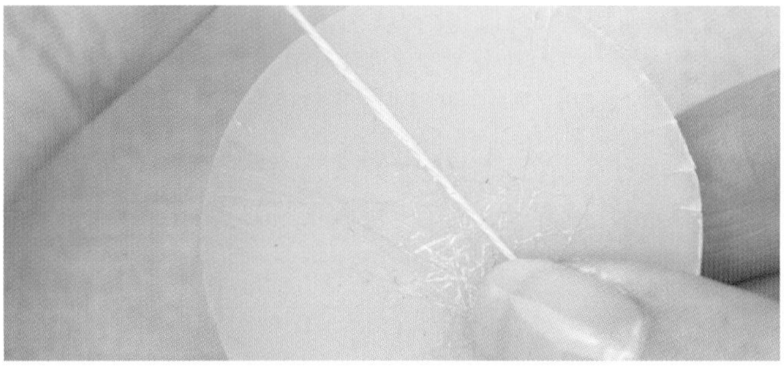

2 Wax the thread thoroughly by pinching it against a block of beeswax and running it through a few times. Either cut all the required lengths first and then wax, or unfold, wax and fold again.

3 Cast on a double waxed sewing thread in the middle of the shape or at the widest point. Bring the needle up about 1mm ($^1/_{32}$in) inside the design line on one side. Take the thread over the padding and down inside the design line on the opposite side, making the stitch at 90 degrees to the shape.

4 Make another stitch about 3mm ($^1/_8$in) along the shape, again at 90 degrees to the shape. Pull the stitches firmly so that the padding is compacted. Repeat this to the point of tapering, or if the shape does not taper, to 8mm ($^5/_{16}$in) from the end.

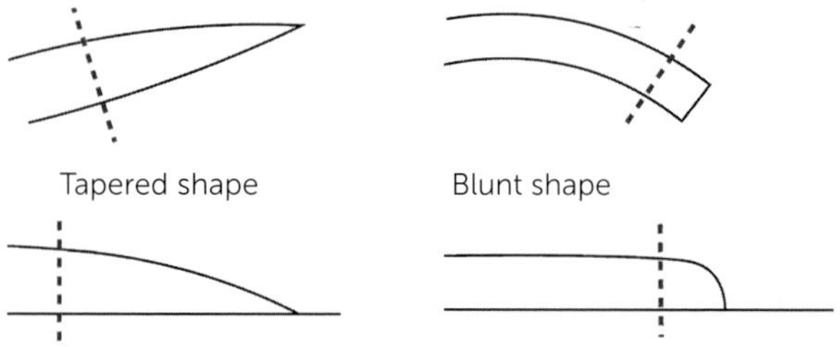

Now you must figure out how to treat the end of the shape. If the shape tapers gradually (for example a leaf shape), then both height and width must be reduced from the point that this begins on the design (i.e. from the red dotted line). If the shape does not taper at all (such as where one shape is overlapped by another), the width will not be reduced, but the height must still be reduced a little at the very end to allow the cutwork to sit properly without showing the padding underneath.

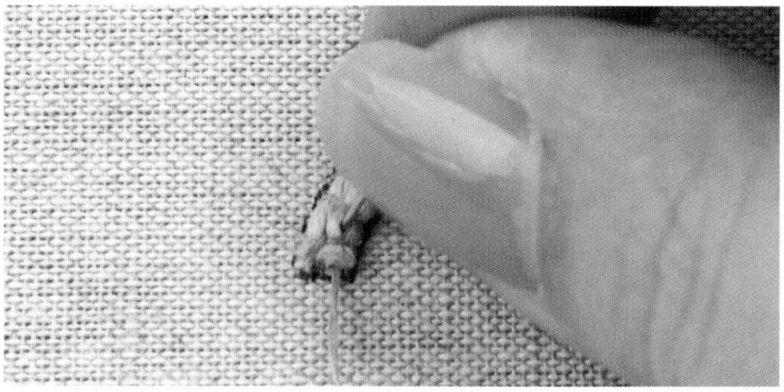

5 If the end is blunt, lift the padding threads up away from the fabric and cut two or three from the underneath (closest to the fabric). Lay the threads back down and continue to stitch. Repeat this once.

6 Keep stitching up to the end of the shape. Trim off the excess padding at the end of the shape, 1mm ($^1/_{32}$in) inside the outline. Bring the needle up at the end of the shape and make a couple of stitches down into the padding threads. Make two or three stitches over the end at 90 degrees to fully secure and neaten the shape.

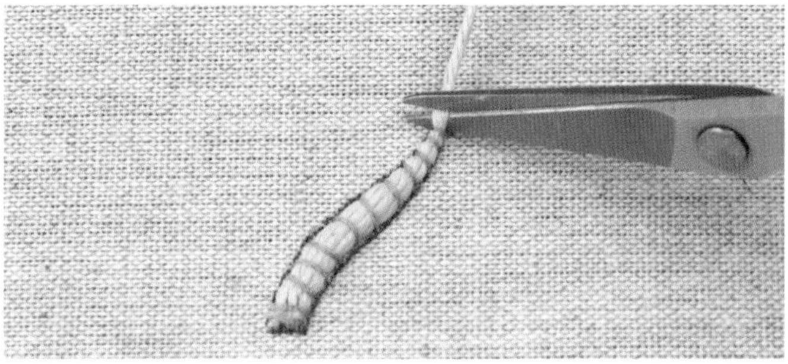

7 If the shape is tapered, as soon as it starts to narrow, lift the padding threads and cut two or three from the underneath (closest to the fabric). Lay the threads back down, check the shape, and keep stitching. Repeat this as necessary to create the shape.

8 Once the string is stitched in place, go back along the whole length, stitching once or twice between each original stitch. This makes the padding more solid to better support the gold threads.

PADDING WITH INTERFACING

Padding with firm interfacing is fantastic for giving very defined edges with just a little bit of height.

Interfacing can be dyed or painted to match the metal threads.

This type of padding can be worked directly on to the fabric, or applied over felt padding.

Choose a firm interfacing that is reasonably thick, such as pelmet interfacing. It should be densely meshed so that it can be cut into shapes easily and will give clean, crisp edges.

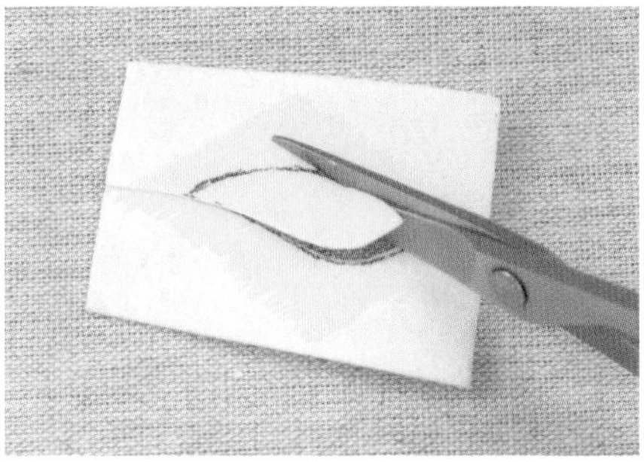

1 Transfer your outlines on to the interfacing. You can either prick and pounce (no need to draw, as the pounce will stick), or create paper templates to cut around. Cut out the interfacing about 1mm ($^1/_{32}$in) inside the lines.

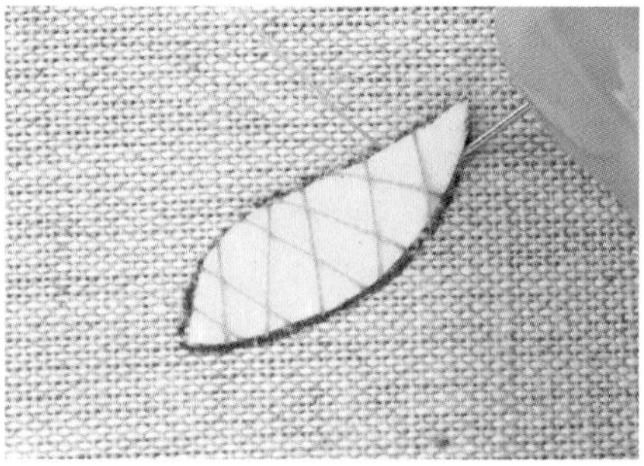

2 To secure the interfacing, use a single thread to stitch over the interfacing in a criss-cross pattern. No stitches should pierce the interfacing.

CHAPTER 5

COUCHING

'Couching' is the word used to describe any stitching where one thread is used to stitch over another, thus securing it to the fabric.

In goldwork, this is a way of attaching gold threads that could not be embroidered with in the typical way because taking them through the fabric repeatedly would cause damage.

Metal threads with a core such as Japanese thread or smooth passing are applied with standard couching, with the stitches remaining visible. Pearl purl, on the other hand, because of the nature of the wire, is couched invisibly.

Couching often makes up the bulk of a traditional goldwork project. Historically it was a relatively cost-effective way of using the metal, compared with cutwork or chipping, and it is quite stunning in appearance. When worked over padding and along directional lines, couching can be used to create wonderful depth in a design.

In traditional goldwork, couching is almost always stitched in a brick pattern, which allows the rows of gold to sit tightly together. This is known as 'bricking'.

Hair ornament with couched Japanese thread, twist, pearl purl and overstretched pearl purl. Coloured threads and appliqué techniques have been used to enhance the design.

BASIC COUCHING

Basic couching is the simple technique used to stitch down any of the metal threads with a cotton or silk core, using the traditional 'bricking' technique which allows the gold to shine through while keeping it secure and enabling the rows to sit tightly and neatly next to one another.

There are many additional techniques that come in useful when considering couching these threads. Finishing threads by 'plunging', turning corners, working along curves and filling awkward spaces will be covered in the following pages.

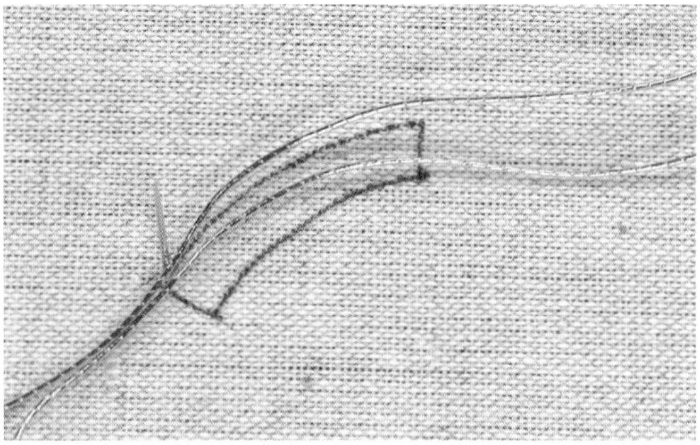

1 Begin with a single waxed sewing thread in a small embroidery needle. Bring the needle up about 2mm (1/16in) from one end of the design line, just outside the line so that it will be covered with the gold. Bring two gold threads together into a pair (either from two reels, or one cut length folded). Position the gold threads so that there is at least 50mm (2in) excess for 'plunging'.

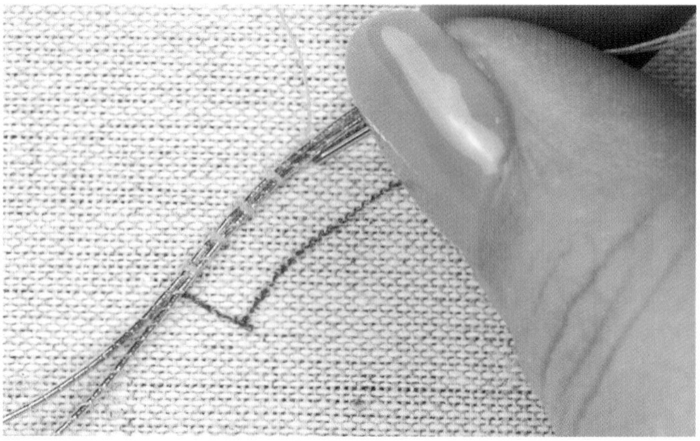

2 Make a stitch over the two threads at 90 degrees. The stitch should be short enough to hold the threads securely without any sideways movement, but not so tight that they appear pinched or twisted. Make another stitch further along the line. Stitches are typically placed about 4mm (1/4in) apart, but this can vary depending on the design.

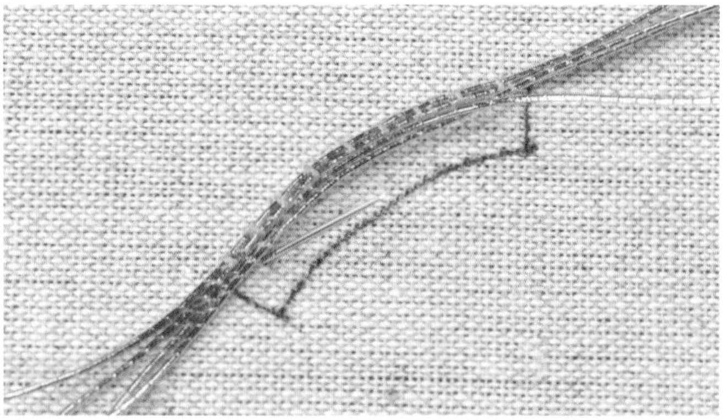

3 Continue to stitch along the line. Hold the gold threads at a slight tension all the while, to give a neat finish. At the end of the line, cut the gold threads with at least 50mm (2in) excess. Hold two gold threads together to start a second row of couching. Bring the needle up accurately, leaving just enough room for the pair of gold threads to sit between the needle and the previously stitched row. The stitch should fall between two stitches of the previous row to create the traditional brick pattern known as 'bricking'.

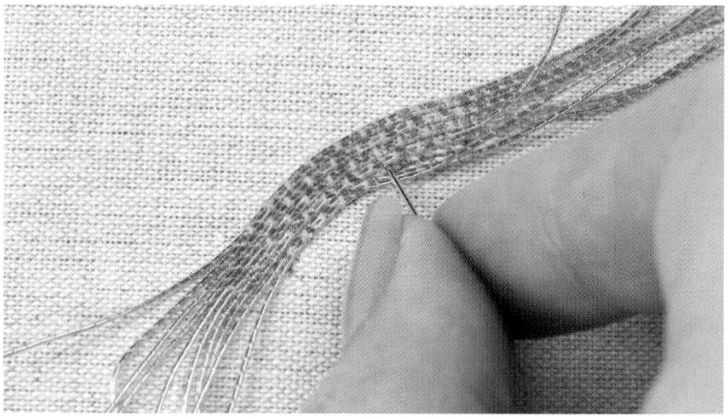

4 Take the needle down between two stitches of the previous row, tucking it slightly underneath the gold threads. This pulls the two rows neatly together, avoiding unsightly gaps. Continue this along the row, and for as many subsequent rows as necessary to fill the space.

STARTING WITH A FOLD

Sometimes it is useful to start the gold threads with a neat fold, rather than as two separate threads. This technique can be particularly useful when working on sheer fabric or three-dimensional pieces where plunging may look untidy.

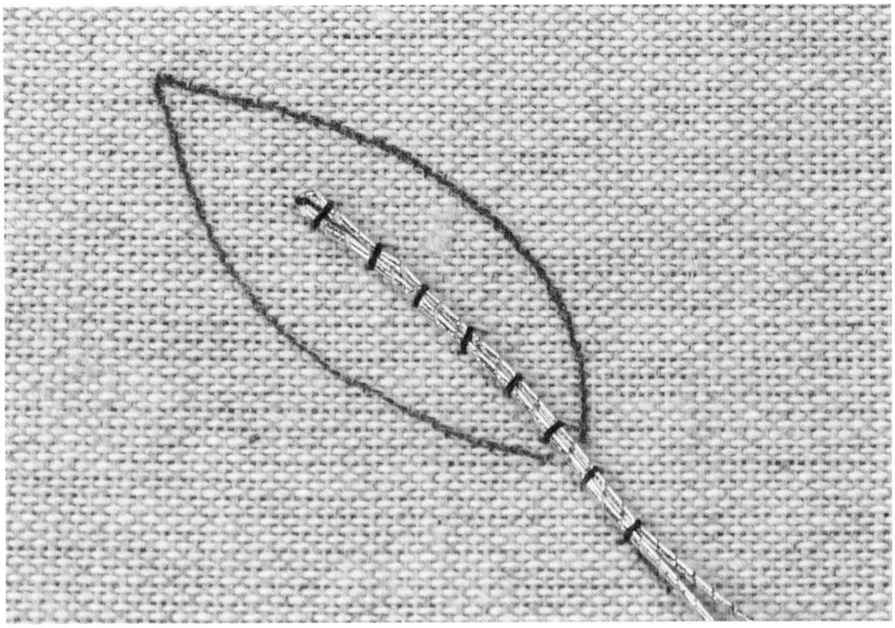

Bring the needle up right at the required starting point of the couching. Fold the length of gold in half, being careful not to damage the gold covering, and make a tiny stitch over the fold in the same direction as the design line. Pinch the two halves together and position the first couching stitch close to the fold to hold them together neatly. Continue to couch the line as usual.

TURNING AT THE END OF A ROW

When filling a solid shape, particularly a square such as a background for Or Nué, it can be useful to turn the gold threads at the end of a row. Done well this can look very pleasing, and it avoids excessive plunging.

It is possible to turn both threads at the end of each row, but the method of plunging one and turning one tends to give a better finish overall, and means that you can use shorter pieces of gold thread.

Couch to the end of the line so that both threads are securely attached close to the end. Cut the outer thread ready for plunging (leaving about 50mm, or 2in, excess). Turn the inner thread by bringing the needle up on the inside of the turn and pulling the gold quite hard back against the thread. Make a tiny stitch over the turn to hold it secure, and add a new length of gold to couch with the inner thread as the next pair. Work back along the row creating the traditional brick pattern with the stitches.

PLUNGING AND FINISHING

Once gold threads are couched, they must be finished off, both to neaten the appearance on the front, and to secure them and prevent unravelling.

A long tail of about 50mm (2in) should be left for plunging. A shorter tail can be used, particularly by more experienced embroiderers. However, a long tail is easier to thread and handle, which can avoid the gold wrapping being stripped from the core thread, which is tricky to rectify.

If a large area is to be filled with couching, it may be a good idea to plunge and tie back the threads in bundles as you go along so that it doesn't become an arduous task at the end.

Use a large chenille needle for plunging, size 22 to 18, depending on the thickness of the gold.

Only plunge one metal thread at a time, each into a new hole.

Determine the 'plunge point' by following the line of the thread carefully to the end of the line where you want it to disappear – it shouldn't waver off to one side.

If necessary, create an extra stitch closer to the plunge point to hold the couching more securely – particularly if the brick pattern leaves a large gap.

If the couching sits against another shape that overlaps it, make sure that the plunge points allow you to still see the outline of that shape clearly so that it will not be forced off course later.

1 Take the needle through the fabric at the plunge point once without threading it, to create a pilot hole. Then, thread the very tip of the gold into the needle and take the needle down again into the same hole, taking the gold through.

2 OR: Take the needle through at the plunge point and then thread the needle with a loop of strong thread. Take the needle through so that only a little loop of thread shows. Pass the very tip of the gold through this loop, and pull the loop to carry the gold through.

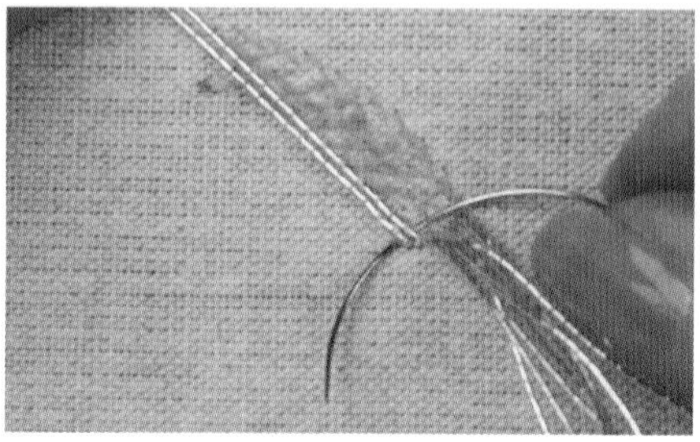

3 To fasten off the gold threads on the back, first position a pair of gold threads over the back of the worked stitches. Start a double waxed thread by catching into the fabric on the back. It is useful to have a curved needle for this, but it is possible with a straight needle.

4 Work an overcast stitch over the pair of threads, catching the needle into the back of the stitches and the fabric. Make sure the needle doesn't pass to the front.

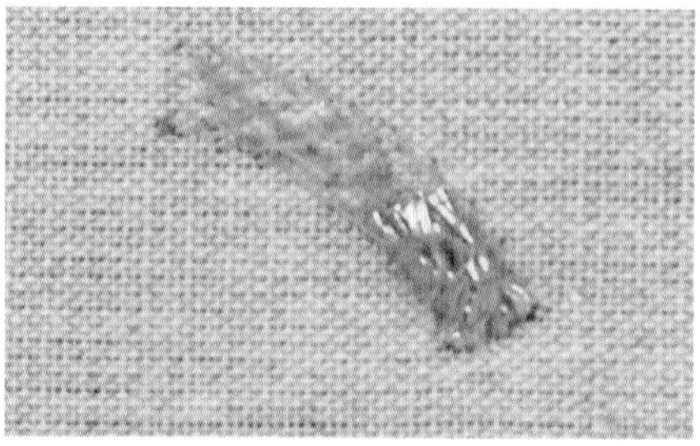

5 Continue to overcast for about 10mm (3/8in), then go back over a few stitches to secure the thread. Cut the sewing thread, and then trim the gold short. Repeat for any other gold threads. When there are lots of threads, tie back four at a time if necessary.

Notes

Larger twists, cords and braids may have to be separated before plunging. Unravel the strands of gold or thread to the plunge point, and try to take each strand into a separate but nearby hole wherever possible.

Curved needles take some getting used to, but with a little practice they make the process of tying back the threads much easier, and cause less strain on the fabric.

TURNING CORNERS

There are various methods for turning corners; which one you choose depends on the shape you are filling.

Some corners will require only turning the threads, others will mean some threads need to be plunged.

RIGHT ANGLE (OR OBTUSE) CORNERS

Use this method for any corner that is a right angle, or an obtuse (wide) angle. No threads are plunged in the corners for this technique.

1 Bring the needle up in the corner between the two gold threads. Leaving the inner one out of the way, fold the outer thread fairly hard against the sewing thread, and then make a diagonal stitch over the outer thread at the corner.

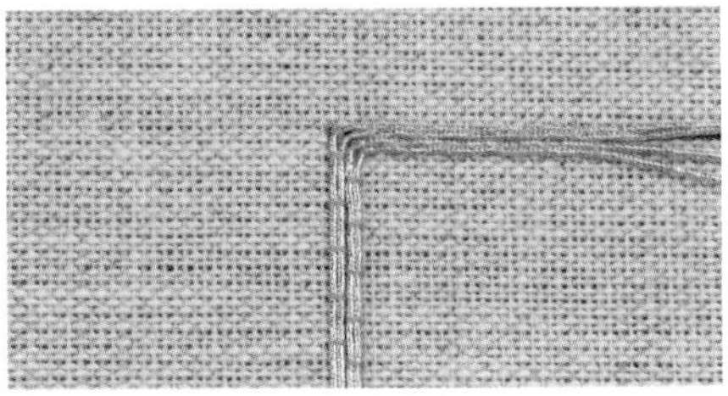

2 Repeat the same method for the inner thread, bringing the needle up inside it to create the bend. If the corner is very close to the last couching stitch, manipulate the inner thread into place and make the next couching stitch close to the corner.

ACUTE CORNERS

Use this method for corners that are less than a right angle, but not particularly tight.

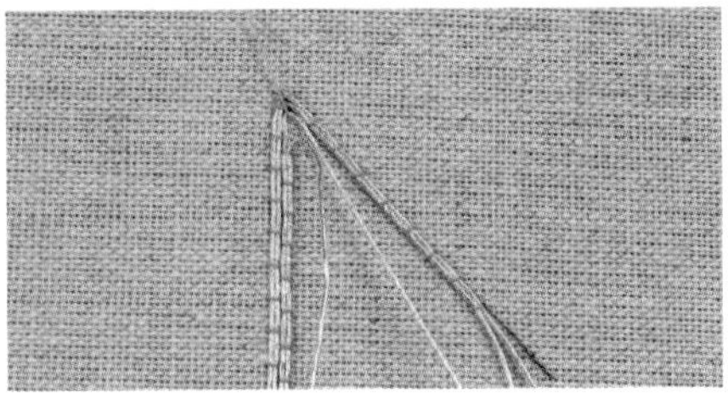

1 Bring the needle up in the corner between the two gold threads. Leaving the inner one out of the way, fold the outer thread quite hard against the sewing thread, and then make a diagonal stitch over the outer thread at the corner.

2 Make a stitch over the outer thread very close to the corner, taking in both sides of the corner. This stitch preserves the alignment of the outer thread.

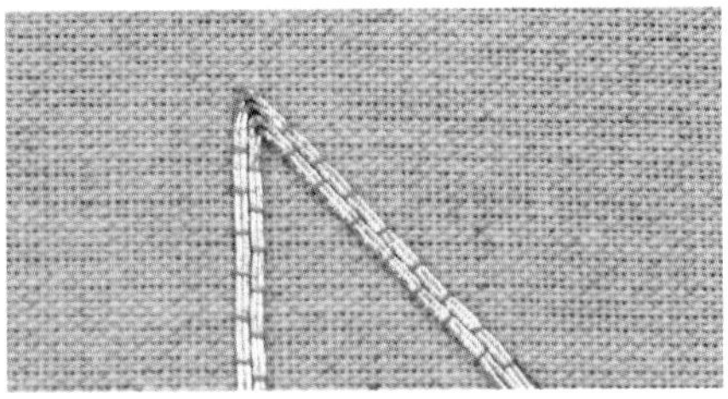

3 Turn the inner thread with a diagonal stitch into the corner, folding it tightly against the sewing thread.

VERY ACUTE CORNERS

Use this method for corners that are much less than a right angle, leaving particularly tight spaces.

In this method, some of the gold threads must be plunged into the corner as there is not enough space to turn them without fabric showing between the rows.

If possible, turn the outer thread without plunging to get the neatest outline. After that, all the threads may be plunged, or rows may be turned and plunged alternately.

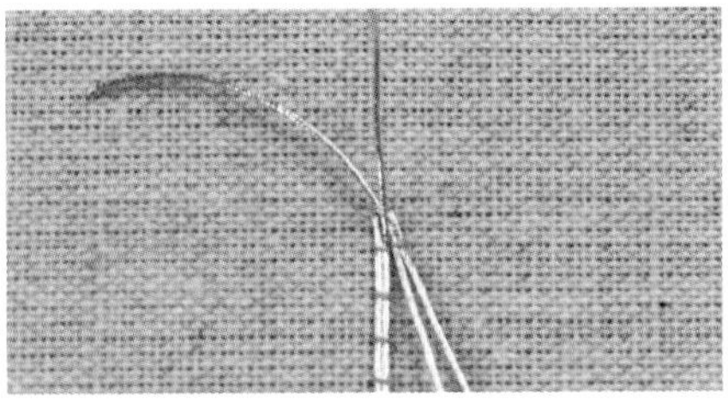

1 Turn the outer thread as for an acute corner, with a diagonal stitch. Cut the inner thread ready for plunging, with at least 50mm (2in) excess. Start a new thread to continue around the corner in a pair.

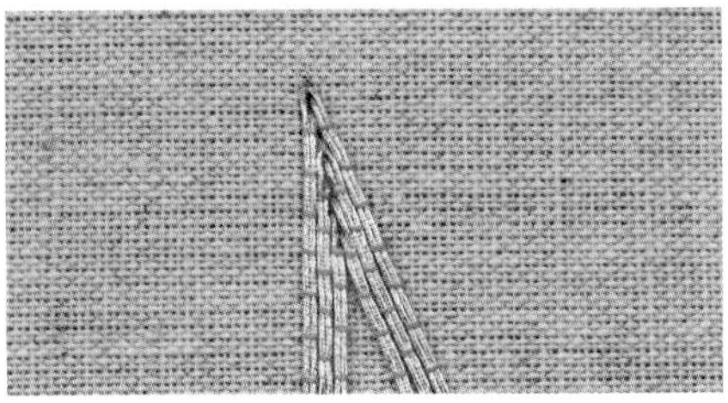

2 Continue to stitch more rows of couching. Plunge the inner threads in a stepped pattern, one at a time, starting from the outside. Plunge as close to the corner as possible and tie the threads back.

COUCHING IN A CIRCLE

Couching in a circle should almost always begin on the outside edge. This is because the most important shape in this case is the outline.

The same is true for most geometric shapes, but a circle presents particular challenges because there are no corners.

Usually a brick pattern is the best because it is the most robust, but the design may require something different.

Generally, a pair of gold threads should be used, but if using a thick gold thread, couch a circle with a single thread for accuracy.

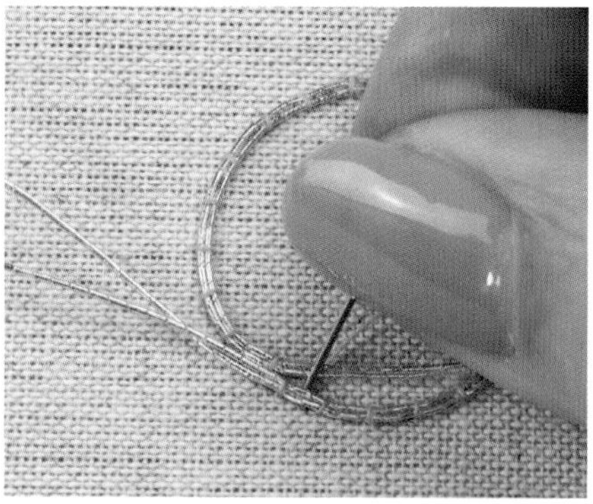

1 Begin with a row on the outline of the circle. Place the stitches 5mm (3/16in) apart. Once you reach the beginning again, bring the needle up with just enough space for the gold threads, and tuck the needle under the previous row, as for basic couching.

2 For the most robust surface, maintain the brick pattern as far as possible towards the centre of the circle. In the very centre, finish off with just a single gold thread.

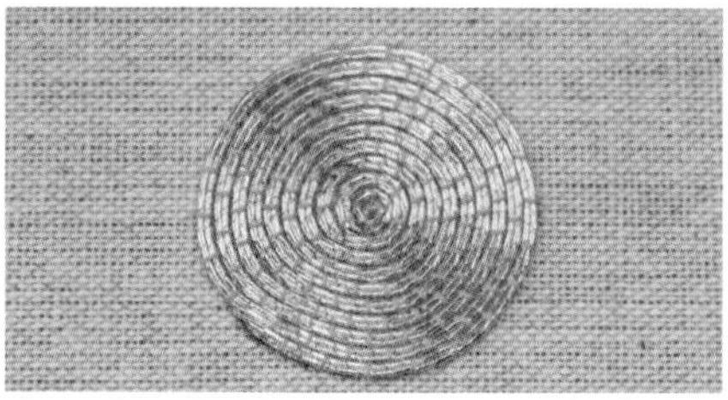

3 Plunge the threads in the middle, filling as much space as possible. On the outer edge, plunge the threads in a staggered manner so as to create the smoothest possible edge.

4 Tie back the ends with overcasting stitches on to the back of the worked area. Stitch down at least 10mm (3/8in), and then trim the ends away neatly.

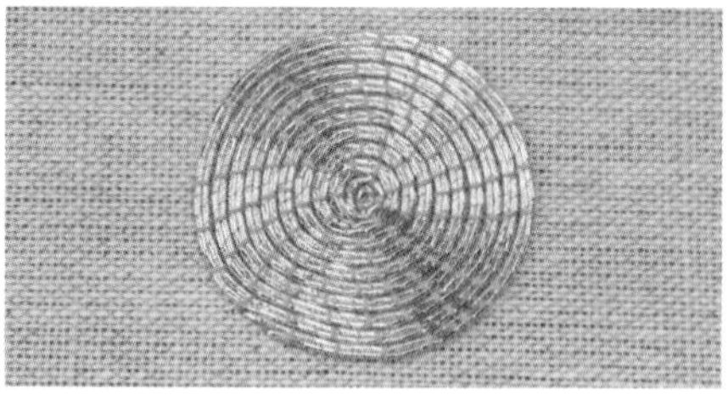

As an alternative, instead of a brick pattern, try lining up the stitches to make a decorative pattern. This can be a very useful effect in some designs, drawing the eye towards the centre of the circle.

FILLING SHAPES

A lot of the time, starting on the outside of the shape and working towards the middle gives the neatest effect; however, this is not always the most visually interesting method of couching.

Before you start a project, consider whether you can add directional flow or interest to a design through the pattern of the couching.

STARTING IN THE CENTRE

Rather than starting at the edge, consider starting in the centre of a shape.

Starting in the centre can be very useful for uneven shapes, and can allow you to choose one or more focal points in the design.

Shape stitched starting at a focal point.

DIRECTIONAL LINES

By establishing a particular directional line, you can add to the flow of a design. Directional lines were traditionally used to enhance the musculature of beasts on family crests, and the same principle applies to modern goldwork.

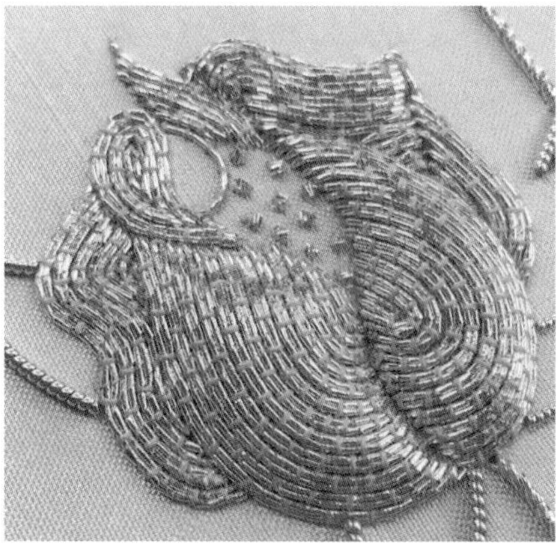

Each rose petal is couched with Japanese thread so that the directional lines enhance the design.

Sometimes the best way to construct the couching is to choose a variety of directional lines and work them together to create texture and light play in the design.

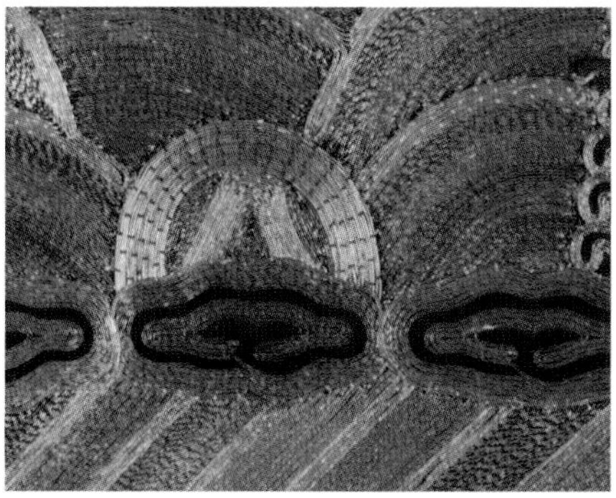

In this example, silver Japanese thread is couched with simple bricked stitches, but the sweeping curves contrast with the straight lines to add an extra dimension.

COMBINATION COUCHING

A really good way to encourage light play across the surface of a design is to use a variety of different threads within a couched area. This is known as 'combination couching'.

All the couching threads are suitable for use in combination couching, but Japanese thread, smooth passing, check thread, rococco and twist are the most typical components.

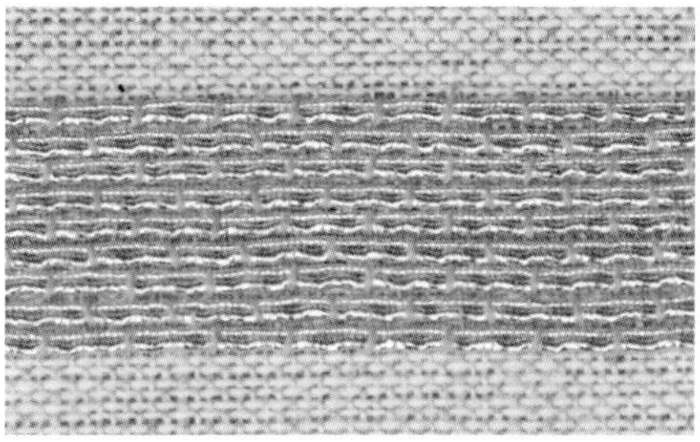

Threads may be worked in pairs; it usually helps if they are similar in size, if not in texture. In this example, smooth passing No. 4 and 8 x 2 check thread are stitched together. It works well because they are similar in width and sit comfortably side by side.

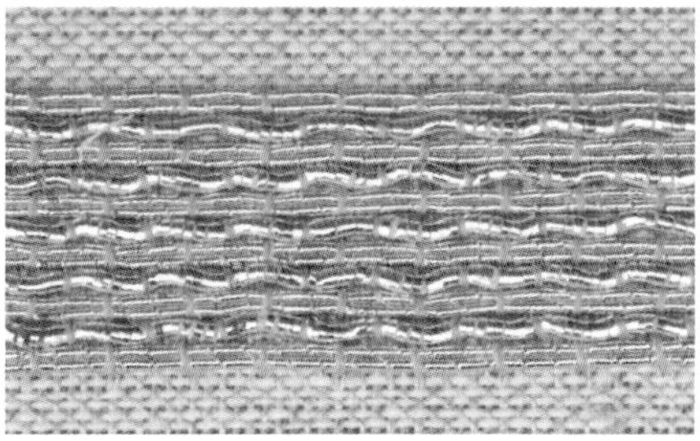

Other threads are better worked as alternating rows to create a pattern. Here, Japanese thread (K4) is stitched in pairs, with a single line of medium rococco every other row. The rococco is much thicker than the Japanese thread, creating a more obvious texture.

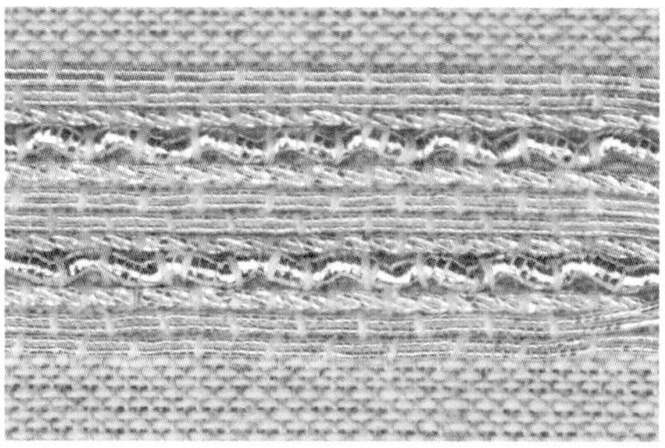

Try many different combinations to work out what best suits your design. Here the pattern is more complex: a row of paired smooth passing No. 4, then a row of 1½ twist, then large rococco, then twist, then smooth passing again, and so on.

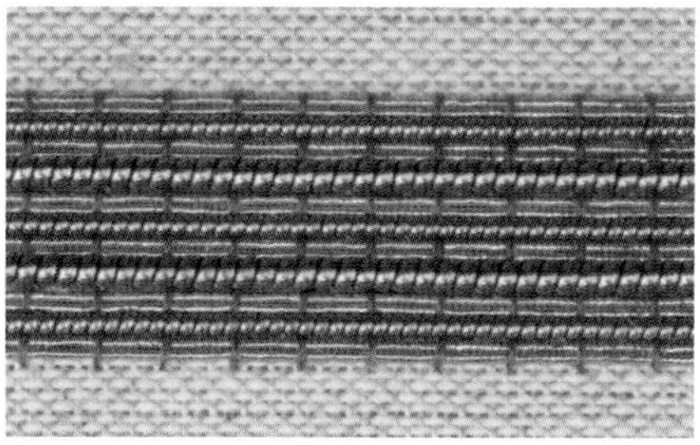

Incorporate pearl purl for a different texture. In this example, smooth passing No. 4 is alternated with pearl purl No. 2 and super pearl purl.

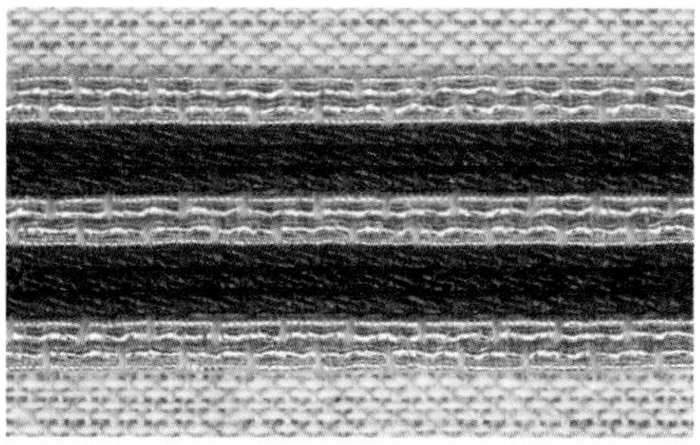

Add different coloured metal threads for even more variation. Here, smooth passing No. 4 and 8 x 2 check thread are stitched together, then the same back-to-back, then 1½ twist in red, and then burgundy; then the pattern is reversed.

COLOURED COUCHING

Coloured couching is a brilliant way to bring colour into a goldwork design. Use stranded cotton, silk or rayon threads.

DIAPER PATTERNS

Diaper patterns diverge from the usual brick pattern of stitches.

On a small scale, the stitch pattern may be enough to secure the gold. On a larger pattern, it may be necessary to create the pattern with a contrasting colour and supplement the main stitching with extra stitches in a thread to match the metal.

In this example, the diagonal pattern of the stitches is enough to secure the metal because the stitches are still sufficiently close together. Therefore, the thread can match the metal to give a subtle effect.

This pattern is created with a contrasting thread, with extra stitches in gold to keep the metal secure. The dominant pattern is bold, but the stitches are still arranged in a brick pattern for security.

ITALIAN COUCHING

Italian couching involves the use of coloured threads (historically silks) to add patterns or shading to an area of couching. The metal threads follow the directional flow or contours of the couched area, with each coloured stitch sitting at a right angle to the metal.

Shading is achieved by the density of the coloured stitches, which might be anything from 5mm ($^1/_4$in) apart, to right next to each other with no metal showing. It may be worked flat or over padding, depending on what the design requires.

The design is either worked from an illustration, or first painted on to the fabric or padding, with all the details of colour and shading. This is then copied with the stitches on the couching threads as the design is filled.

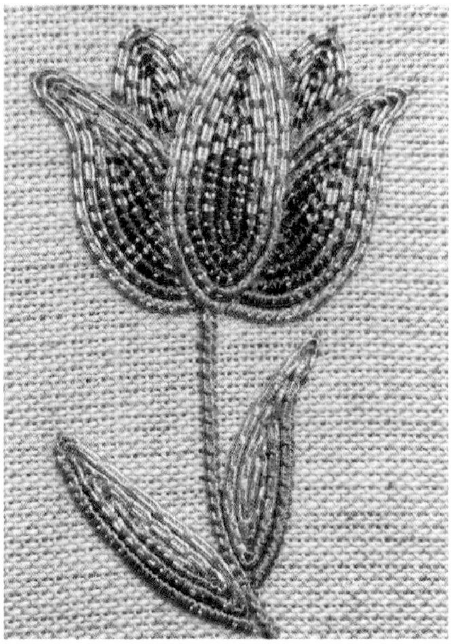

A design worked with Italian couching. Note that there is only a limited palette of colours, and the shading is created by varying the density of the stitches.

OR NUÉ

Like Italian couching, Or Nué involves coloured threads. The first important thing to note is that in Or Nué all the metal threads are laid horizontally, and a great deal of the metal thread is eventually covered with stitches.

Or Nué uses a range of tones in each colour to create shading, allowing for extremely realistic depictions of drapery in Renaissance embroideries.

Or Nué should be worked with no padding, and for traditionalists the gold should be turned at the end of each row.

Each stitch must lie at a right angle to the gold threads, and parallel with its neighbours to give a perfectly neat appearance.

The design is first painted on to the fabric, with all the details of colour and shading. This is then copied, row by row, with the stitches.

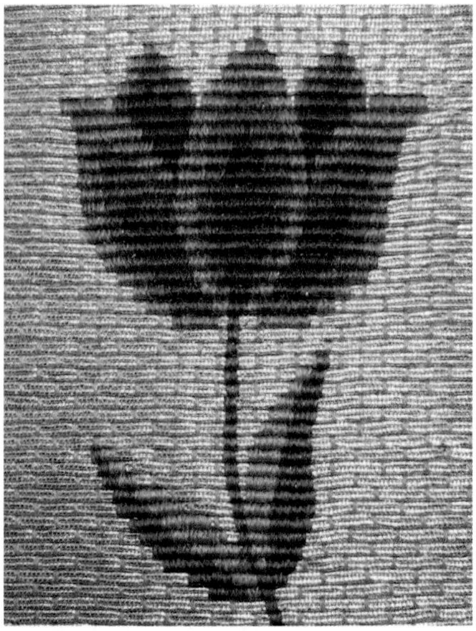

A design worked with Or Nué. Within each hue, a range of tones is used to create depth. The trick with Or Nué is to keep the rows perfectly evenly spaced and close together so that no fabric shows in unshaded areas.

BASKET-WEAVE COUCHING

Basket-weave couching gives a beautiful texture, and can be worked with all sorts of patterns. It is traditionally stitched with either Japanese thread or smooth passing, but do experiment with other threads if you like.

To prepare for basket-weave couching, first stitch hard string padding over the area. Traditionally, basket-weave is worked in straight lines across the shape, so it is always a good idea to start in the middle of the shape, at the widest point.

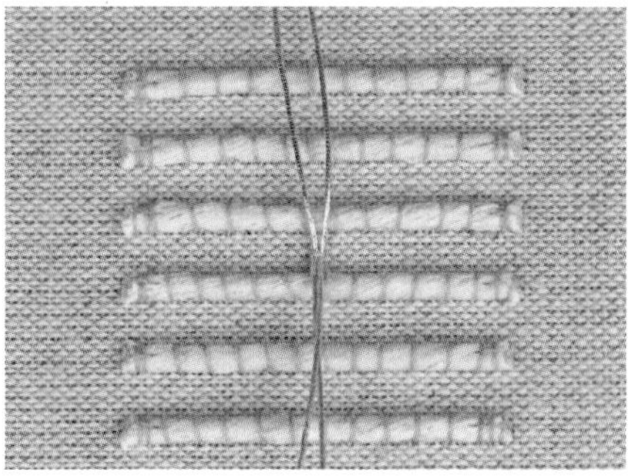

1 Bring the needle up exactly halfway between two strings. Lay a pair of gold threads at right angles to the string and make a stitch over the pair as you would for basic couching. Pull tight so that the gold falls between the strings.

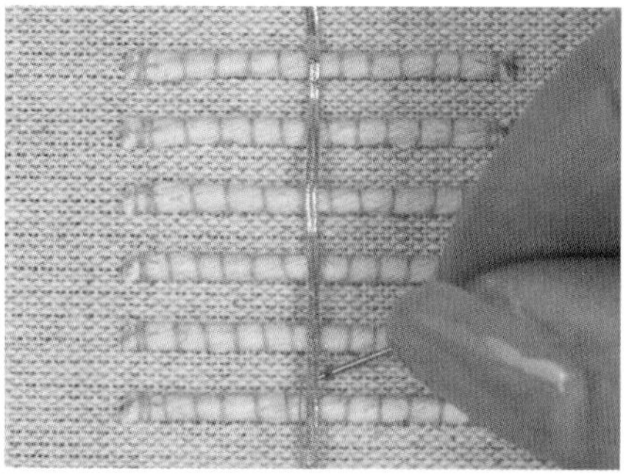

2 Carry the gold threads over the strings, holding them taut. Skip two strings and make another stitch. Remember to pull it tight so that the gold falls between the strings. Repeat this all the way to the end, and then go back to the middle to complete the row.

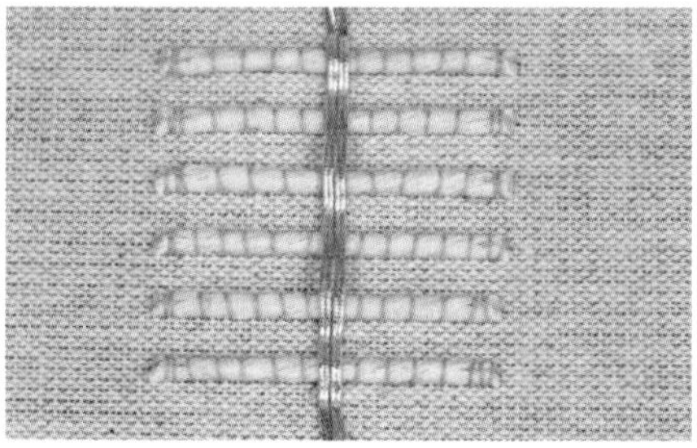

3 Traditionally, the pattern is made from blocks of two pairs stitched the same. Stitch another row the same, right next to the original row. This time you can work from end to end, just be careful to keep the line straight and very close to the first row so that no string or fabric shows through.

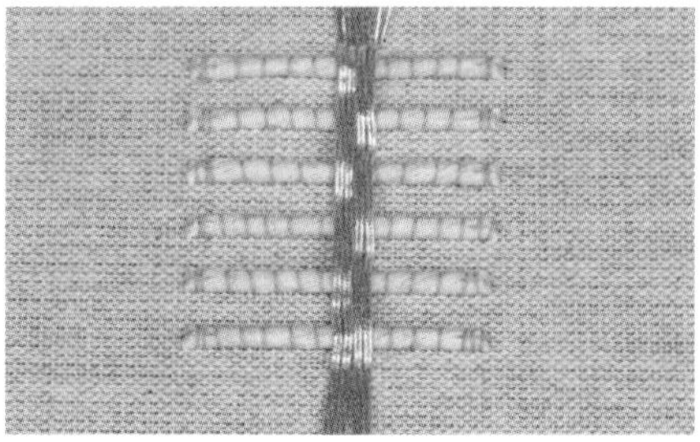

4 To continue the pattern, make the next row alternating with the first. It is more difficult to keep the row straight, so if it proves to be a problem, start in the middle of the row. On each row there should be a stitch on the outside of the last string to secure the gold.

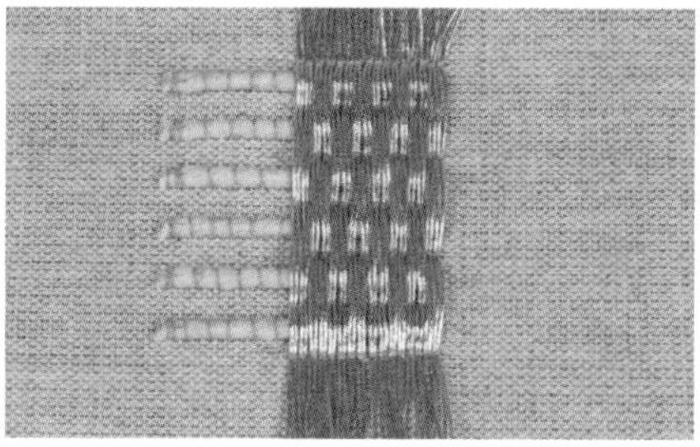

5 Continue to lay rows next to one another until the shape is completely filled. The last row is often the trickiest because the gold can try to fall off the end of the string: make sure that it is completely straight, and hold it at very good tension.

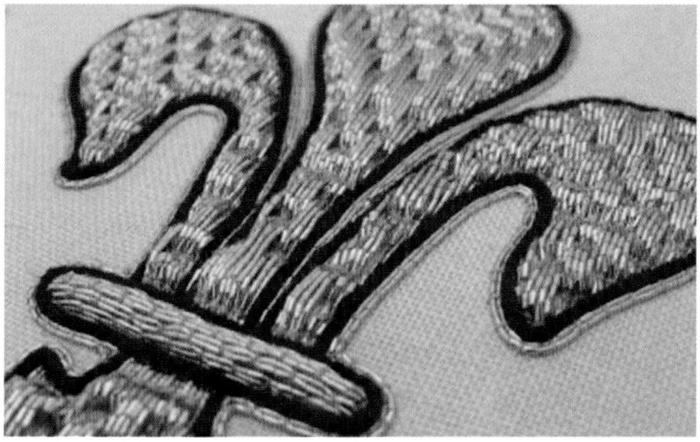

A fleur-de-lys worked in patterned basket-weave with outlines of red cord and Japanese couching. This is one motif of three from an ecclesiastical basic goldwork sampler. Worked by the author in the first year of her Royal School of Needlework apprenticeship, 2007.

Note

Make a holding stitch (a small 'up, then down close by' with the sewing thread) between couching stitches to keep the tension whenever you feel it necessary.

COUCHING OVER CARD

Though this method is referred to as 'couching over card', it is really better done over stiff interfacing, because that will wear better and it can be dyed/coloured to match the metal threads.

Couching in this way can add defined shapes into an area of plain, straight couching done with plain threads. It can be used on its own to create a design, or incorporated into a design with mixed techniques.

First, apply any overall felt padding to the design, and then apply the interfacing shapes over the top.

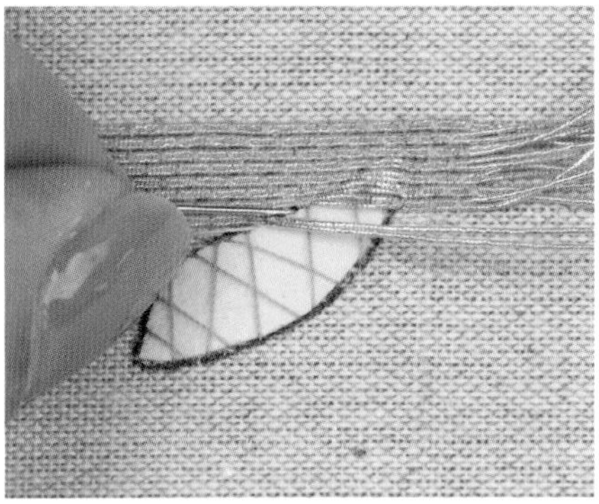

1 Couch the background as usual, with a brick pattern over pairs of gold threads. Using a contrasting thread will give extra definition to the design. At the edge of the interfacing, place a stitch as close as possible to the edge, following the angle of the shape.

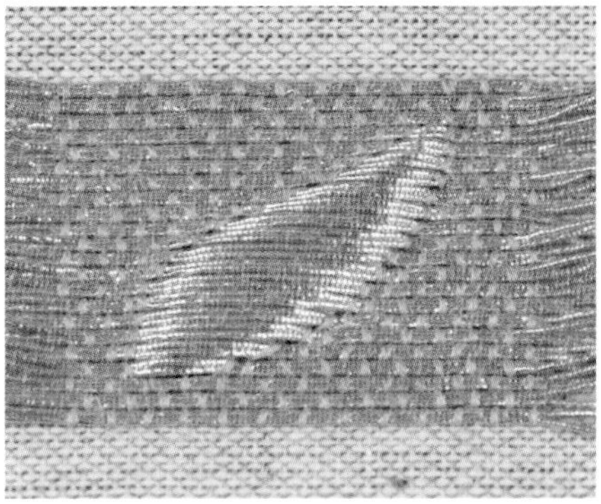

2 Carry the gold threads over the interfacing with no stitches, and then make a stitch as close as possible to the edge on the opposite side. It is important to keep a straight line over the card, because there are no stitches to hold it securely in a curve.

Three ecclesiastical symbols: the pomegranate, crown and the fleur-de-lys. Stitched by the author during her first year on the Royal School of Needlework apprenticeship. Techniques used include basic couching, Elizabethan twist, basket-weave couching, invisibly couched twist and cord, cutwork, chipping, s-ing and silkwork.

COUCHING TWIST INVISIBLY

Twist may be couched in pairs or singly in the same way as any of the other core threads (basic couching), but sometimes it is useful to couch it invisibly.

If the twist is to be seen on its own, for example as an outline or tendril, it is subtler to use this method.

The same process may be used to attach a cord (whether gold or another type of thread), which can look very nice combined with goldwork.

Use a single waxed sewing thread to couch twist in this way.

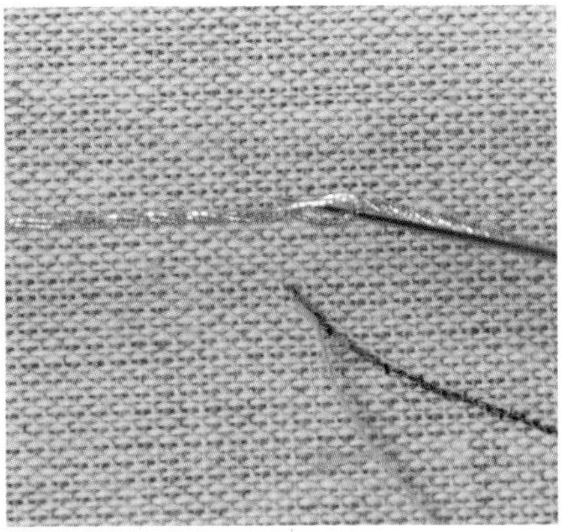

1 After casting on, bring the needle up close to the start of the line. Leaving at least a 50mm (2in) tail for plunging, pass the needle through the twist, under the top two strands and over the bottom one.

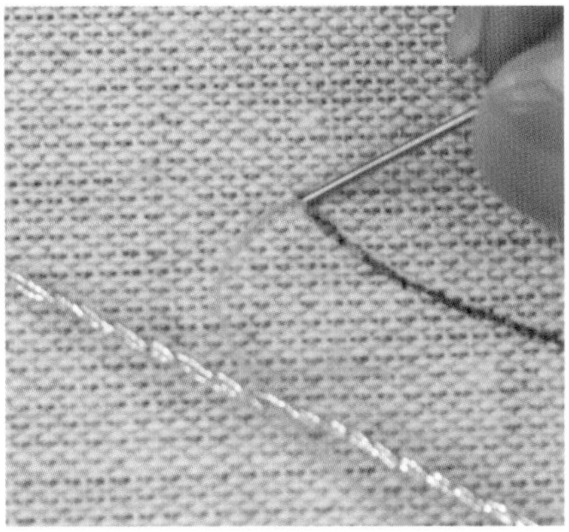

2 To complete the attachment, take the needle down very close to the starting point in the ground fabric, resulting in a tiny stitch. Once pulled tight this stitch should be invisible.

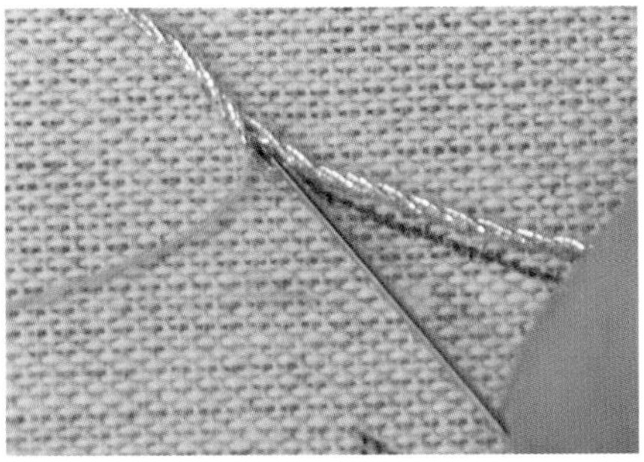

3 Lay the twist along the line and bring the needle up on the line about 4mm (1/8in) from the first stitch. Gently unwind the twist a little bit so that you can pass the needle through the twist, angled along the line. Make sure to retwist the gold thread as you complete the stitch.

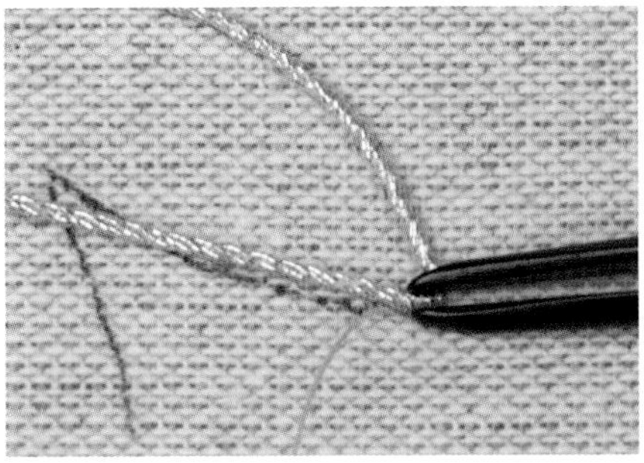

4 When turning a corner, make a stitch as usual right on the turning point. Twist the gold thread more than usual, and manipulate it into shape with a mellor or tweezers. Carefully make the next couching stitch closer than usual, and continue to couch.

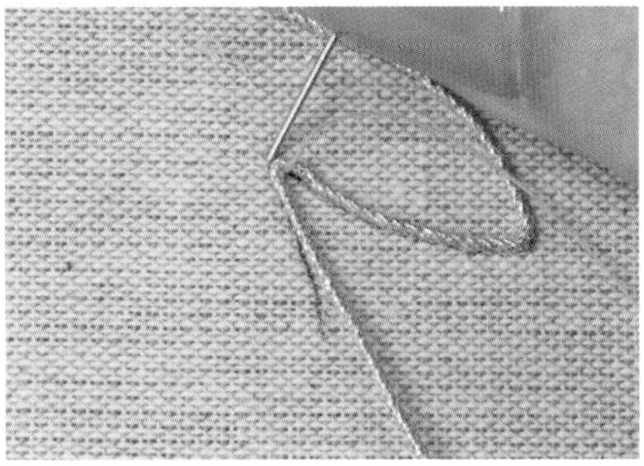

5 If a corner is particularly tight and will not hold its shape well, place a stitch right in the corner over all three strands (a normal couching stitch). Note that this stitch will be visible.

A traditional pomegranate design stitched by the author at the Royal School of Needlework as part of an ecclesiastical goldwork sampler. This design features basic couching, invisibly couched twist and Elizabethan twist.

Detail of the Elizabethan twist on the ecclesiastical pomegranate embroidery.

ELIZABETHAN TWIST

Elizabethan twist is a very fine two-ply twist. It may be couched in the usual way, but used like that it is best reserved for the outlining of small details.

More often, it is used in a completely different way to the other threads in this section. Rather than couching at regular intervals along the thread, this method involves stitches placed at either side of the area and on any design line through the centre. For the gold to be sufficiently secure, these should be no more than 6mm ($^1/_4$in) apart, so make sure to plan the design carefully.

Use a contrasting stitching thread for this technique to get the most dramatic appearance.

To make it seamless, measure the amount of gold needed and start couching halfway along the thread. Once complete, the ends should be plunged neatly.

Areas of Elizabethan couching are often outlined with a larger gold thread to match them in better with other types of gold. This can be useful in a design with mixed techniques.

The same technique may be worked over padding – in such cases this side-to-side couching is otherwise known as 'strapping' the gold.

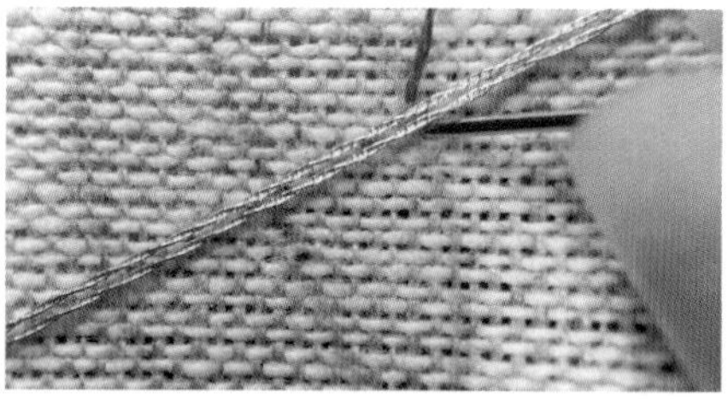

1 Begin partway along one side of the shape (the widest point is the best place). Place a pair of gold threads so that they sit at right angles to the shape. Bring the needle up on the outline, and down again on the outline, catching the gold in a small stitch.

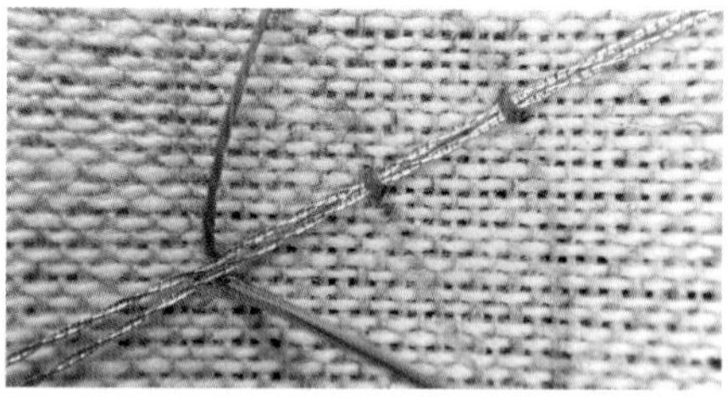

2 Holding the gold taut, make another stitch at right angles to the gold on the next design line, with no stitches between. Repeat to the other side of the shape, finishing on the outline.

3 Turn the threads tightly and make another stitch on the outline to secure. There should be no stitch on the turn itself.

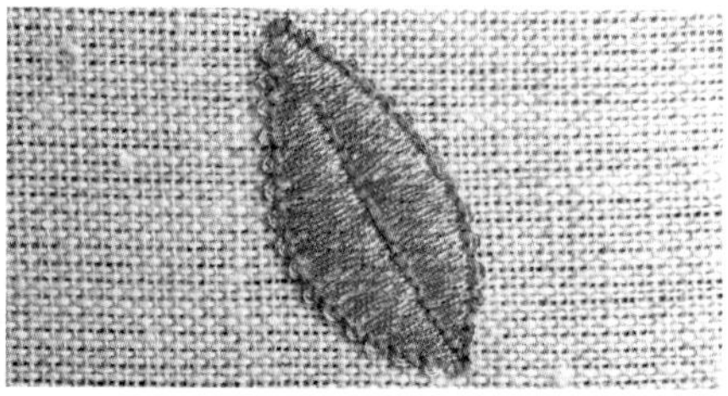

4 Continue to stitch, following the pattern. All the stitches should be at right angles to the gold, and the gold should sit parallel and very close together. Once the first half is finished, start again in the middle to stitch the rest.

UNDERSIDE COUCHING

This type of couching is what you see in the famous Opus Anglicanum (English work) of medieval Britain. It was often worked as the background of garments that would drape, such as copes. This manner of stitching gave great flexibility compared with standard couching.

For a background, metal threads are usually laid in vertical lines along the warp of a strong linen ground. A pliable gold thread that is roughly the same thickness as a thread of the linen must be used: smooth passing is a good choice.

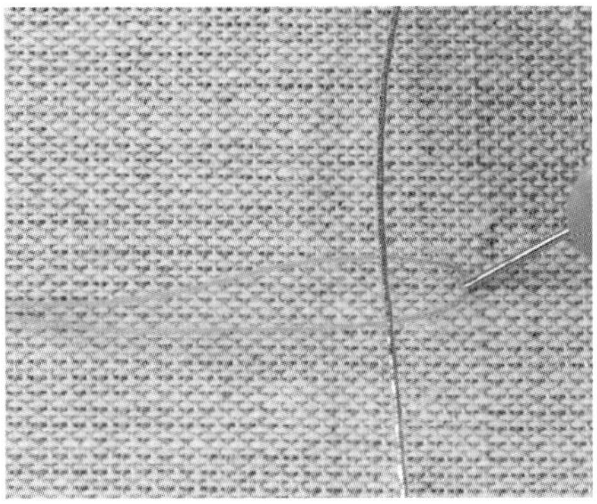

1 Use a double waxed sewing thread, or a single extra-strong thread. Bring the needle up through a hole in the linen (use a small tapestry needle), and take it back down through the same hole, catching one gold thread underneath.

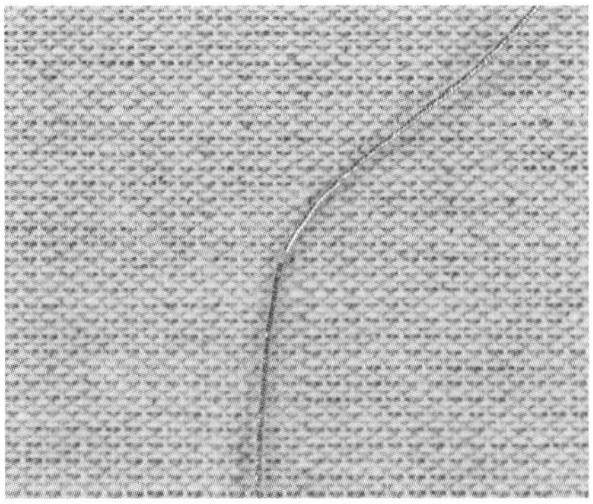

2 Holding the gold thread in place, pull the stitch closed so there is only a small loop of the stitching thread on the surface.

3 Pull sharply on the stitching thread. A small loop of gold thread should pass through to the back. Continue to couch, making a stitch every 5mm ($^{3}/_{16}$in).

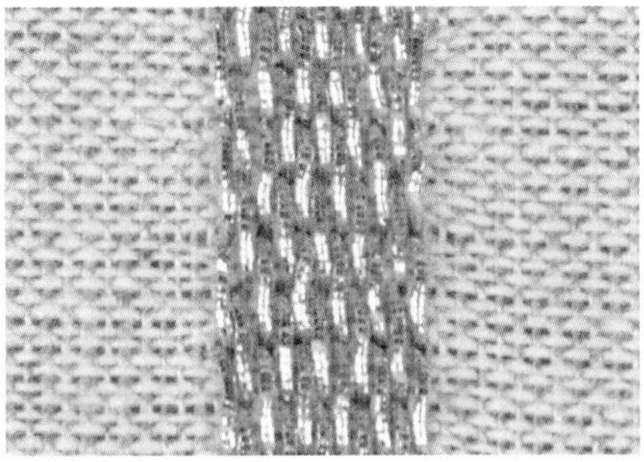

4 For each subsequent row, alternate the stitches in a brick pattern as you would for basic couching.

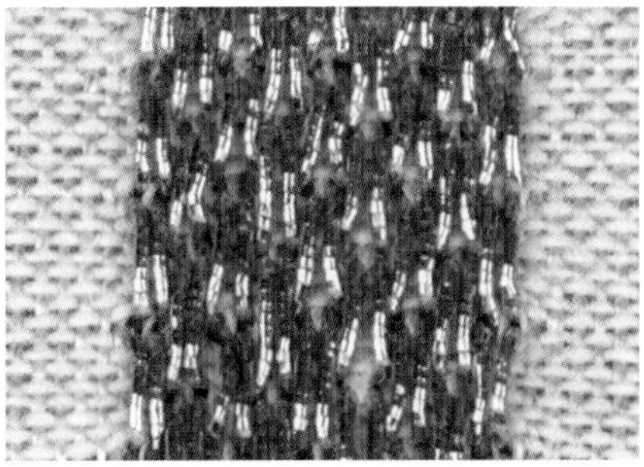

Underside couching may be stitched with diaper patterns, to create subtle texture in the area.

Underside couching may also be used within the design. The method of stitching is the same, but the gold may be stitched along a curve, in single rows, or to cover areas.

It was traditionally used to highlight the folds on the draped garments on figures stitched with split stitch or silk shading, or to add a rich gold trim to an important figure's cloak.

Where backgrounds remained unstitched, silk was often laid over the linen to give an overall colour (be it plain or textured, such as damask). This adds a level of challenge to the technique, but means that a design can be worked in underside couching to great effect, with no need to stitch a whole background. This must have saved a lot of time and a great volume of the precious metal.

When stitching underside couching in curves and amongst other types of stitching or through two fabrics, you must be very careful to ensure the gold does pass through a hole in the ground fabric and create the loop on the back; this is more difficult when there is other stitching involved.

PEARL PURL/ LIZERINE

Pearl purl and lizerine are made as a tight coil of wire with no core thread, which means that when couched they sit on the surface of the fabric without the need for plunging. This makes them ideally suited for outlines, or design lines such as tendrils, which extend into the background fabric.

These threads are the perfect border for an area of chipping, as they sit fairly proud, giving a neat finish to the edge.

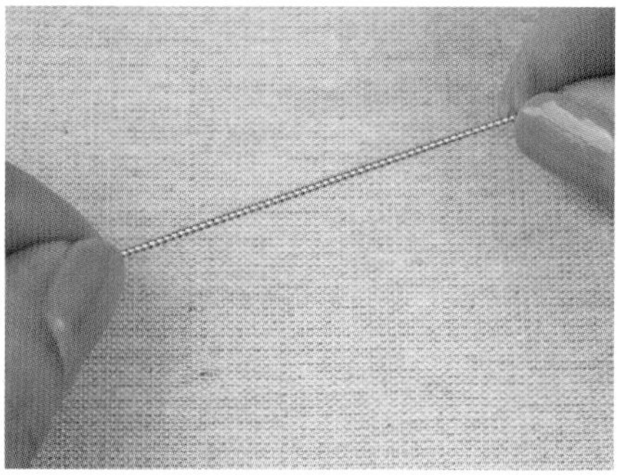

To stretch pearl purl, pinch both ends between finger and thumb (or use tweezers to grip). Pull very gently on the purl, repeating in a sort of bouncing motion. When it is sufficiently stretched, you can feel it relax slightly, as if it is no longer springing back.

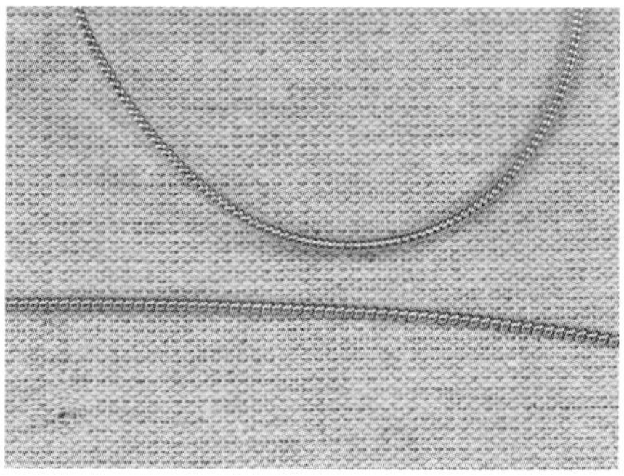

It will look slightly different too – rather than naturally curling up in a spiral it should lie reasonably straight, as shown above. Make sure to cut the end neatly before you stitch it down.

Pearl purl once stitched is a very robust wire that will keep its beautiful shine and enhance many designs. However, during the stitching process it can be kinked or dented by handling or by mistaken stitches.

If you need to unpick any stitching, do so very gently to avoid having to start again. With practice this is not much of a problem, but to start with do take extra care.

Make sure that you complete the line of pearl purl you are stitching before moving your frame around, as pearl purl can be damaged if it is part stitched.

Due to the way they are manufactured, these wires are very tightly coiled and so are quite springy. They must be stretched before stitching.

This monogram embroidery makes use of different sizes of pearl purl within the design, and incorporates overstretched pearl purl with coloured thread, chipping, couched Japanese thread and surface embroidery.

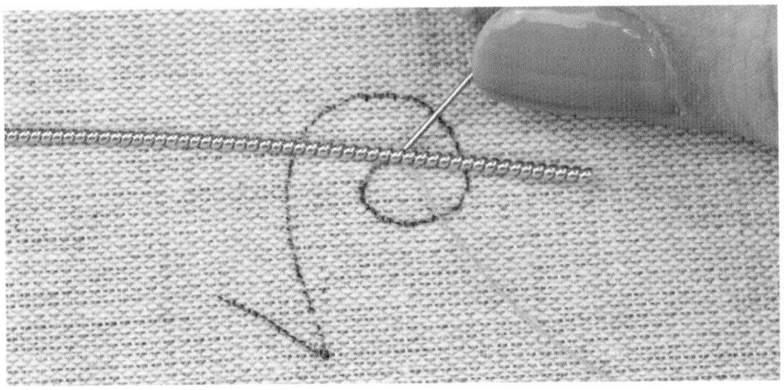

1 Use a single waxed thread. To start a length of pearl purl, bring the needle up on the design line about 2mm ($^1/_{16}$in) from the start. Lay the pearl purl along the line (but don't worry about lining up the end). Make a small stitch over the purl, at a slight angle to match the coils.

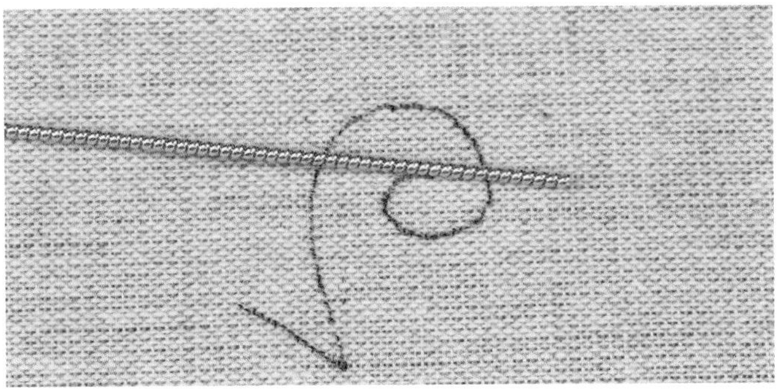

2 Pull the stitch firmly, but not too hard. The stitch should pop through between the coils of wire – the pop is often audible. If you pull too hard, the pearl purl may kink and this cannot be undone, so be careful.

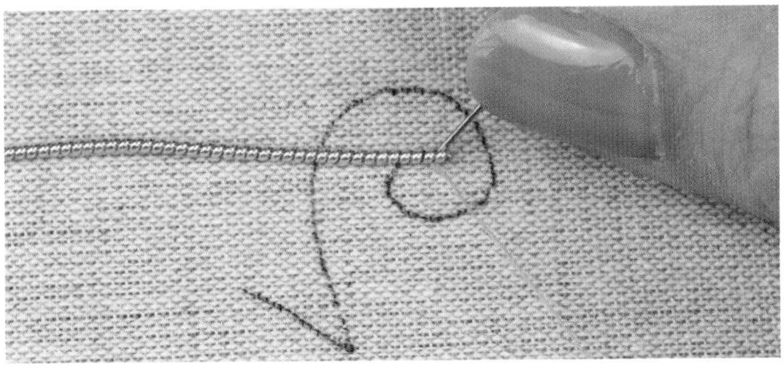

3 Once the first stitch is complete, you can spin the wire so that the end matches exactly with the end of the design line. Make another stitch in the first gap, and one over the cut end if necessary to hold it firmly.

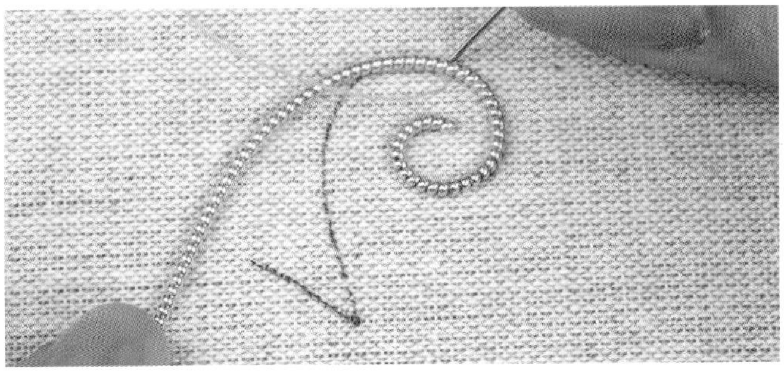

4 Make the next stitch three or four coils along, and repeat this along the line. If the purl needs to follow a tight curve, stitch every one or two coils for accuracy. Encourage the wire to follow the correct course with your fingers and/or a mellor.

5 To turn a corner, bring the needle up on the inside of the purl. Use your fingers to start bending the purl into shape, and then use tweezers to pinch the corner. It is a good idea to bend it a little more than necessary, and then ease it back to the correct angle.

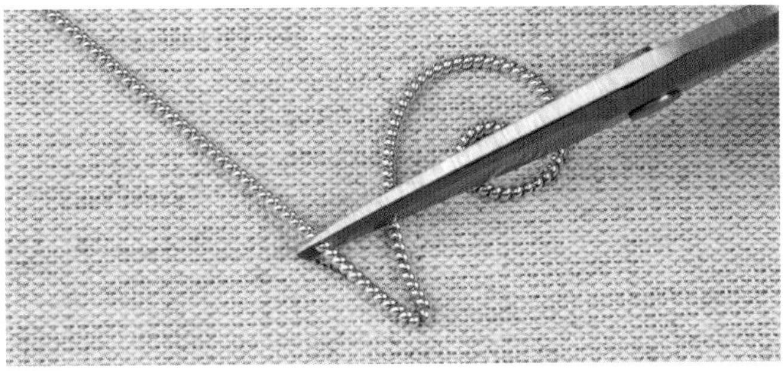

6 To finish pearl purl, first stitch up close to the end of the line – within 10mm ($^3/_8$in). Use a very sharp pair of scissors to cut the purl exactly at the end of the line. Continue to stitch up to the end, finishing with a last stitch over the cut end..

OVERSTRETCHED PEARL PURL

This technique may sound like a mistake, but actually it is a very attractive way of using pearl purl or lizerine. Add a coloured thread within the coil of wire to give a striped, candy-cane effect.

Any size of pearl purl and any type of thread may be used (for example, stranded silk or cotton), as long as the thread passes comfortably within the purl. The smaller sizes of pearl purl are tricky to wind with colour because they bend very easily, so it is best to try with sizes No. 1 and upwards first.

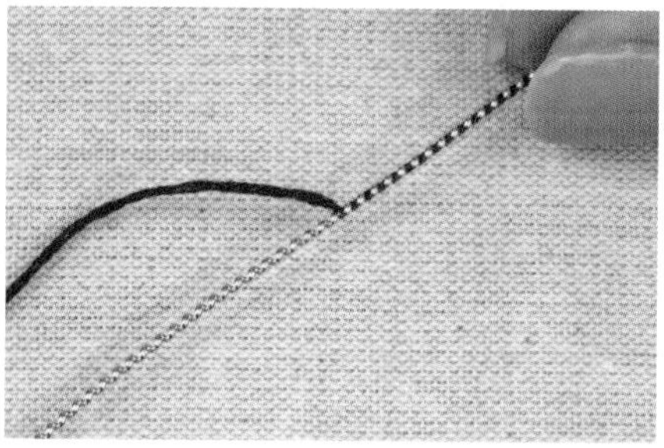

1 First stretch the pearl purl more than usual. How far you stretch is up to you, but it should generally be stretched evenly along its length. Take a length of thread longer than the purl by at least 10cm (4in) and wind the two together, keeping hold of one end.

2 With a matching thread, couch down the purl and thread. Make sure the stitches fall into the gaps, and place the stitches every two or three coils, closer for tight curves. At the end of the line, unwind any excess purl. Cut the purl and plunge the thread at each end.

CREATIVE USES OF PEARL PURL

Because pearl purl (and lizerine) can be cut cleanly with no extra finishing, they are ideal for all sorts of other surface embellishments.

Experiment with different sizes and combinations to achieve all sorts of varied effects for your designs. You can get really creative with these techniques, so these are just a few ideas to spur the imagination. These non-traditional methods can be a good way to use up scraps of metal wires, so be sure to save any odds and ends.

1 Twist two lengths of pearl purl together to form a cord. Fold a length of the metal wire in half and hold the two ends firmly. Use a knitting needle or pencil to twist the looped end, while gently stretching the wire to set the cord.

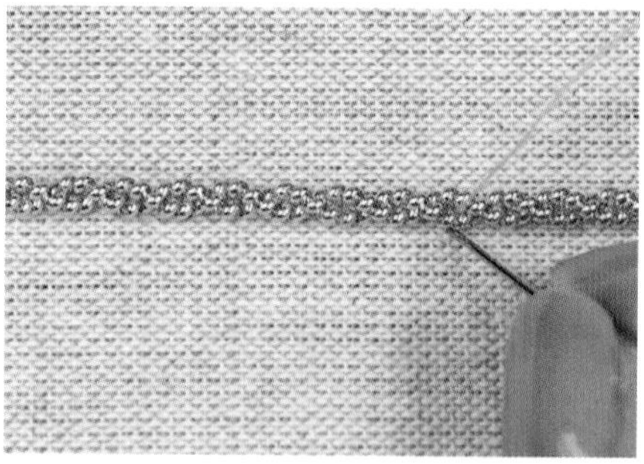

2 Secure the cord with tiny stitches using a single waxed thread, wherever it touches the fabric.

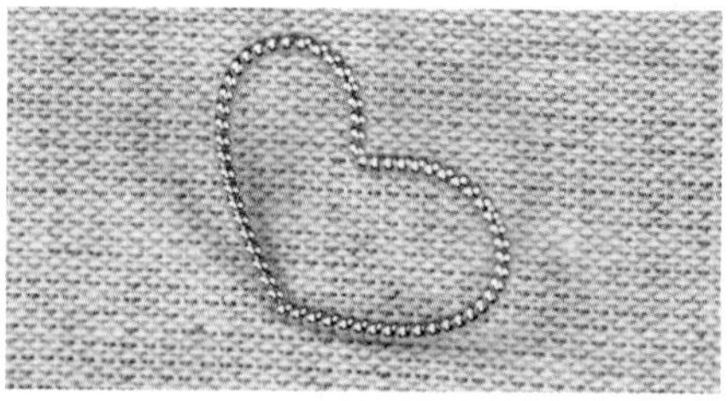

Pass fine beading wire through pearl purl, and manipulate into a shape. Secure with tiny stitches at the base of the shape, and cut the beading wire.

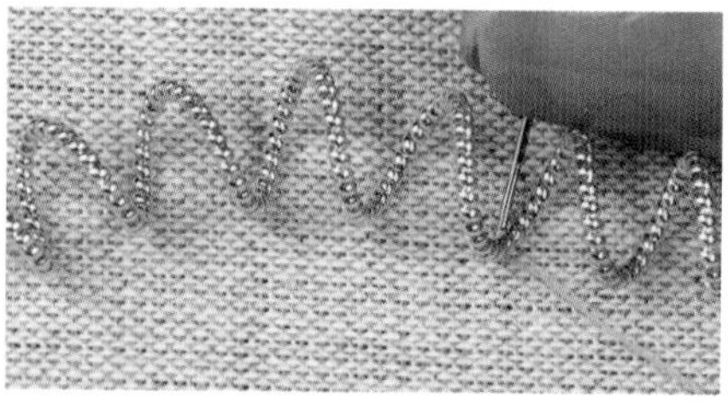

Wind pearl purl around a knitting needle or similar to create a larger coil. Stitch the wire down as it falls with tiny stitches where it touches the fabric. Please note this technique is not very robust.

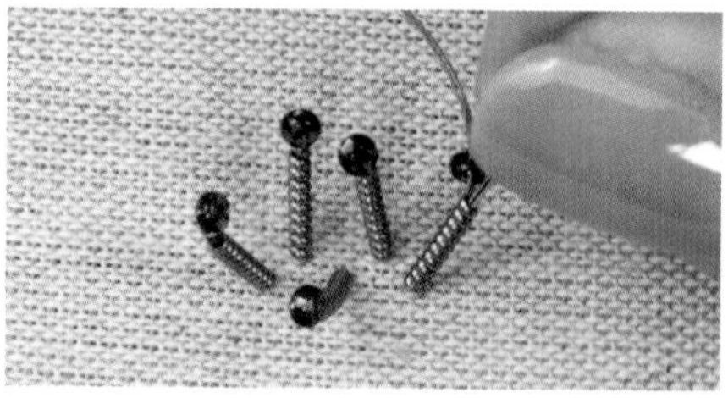

Cut short lengths of pearl purl. Bring the needle up and take it through the length of purl. Pass the needle through a bead, and then back through the purl again. Take the needle into the fabric to make a tiny stitch.

MILLARY WIRE

Millary wire is a combination of a wrapped thread and a stiff wire – like an overstretched pearl purl with a Japanese thread running through the middle, bound together with a thin metal thread. It does not need to be stretched.

Millary wire can be used to add eye-catching texture to a design, and can be a lovely addition to combination couching.

1 Couch over the wire with the stitches falling between the loops of wire and over the metal-wrapped thread inside. The stitches should be very small so that they are not noticeable.

2 At the end of the line, cut the looped wire with a clean end, but plunge the metal-wrapped threads through the fabric with a chenille needle, and tie back neatly.

TRELLIS FILLING

Trellis filling is traditionally a crewelwork stitch, but it can be very effective in goldwork.

Use it to create interest over a large open area. Try the denser version, battlement couching, to create a variety of textures. Experiment with chips of purl on the intersections.

Any of the metal-wrapped threads may be used for a trellis like this, and a combination of threads can be lovely. The finer threads are easier to start with, as they lie reasonably flat – Elizabethan twist or No. 4 smooth passing are good choices. In this example, 1½ twist has been used.

For battlement couching, add further trellises on top of the first, as many as are needed to achieve the desired effect. Try using different types of gold and/or different colours. Hold each layer down with a catching stitch, and try securing the last layer with a chip of purl as an accent.

Because so many threads are plunged, it is useful to reduce the tail to 25mm (1in) to conserve thread, but use longer tails if preferred.

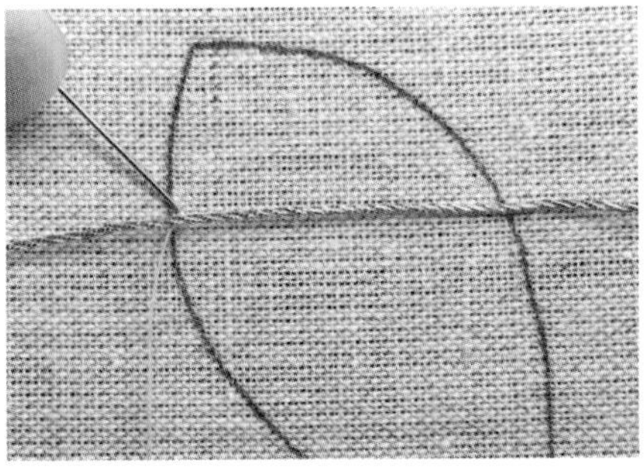

1 Start with two single waxed threads on the go at once – one on either side of the shape, at the widest point. Lay a gold thread taut across the shape, and make a small couching stitch just inside the design line at each end.

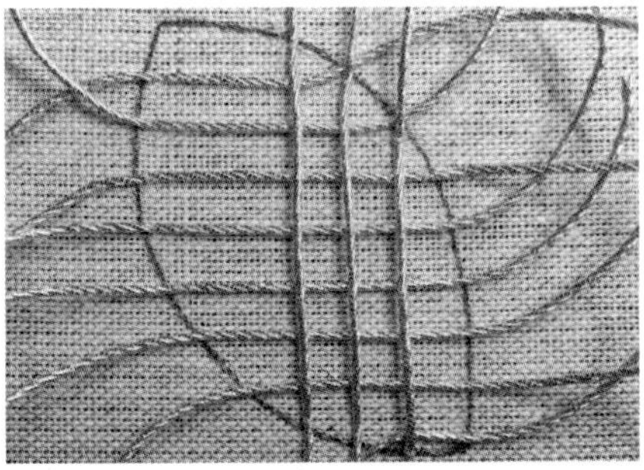

2 Repeat at even intervals across the shape. Add another layer of gold threads, crossing the first to form either squares or diamonds. Cut each one with at least 25mm (1in) for plunging at each end.

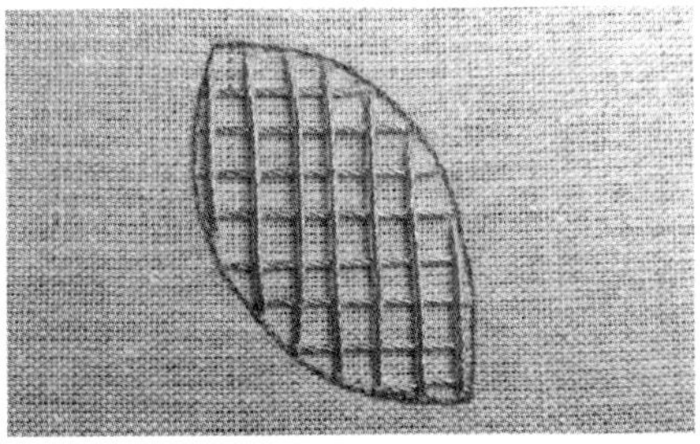

3 Once the trellis is complete, plunge all the ends and tie them back carefully.

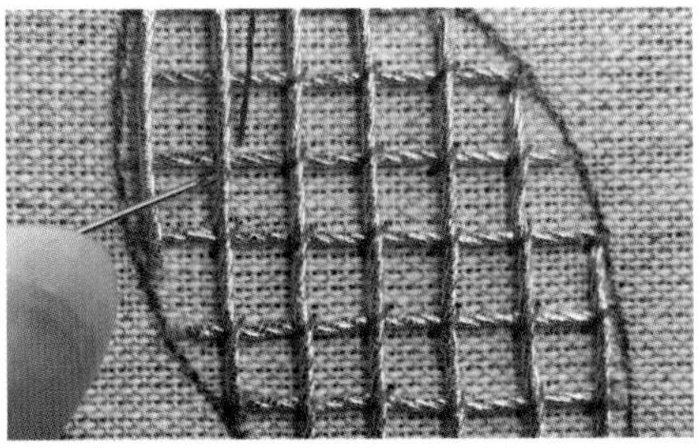

4 Cast on a matching or coloured thread on the edge of the shape. At each intersection of gold, make a small stitch (or two) to form a cross. The stitch should be snug enough to hold the gold securely, but not so much that it pinches the threads and pulls them out of alignment.

CHAPTER 6

CUTWORK

Cutwork is the umbrella term for any goldwork technique using cut purls. It is also the name for a specific technique that is rather like satin stitch but with gold wires.

Bear in mind that cutwork is one of the more fragile techniques while stitching, though it can be quite robust once complete as long as it is stitched correctly. It can be seen on many pieces of antique needlework in fine condition, which shows how well it stands up to damage over time.

The techniques should be worked in the order listed here due to the fragility of the work.

Cut purls can be used in a variety of ways to bring texture to a design and to encourage light play across the surface.

The purl wires used for cutwork cannot be stitched through the fabric – they simply aren't designed for it. They are all made in a similar way, as a coil of very fine wire, and are therefore applied to the surface of the fabric or padding in a similar way to beads – the needle and thread pass through the gold. The pieces of cut gold are known as 'chips'.

These wires are very delicate (at least until they are stitched down) and so should be treated with care and respect.

When cutting the purls, it is a good idea to use a velvet-covered board or beading mat to keep the wires under control – they can be very springy.

If a wire gets dropped on the floor, be careful when retrieving it – if it gets stuck and ends up stretched or kinked, it is rendered useless for traditional work (though it can sometimes be used for more creative pieces).

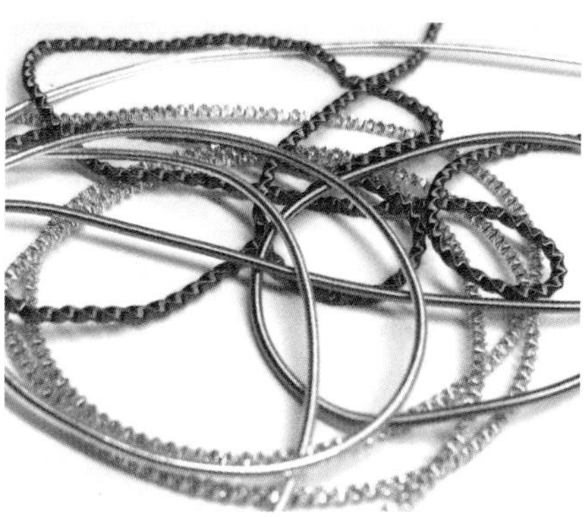

Purl wires: lilac rough purl, silver smooth purl, rust-red wire check and gilt bright check.

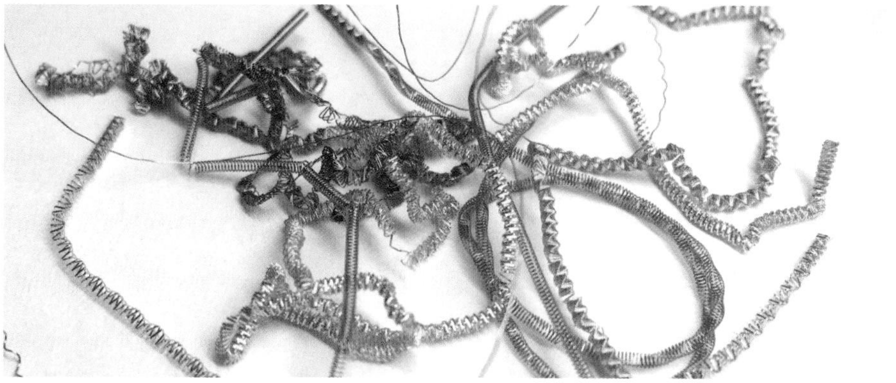

Purl wires of various types that have been damaged either by stretching or breaking, which creates kinks. These can be useful for creative projects so it is worth storing them.

CHIPPING

TRADITIONAL CHIPPING

Chipping is a beautiful technique that lends a lovely sparkle to a design. It is traditionally worked in bright check to give the greatest shine to the surface, but it is equally effective in wire check, or even with smooth or rough purl.

Chipping may be stitched in almost any area – because the pieces of gold are so small they can fit in the smallest and most awkward spaces. A layer of matching felt underneath helps the eye to fill in any tiny gaps between chips with colour, but padding is entirely optional. A border of couched thread helps keep densely packed chips in place within their shape.

Use a double waxed thread in a small embroidery needle, and make sure that this passes comfortably through the gold.

1 On a velvet board, use sharp scissors to cut a few very small pieces of bright check. The pieces, known as 'chips', should be as long as they are wide – like little cubes. Make sure to cut cleanly so there are no stray tags of wire sticking out – the scissors should sit straight across the purl at a right angle to achieve this.

2 Bring the needle up in the middle of the area. Pass the needle through a chip and gently slide the chip down to the surface of the fabric or felt. Take the needle down, making a small stitch – this should be just big enough to allow the chip to sit comfortably flat on the fabric, but not long enough for it to move about. Use a mellor to guide the thread through, avoiding tangles, which may damage the gold wire or cause the chip to stand on end (so that you look down the hole in the middle).

3 Make each subsequent stitch by bringing the needle up a chip's length from the existing chips, and angle the needle back towards the existing chips. Add the chips at random angles as much as possible to achieve the best sparkle and the most consistent surface. Remember to use a mellor to guide the thread down to the fabric. Around the edges, cut chips slightly short if needs be to fill tiny gaps.

SHADED CHIPPING

Chipping doesn't always have to use just one type of purl wire. It can be lovely to shade from bright check to wire check, or to fade gradually from silver to blue, for example.

Shaded chipping is a simple technique that just takes a little thought as it is worked.

It is a good idea to plan where the transition between shades or colours should occur – try it out on a copy of your design with coloured pencils or paints first.

1 Begin to stitch chipping in an area of one solid colour, to establish the technique. Work towards the transitional area.

2 Begin to introduce one or two chips of the new colour into the chipping at first, and gradually increase their number.

3 As you work through the transition, add more and more of the new colour until only a few chips are in the original colour.

4 Eventually, stitch only in the new colour. Repeat for further colour changes. Ensure that you completely fill the shape right up to the edges with the appropriate colour.

TEXTURED CHIPPING

Sometimes it can be useful to have a more rough-textured effect for a chipped area. Use chips that are longer than usual so they must curl into an arched shape when stitched. The length of the chip can be up to three times its width, but the stitch should be the normal length. The chips should be stitched at random angles and densely packed to fill the space, with no padding or fabric showing through.

When stitching these chips, pull very gently on the thread so that the chip curls over – it may be useful to hold the tip of a mellor under the stitch as you complete it, to encourage the chip to bend, rather than break.

LONG CHIPPING

Long chips give a different texture again. This can be particularly interesting in smooth or rough purl, which lend themselves to longer pieces.

Stitch the chips so that they lie flat on the fabric or felt, and leave none of the fabric or padding showing. Aim for random angles as you would for traditional chipping, but note that it is harder to do this as the long, thin shapes don't fill the space as easily. You may find that some of the chips curve slightly, which helps them to fill the space: this is to be expected, and adds to the choppier appearance.

SCATTERED CHIPPING

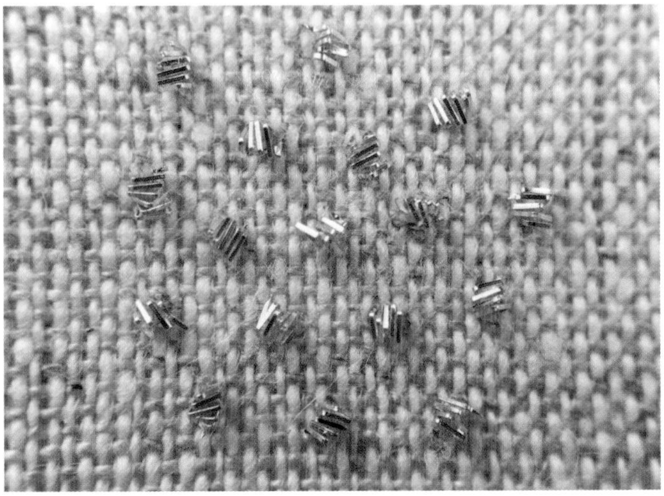

Scattered chips worked straight on to the background fabric are very useful and can be quite striking on a highly contrasting fabric. Chipping like this can be a good way to introduce shading, by varying the density of the chips. You can start off with dense chipping over padding, then fade into scattered chipping on the background, and finally into very sparse chips.

Apply each chip in the same way as traditional chipping, but space the stitches apart.

This technique looks particularly spectacular on dark fabrics. It is lovely on velvet, but do be very careful as velvet tends to mark, so you must place each chip correctly the first time.

CUTWORK

FLAT CUTWORK

Cutwork involves cutting long pieces of purl wires and stitching them down to cover an area. Smooth purl, rough purl, bright check and wire check are all suitable for this technique.

Traditionally the purls are laid at 45, 90 or 135 degrees to the shape, depending on the style of the design and the shape itself.

Flat cutwork may be stitched straight on to fabric, or on to an area of felt padding.

Always use a double waxed sewing thread for cutwork.

1 Start in the middle of one side, bringing the needle up just outside the design line. Lay a length of purl across the shape, and measure how long it will need to be to cover the distance. Use scissors to make a dent in the purl. On a velvet board, cut the purl to size with sharp scissors.

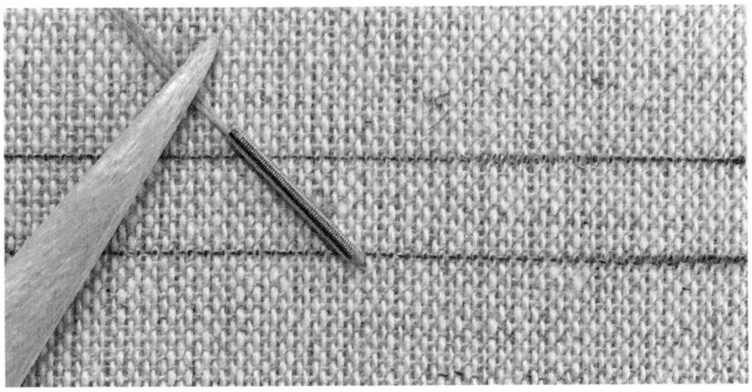

2 Pass the needle through the length of purl and slide it down to the surface of the fabric. Use a mellor to push the thread down, and check the length of the purl. If it is too short, use it to measure a new one, and if it is too long, trim it to size.

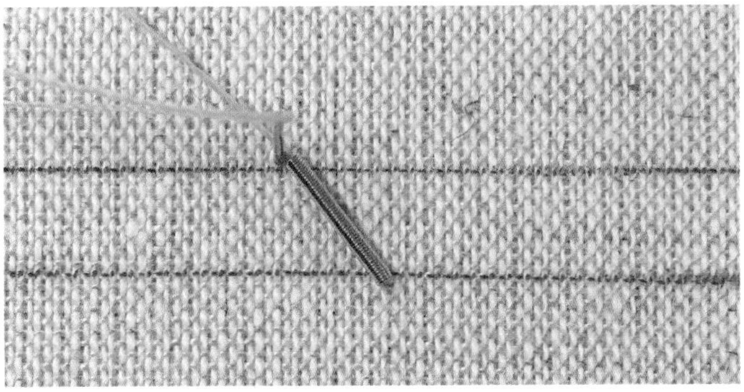

3 Use the first purl as a guide to cut some more purl chips (even if the shape narrows). Pass the needle through the chip again and slide it down to the fabric. Carefully take the needle down at the end of the purl. Once stitched the thread should not show.

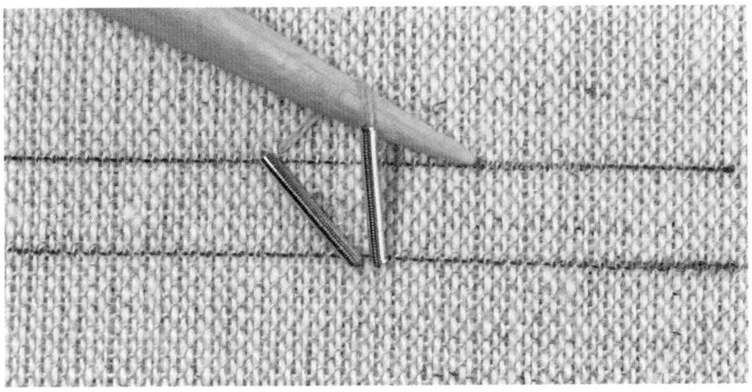

4 Repeat the process, bringing the needle up next to where you started, leaving enough room for a purl to sit comfortably (this is usually further away than you think at first). Take the needle down close to the previous chip. Use a mellor to guide the chip down to the fabric.

5 When working cutwork, it is important to remember always to stitch into the acute angle, thus leaving a long stitch on the back, which improves the tension. To finish the shape, return to the middle but stitch in the opposite direction.

RAISED CUTWORK

The more traditional form of cutwork is raised over soft string padding. Smooth purl, rough purl, bright check and wire check are all suitable for this technique.

The purls are usually laid at 45, 90 or 135 degrees to the shape, depending on the style of the design and the shape itself.

Though soft string padding is the most traditional, sometimes felt is useful for a less dramatic curve.

Always use a double waxed sewing thread for cutwork. A mellor can prevent damage to the threads by guiding the cut purls into place, and so is a very useful tool to have for cutwork.

Try alternating the purl threads to achieve a striped or shaded effect.

1 Start in the middle of one side, bringing the needle up on the design line. Lay a length of purl across the shape, and measure how long it will need to be to cover the distance. Cut the purl to size with sharp scissors (take it aside to a velvet board if you like, rather than risk cutting your background fabric).

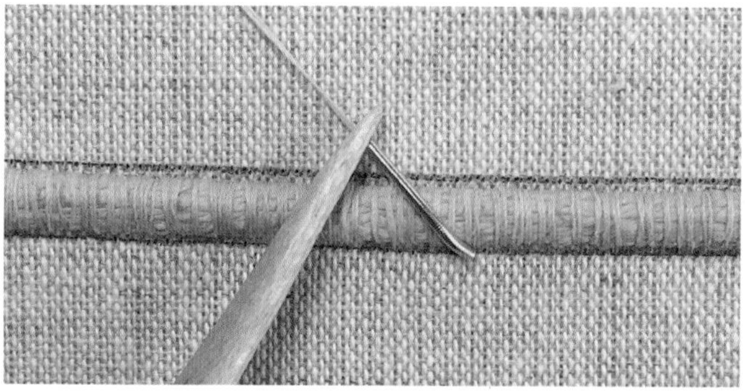

2 Pass the needle through the length of purl and slide it down to the surface of the fabric. Use a mellor to push the thread down, and check the length of the purl. If it is too short, use it to measure a new one, and if it is too long, trim it to size.

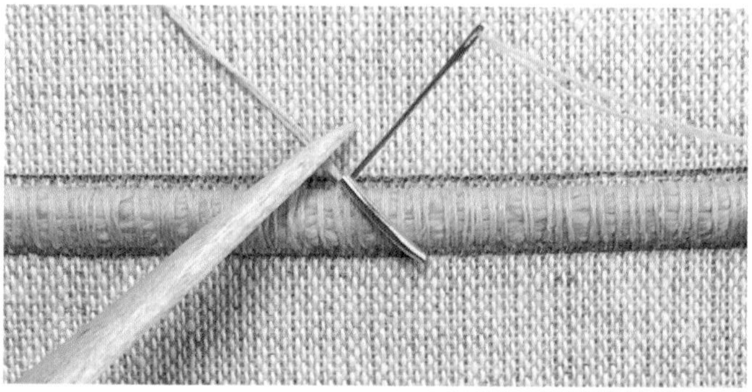

3 Use the first purl as a guide to cut one or two more chips. Then, pass the needle through the chip and slide it down to the fabric. Carefully take the needle down at the end of the purl, on the design line. Once stitched, the end of the purl should sit flat on the fabric.

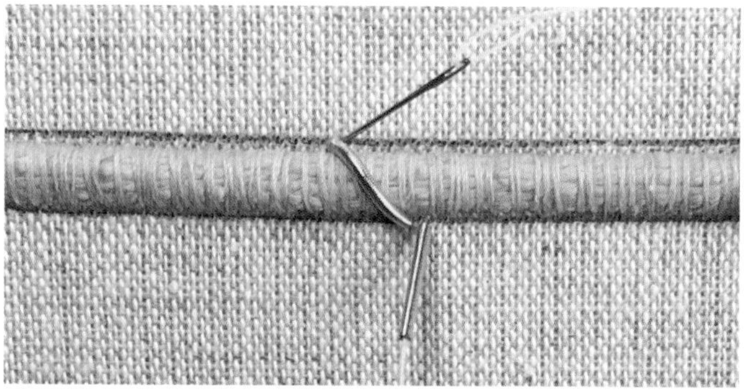

4 Repeat the process, bringing the needle up next to where you started, leaving enough room for a purl to sit comfortably. Take the needle down next to the previous chip, angling the needle towards that chip to achieve the best angle.

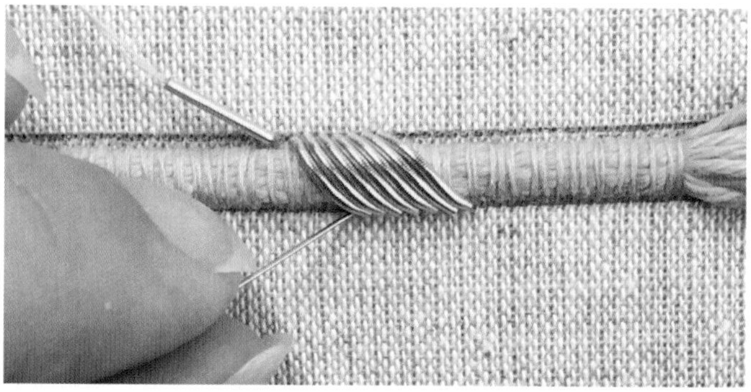

5 When working cutwork, it is important to remember always to stitch into the acute angle, thus leaving a long stitch on the back, which improves the tension. To work in the other direction, start in the middle but stitch the opposite way.

WORKING ON A CURVE

Whether you are stitching flat or raised cutwork, sometimes you need to change the angle of the stitches to flow gently around a curve.

In order to do this, you must alter the spacing of the chips ever so slightly, leaving a bit more space on the outside of the curve and a bit less on the inside.

The trick here is to achieve the turning angle without either cramping the chips or leaving significant amounts of padding showing. It is often easier with finer purl, such as No. 8.

Please note that you can't necessarily change the angle a huge amount: it all depends on the purl used and the degree of curve. Expect a little trial and error.

1 Begin in the same way as for flat or raised cutwork, at the widest point. Set the first chip at the desired angle. Sometimes on a long, curving shape a steeper angle can look more attractive.

2 For the second chip, leave a tiny bit more space on the outside of the curve, but not so much that a gap will show. Thread on the chip to check the spacing. Make sure you are also cutting the chips to the right length.

3 Once you are happy with the positioning, take the needle down on the opposite side. To tuck the chip even closer than usual, make sure that the angle of the needle is exaggerated, and that the tip of the needle disappears under the previous chip.

4 Repeat the process, adjusting the spacing of the chips to allow for the changing curve of the shape.

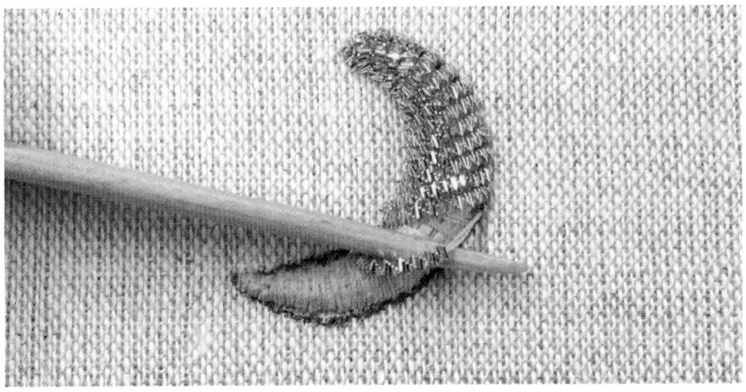

5 When the first half is complete, begin again in the middle, stitching in the opposite direction (into the acute angle). If the shape were to begin to curve the other way, gradually switch the spacing around.

POINTED SHAPES

Shapes worked in cutwork often have pointed ends, such as the tips of leaves. These must be handled correctly to ensure a beautiful finish to the work, with a sharp point rather than a rounded shape.

Usually, pointed shapes with padding work best with angled cutwork (rather than at 90 degrees) because it is tricky to reduce the length of the chips enough if they go straight across the shape. This is less of an issue with flat cutwork as the chips do not have to bend and can therefore be cut very short if necessary.

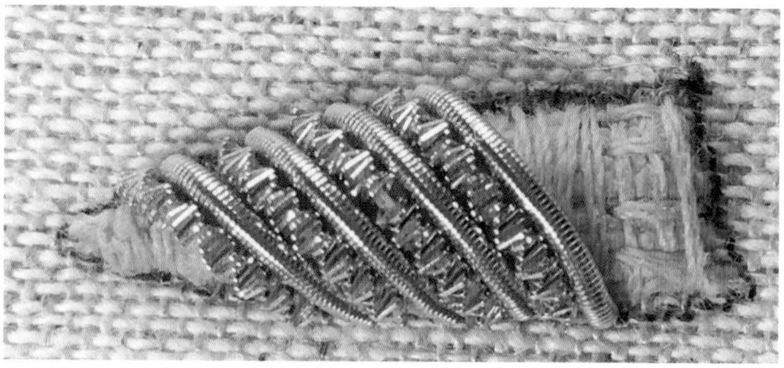

1 Work up to the point of the shape in flat or raised cutwork. When you get close to the tip, adjust the angle ever so slightly so that it is a little steeper.

2 For the very last chip, bring the needle up at the very end of the shape, a tiny bit outside the design line. This will emphasize the sharp point. Take the needle down as usual, taking extra care as you complete the stitch.

CORNERS

A true corner is not all that common in cutwork, but they do sometimes occur, so it is worth knowing how to tackle them.

It is more likely that you might come across a point where two pieces of cutwork join, such as the tip of a veined leaf.

The simplest way to tackle a true corner is to keep the angle the same on both sides, but it can be turned if necessary.

For a shape such as a veined leaf, the best way to tackle the join at the tip is to start there. Place the first chip right in the tip of the leaf (extending a tiny bit past the design line to get a sharp point), and work to either side from there.

For a true corner, there are two options. If string padding is used, a gap must be left with enough space to complete each side without overlapping (the amount of space depends on the size of the purl used – allow twice the width of the purl). Alternatively, if worked flat or on felt, the corner may be filled with a herringbone pattern.

BASKET-WEAVE CUTWORK

This cutwork technique may be used to fill areas with striking basket-weave patterns. Brick patterns, alternating horizontal and vertical blocks, diagonal blocks, and many more patterns can be created with cutwork. The patterns can be subtle if worked in one type of purl, by just changing the angle of the stitches.

For a more dramatic effect, try using a combination of purls, or even mixing colours.

This technique works best over at least a little felt padding, as the slight curve of the cut purls adds to the woven appearance of the work.

As for all cutwork, always use a double waxed sewing thread for this technique.

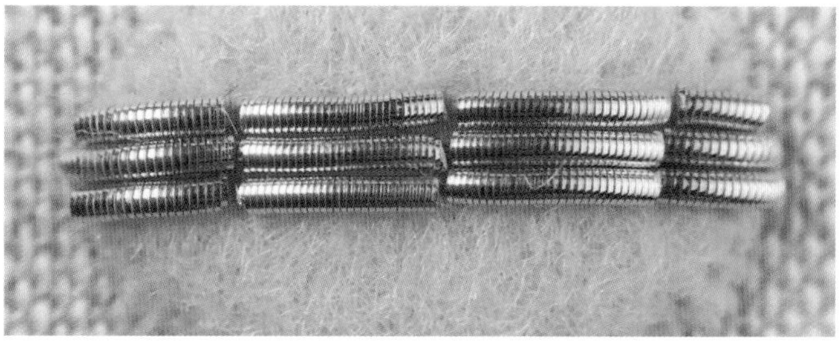

1 First determine the pattern you want to follow. This basic brick pattern is quite simple to stitch. Cut a few purls all the same length, and keep one back as a guide. Make the first stitch in the middle of the felt. Add another two parallel chips to create a block. Continue to stitch blocks in a row.

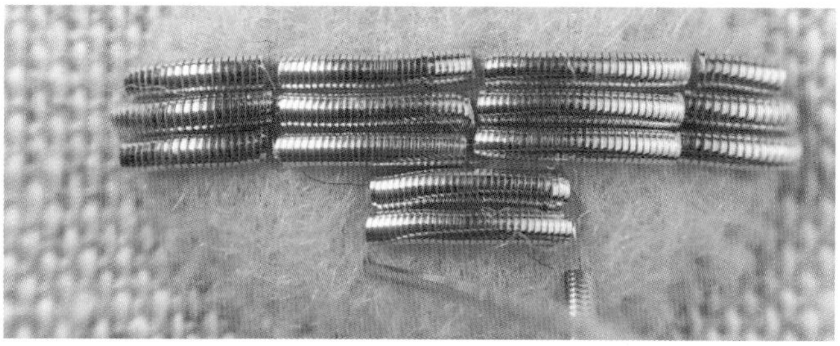

2 To start another row underneath, bring the needle up halfway along a block, and thread on a chip. Keeping the purl parallel, take the needle down at the end of the chip. Stitch another two chips to create a block, and repeat.

SPANGLED CUTWORK

Spangled cutwork is like regular cutwork, but with the addition of spangles. It is worked in a very particular way, however, so that the spangles are attached as part of the cutwork, without the hole or 'dimple' showing.

Usually, the spangles are put on every second, third or fourth purl chip. This depends on the size of the spangle and the size of the purl, and on whether a gap or overlap is desired in the spangles.

Spangled cutwork looks best over padding, because the chips butt up neatly to the spangle. However, it can be done with flat cutwork, too.

1 Work the first one, two or three chips as regular cutwork. For the next stitch, cut the purl slightly longer – about 3mm ($^1/_8$in). Place a spangle next to the padding, with the dimple facing the padding. Take the needle through the purl, and lie the purl over the padding so that the end lines up with the hole in the spangle, to check the length.

2 Take the needle down through the hole in the spangle to complete the stitch. Make the next one, two or three stitches without a spangle, and then repeat the process of adding a spangle. Experiment with different densities of spangle.

POTENTIAL PROBLEMS – AND FIXES

Cutwork has a reputation for being a difficult technique. However, this doesn't have to be the case. Cutwork is really a case of trial and error. With practice comes accuracy, and that is what is needed for cutwork.

Knowing how to get round the issues you may face is an important part of learning cutwork (whatever form it takes – flat, raised and so on).

First you need to know how to judge whether the chips are sitting correctly, and how to reverse a stitch that didn't work out quite as expected.

There is also a popular misconception that cutwork is very fragile and vulnerable. In fact, when cutwork is worked correctly it is quite robust.

Shadows: These usually appear when the chip is slightly too long for the space. The metal coil compresses when the thread is pulled tight, and this causes small areas of damage. Usually shadows appear at either end of the chip, but they can be in the middle.

Cracks: These appear for a few reasons – the chip could be significantly too long, it could be too short and pulled too much against the padding, or the damage could be sustained after the chip is laid down by catching it with a mellor/scissors/fingernail.

Chips too short: When the chips are too short, either padding or fabric will show through. The stitch itself should be invisible. Keep an eye on all sides, especially if you are working at an awkward angle.

Removing Damaged Chips (Just Worked)

When it is immediately obvious that the chip you have just stitched isn't quite right, there is a simple way to fix it.

However, it isn't quite as easy as just unthreading the needle and pulling out the thread, because you are working with a looped thread. Remember, the loop is important for sliding smoothly through the cut purl, so it needs to be kept, if at all possible. That said, if this technique doesn't work, the only way to remove the purl will be to cut the needle off and pull it through. If that happens, cast off the threads and start a new looped thread.

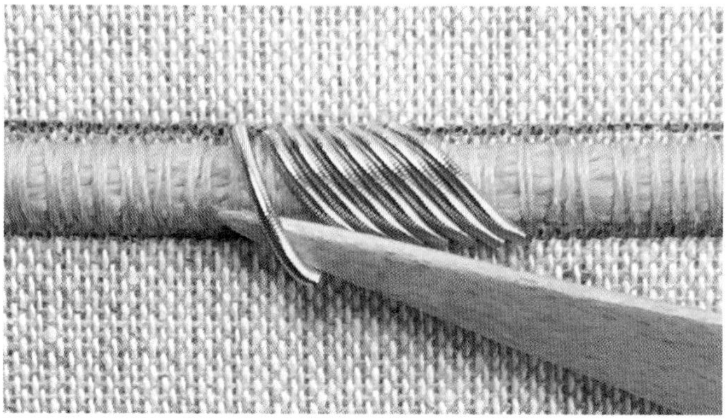

1 To remove a just worked chip, first lift the purl with a mellor: slide the mellor between the last two chips very gently, keeping the tip aimed at the damaged chip. Lift it slowly, until the thread is long enough to get your fingers in, and continue to pull.

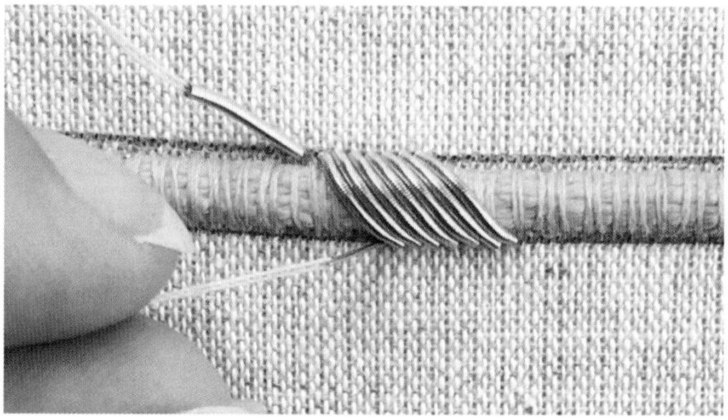

2 To get the needle back out, hold the needle on the back with one hand, angled in the same direction that it was when the stitch was made. Gently pull the stitch on the front with the other hand. The needle should come back out eye first.

Removing Damaged Chips (Once Finished)

Sometimes chips get damaged after the section is finished, or you just don't notice until it is too late. This is a little trickier to rectify, because you have very little space or thread to work with. However, it is possible.

Of course, it wouldn't be ideal to have to remove a large section of cutwork just for the sake of one chip, so it is good to know a method of unpicking just one or two. It isn't a failsafe method, but is well worth a try.

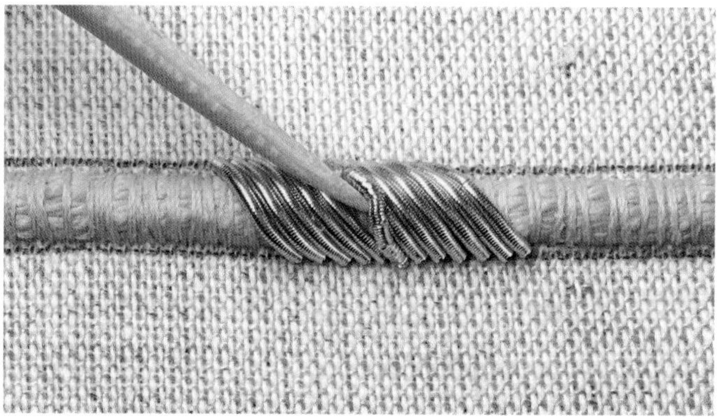

1 First, pass the needle through the fabric at one end of the chip to mark where the chip sits. Turn to the back, and cut the relevant stitch in the middle. Turn to the front and very gently use a mellor to push up the end of the chip.

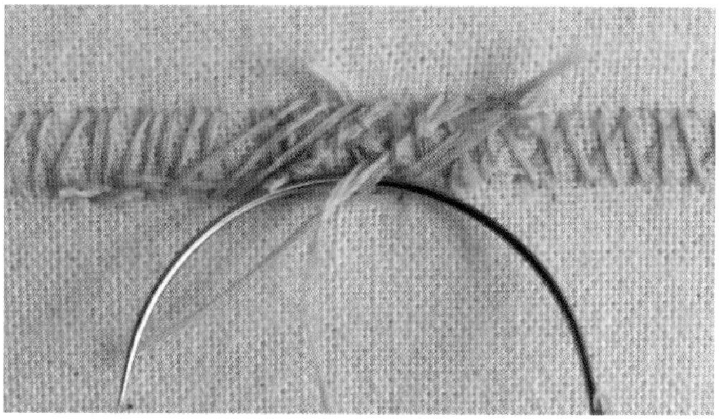

2 Once you can get a hold of the chip, remove it from the thread. Turn to the back and pull the stitch through on either end. Tie back the threads with an overcast stitch. If other chips were damaged in the process, remove those before tying back. Replace the chip(s).

S-ING

S-ing is a lovely stitch, very much like stem stitch (in surface embroidery) but using metal threads. Unlike stem stitch it is worked backwards, with the needle coming towards the existing stitch. This gives greater control.

As for all work with cut purls, a double waxed sewing thread is needed. A mellor is extra helpful for this technique because you must be able to push the stitches out of the way.

The stitches should flow from bottom left to top right, but this is a technicality, so stitch in your most comfortable direction.

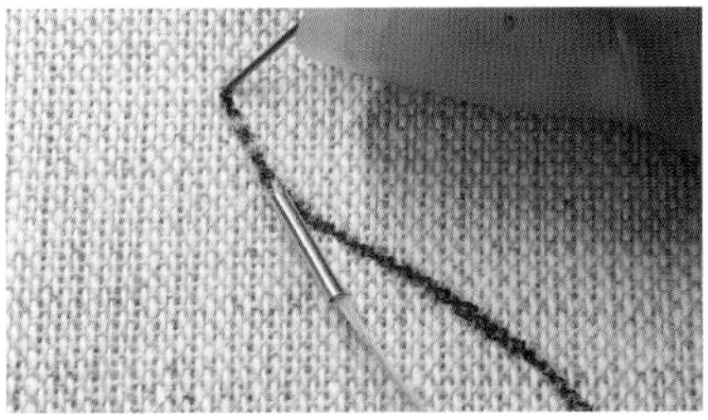

1 Start by cutting a set of purl wires all to the same length, around 6mm (1/4in). Bring the needle up just under 6mm (1/4in) along the design line, and thread on a purl chip. Take the needle down at the start of the design line. The chip should lie nearly flat, but with a tiny bit of curve (don't pull too tight or it may crack).

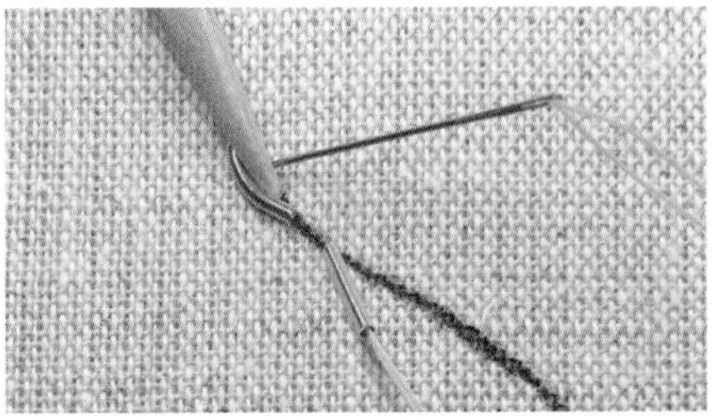

2 To form the second stitch, bring the needle up half a purl-length from the end of the first stitch. Slide the chip down to the fabric. Use a mellor to budge the first chip gently out of the way, and take the needle down halfway along the first stitch, on the line.

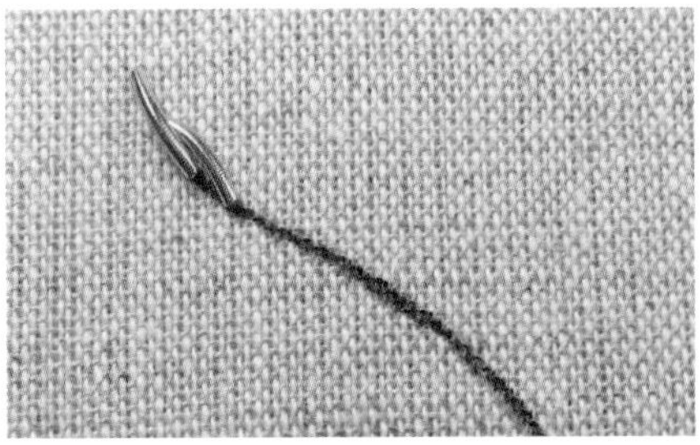

3 Use the mellor underneath the stitch as you pull it, and gently ease the new purl against the first, which should curve to fit around the new chip.

4 Repeat the same process again, bringing the needle up another half-purl length along the line, and using the mellor to guide the stitch. Make sure that the needle goes into the same hole as the end of the stitch before, or as close to it as possible.

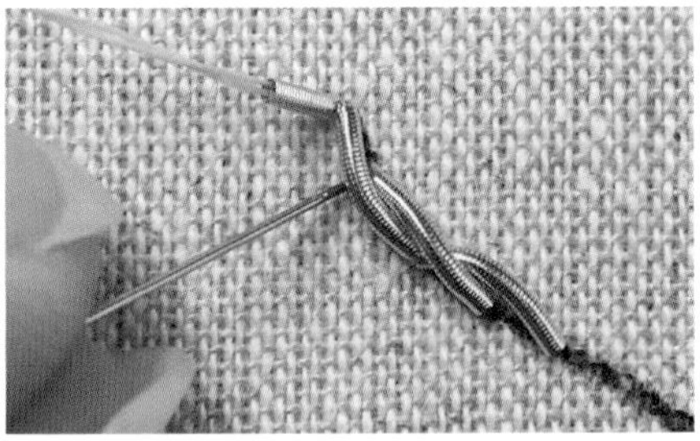

5 Go back to the beginning of the line to encourage the first purl to 'S' curve. Cut a half-length of purl. Bring up the needle at the end of the first stitch, and down halfway along the stitch, meeting the second purl. Do the same at the other end of the line.

Left: S-ing as veins in the laurel leaves of a Coronation goldwork sampler, one of the projects stitched by the author during her apprenticeship at the Royal School of Needlework.

Right: Try s-ing with alternating types of purl and colours. Add a spangle underneath each stitch or every other stitch for a different effect, known as 'spangled s-ing'.

CHAIN STITCH

Chain stitch, and its variations, may be worked beautifully with cut purls.

Determine a set length for each chip, and cut a few before you start, reserving one as a guide. Shorter chips will give a tight, curled chain; longer chips will give a more open look (the design line may show between the chains, so consider working without one if possible). The minimum with No. 6 smooth purl, for example, is about 10mm (3/8in) – any less won't allow enough space for the next stitch.

As for all work with cut purls, a double waxed sewing thread is needed.

A mellor is extra helpful for this technique because you must be able to hold the loops of purl gently while making the next stitch.

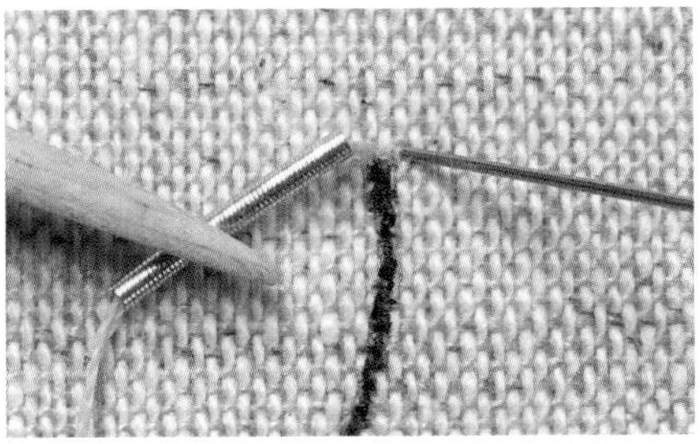

1 Bring the needle up at the start of the line, slightly to one side. Thread on a purl chip and slide it down to the fabric. Take the needle down at the start of the line again, slightly to the opposite side. Hold the thread with a mellor as you complete the stitch.

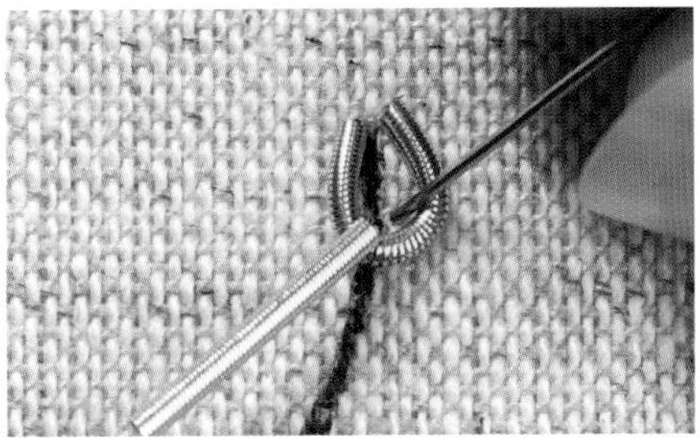

2 First, use a mellor to make sure that the purl touches the fabric, and then encourage the loop to sit flat on the fabric. Being careful not to pull excessively tight, bring the needle up inside the loop, slightly to one side of the line. Thread on a chip and make a stitch, still within the loop.

3 Repeat the process, using a mellor each time to encourage the purl into place. It may be useful to make a holding stitch every so often to avoid pulling too tight and cracking the purl. At the end of the line, bring the needle up and thread on a shorter chip. Make a stitch over the last loop to finish off.

PURL LOOPS

Loops of purl are the building blocks for some useful techniques. For instance, they can be made into simple 'lazy daisy'-style flowers, or worked in concentric circles to form a filling, which is often seen in traditional Indian embroidery.

Any of the soft purl wires, and even softer (smaller) pearl purls, can be used for this method. It is lovely in simple gold or silver, but can be very effective when coloured purls are used.

A double waxed thread is essential, and a mellor will be important to encourage the purl into shape without causing damage.

Fill a space with purl loops to create a texture. Cut the purls the same length for an even appearance, or vary them for different effects. Use a mellor to support the purl as the stitch is completed; this will allow the purl to curl nicely and not kink at the bend.

Lazy daisy with chipped centre and looped purl petals. Note that the loops do not all come together in one spot. There needs to be a space to allow the purl chips to sit well on the fabric and to avoid damage while stitching.

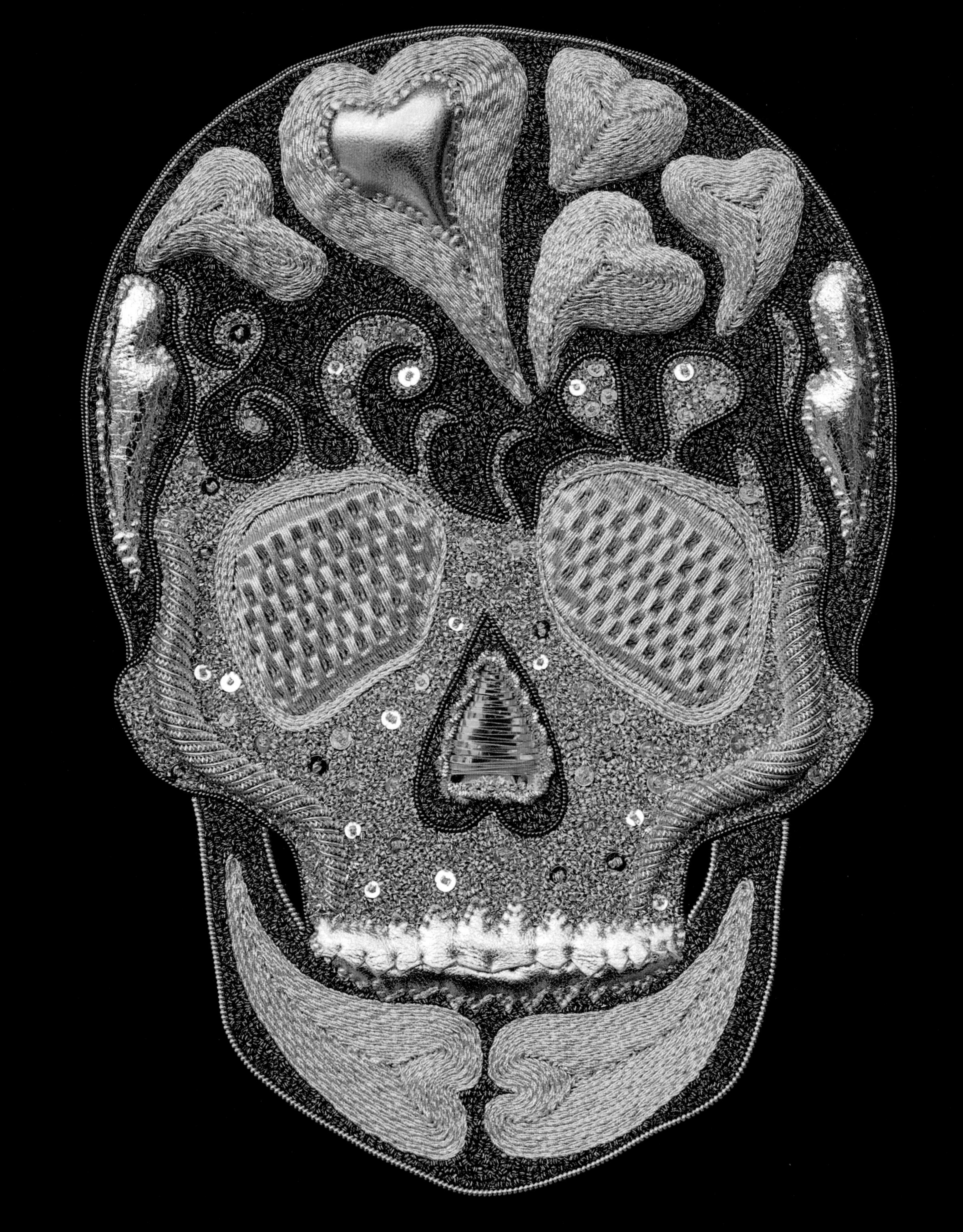

CHAPTER 7

OTHER TECHNIQUES

This section covers the goldwork materials that don't fall under either couching or cutwork: plate, kid leather and spangles.

If used alongside other techniques, plan your order of work carefully to fit these in at the correct times. Plate and spangles are more vulnerable to damage than metal-wrapped threads, but are not as susceptible as soft purl wires.

These materials have a smooth, shiny metallic surface. It is important not to handle them too much with your fingers, because they can tarnish quite easily. It is also important that you are careful with the beeswax and waxed threads, as this can rub off on to the surface of the metal and be difficult to remove.

It is essential not to poke them with anything sharp, as they can mark or dent. Be careful where you put your needles, scissors and mellor when you are working with these materials.

You can have a lot of fun with these materials, and they really can have a big impact on a design even if only a little is used. They are well worth experimenting with.

Copper kid leather, gold spangles and silver broad plate give a beautiful range of textures.

METALLIZED KID LEATHER

Kid leather is very fine leather with a metallized surface. Unlike most fabric, once broken the surface doesn't pull back together. Therefore, it is important to consider where stitches are to be placed, so there will be no need to unpick any. Because the leather marks so easily, do not use pins to hold it in place.

Kid leather is a lovely way to cover a large area with a smooth surface. It works beautifully over padding of any height, and even has a little stretch to it (but do watch out for stress fractures in the surface).

If worked flat, use the exact size of the template. If there is a lot of padding underneath, cut the leather with some extra allowance (a millimetre or two).

1 To transfer the design on to the leather, either draw round a paper template with a fine pen, or use the original pricking of the design to mark the reverse of the leather. Remember to reverse the design so that it will be the right way on the front. Cut the leather with sharp scissors.

2 To position the leather, make long stitches in a criss-cross pattern over the shape starting at the widest point, bringing the needle up and down just outside the shape. Check the leather fits the shape well – if it is too big in places, trim it carefully with sharp scissors. If it is too small, cut a new piece.

3 Using a single waxed thread, bring the needle up in the fabric at the edge of the leather, and take it down making a small stitch into the edge, about 2mm (1/16in). The stitch should be at a right angle to the edge of the leather.

4 Secure the leather in place by repeating the small stitches every 8mm (5/16in) around the shape. Take out the basting stitches.

5 Work further stitches in between the holding stitches, keeping the same stitch length and placing them about 2mm (1/16in) apart.

SPANGLES

Spangles are a dazzling addition to a goldwork design. They are flat and very shiny, and can be applied in many decorative ways. Flat sequins (which are made of plastic) may be applied with the same methods, and some methods work for cupped sequins, too.

The basics of how to apply spangles are quite simple: it is the pattern in which they are applied that makes all the difference – scattered, with beads, fish scale, flowers – anything is possible.

It has to be said that spangles are not cheap, but it doesn't take very many to really enhance a design. They are worth every penny.

To apply a spangle directly to the fabric, bring the needle up, thread on a spangle, and take the needle down just outside the spangle (guiding it so that the stitch sits over the dent). This is useful for lines of spangles which may be set side by side or overlapped. It isn't the best way for individual spangles, as they can sometimes flip over.

To apply a single spangle on its own, bring the needle up outside the spangle and take it down through the middle. Make another two stitches dividing the circle into thirds. Make sure that one of the stitches falls in the dent.

The third way is more decorative and may be used to secure individual spangles. Bring the needle up and thread on a spangle. Take it down to the surface of the fabric before threading on a chip of purl or a bead. Take the needle back down through the hole in the spangle to secure.

Spangles can be worked in a fish scale pattern to fill an area. Apply each spangle individually with a single stitch.

Spangles used to make a flower pattern with a chip of bright check in the centre.

PLATE

Plate is a narrow strip of metal with a smooth surface. One can also buy whipped plate, which has a fine wire wrapped around it to add texture.

Plate can be worked flat, or over various types of padding. The padding must be quite robust to support the plate well, as it is easily dented. Plate must always be started at the narrow end of the shape because the nature of the method means it must increase in width as you work along the shape.

Traditionally plate is used in a similar way to satin stitch – to cover a shape densely. However, it is also very good for creating patterns, especially in combination with other techniques.

1 Cast on a single waxed thread right next to the padding. Begin by using tweezers to create a small hook at the end of the length of plate. Trim the hook if necessary (for example if the shape is very narrow).

2 Line up the plate with the starting point. Bring the needle up next to the plate and make a backstitch to the starting point, leaving it loose. Hook the loop of the plate on to the stitch, so that the hook is underneath, and pull the stitch closed. Make a tiny stitch nearby to hold the stitch tight (a holding stitch).

3 Lay the plate across the padding and make another stitch right across the plate, next to the edge of the padding. The stitch must be accurate in size and position so the plate cannot move about. Pull the stitch tight. Make a holding stitch if you feel it is necessary.

4 Still holding the stitch tight, bend the metal back across the padding. It is important to overlap the previous layer of plate, but also to move along the shape, covering more padding. Make another stitch across the plate to secure it, with a holding stitch if necessary.

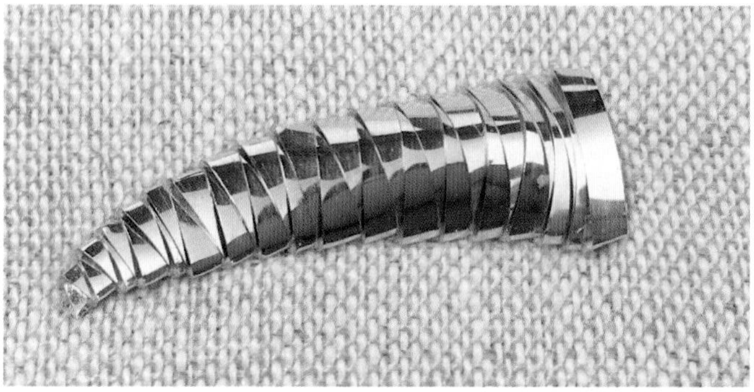

5 Repeat the process of folding and stitching all the way to the other end, using holding stitches regularly to keep the tension. At the end of the shape, cut the plate with just enough excess to bend underneath into a hook. Make a last stitch to secure the hook.

Stitching Plate on Awkward Shapes

When stitching plate in the traditional method, if the shape narrows at both ends, use two (or more) lengths of plate. Begin at each narrow point and work towards the widest point. At the widest point, finish both lengths with one slightly overlapping the other so that the join is as invisible as possible.
For shapes that turn dramatically, plate can be really tricky to use as it tends to overlap too many times on the inside curve, resulting in the outline of the shape being lost or altered. In these cases, you could consider combining plate with another technique, allowing you to leave gaps between the plate on the outer edge and thus preserving the shape – for example, applying fabric or kid leather first, or filling gaps with chipping or lengths of purl.

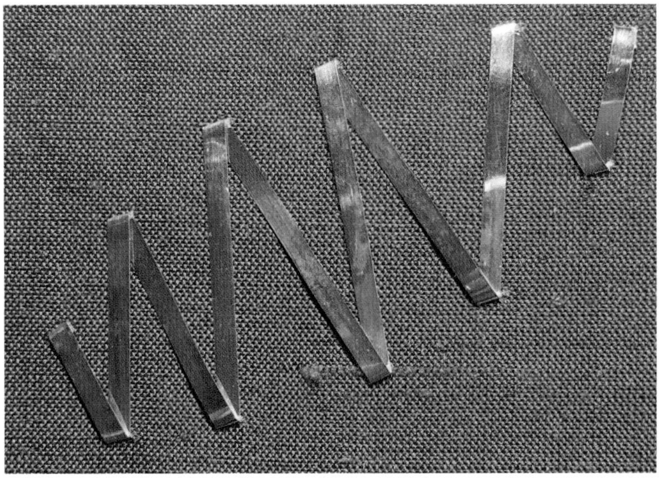

Zigzag stitched with silver broad plate on a contrasting fabric. The plate is started in the usual way with a hook. It is then bent into shape in the right place with tweezers, before a small stitch is placed in the bend to secure it to the fabric. This method can be used for a tight or open zigzag, and looks great over applied fabric.

The various types of plate (broad, 11's and whipped) are surprisingly versatile. The examples on this page are just the beginning – there are all sorts of things you could do with plate. Try plate instead of metal-wrapped threads for basket-weave to create a beautiful texture, experiment with the different metals available, and play with different types of trellis, to which plate lends itself very well.

Trellis filling stitched with 11's plate, with beads and spangles. The plate is secured with a hook at each end, and the intersections are stitched down with a spangle and bead to give a luxurious appearance.

Individual lengths of whipped plate stitched over kid leather to create stripes. The plate is secured with a hook at each end.

CHAPTER 8

ADDITIONAL TECHNIQUES

In this chapter you will find some extra techniques that go hand-in-hand with goldwork. It is not exhaustive by any means – there are many books available on surface embroidery, appliqué and other things, which will combine beautifully with metal threads. The idea is to get you started on your journey with a few key ideas.

If any areas of the design are to be padded, then that padding should be worked first. Padding has a tendency to create fluff, which could get trapped in some of these stitches. These techniques work well over padding, though it should be noted that silk shading in particular needs quite dense padding to properly support the stitches because their tension will pull the padding down.

These techniques are usually best worked before the metal threads in any design, though of course there are exceptions. As a rule of thumb, if appliqué is to be used it should be completed first, followed by silk shading and then other surface stitches.

The stitches in this chapter may be worked with any type of thread. Silk is without a doubt the most traditional accompaniment to goldwork, but cotton is a brilliant substitute. Rayon or other 'faux silk' threads are trickier to handle, but more readily available than real silk, and a great vegan alternative. Crewel wool with its slightly fluffy texture creates a fantastic contrast with the smooth, shiny metal threads. The softness of silk ribbons looks stunning with metalwork. There are really no rules – go ahead and mix it up, see where your imagination takes you.

Silk ribbons, crewel wools and silk threads are all good choices to add interest and colour to a goldwork design. The same stitches can be done with any of these threads, and there are many more to experiment with as you continue your stitching journey.

APPLIQUÉ

Appliqué is a brilliant way to cover a large area with a different colour or texture, so it can be very useful in goldwork designs. Any fabric may be used for appliqué – but if the fabric frays easily it may be best to use lightweight fusible interfacing on the back.

There are many ways to apply fabric, of which this is the simplest method and the most used in goldwork. It must always have an edging applied to cover the stitches and act as additional security for the edge of the fabric – but as one would usually be adding gold anyway, this is no hardship. Couching threads make wonderful edgings, but equally you can stitch over the edge with chipping or cutwork (if doing so, remember to stitch the appliqué before any padding).

1 Use prick and pounce or a template to mark the fabric before cutting with very sharp scissors to get a clean edge. (If using fusible interfacing, apply this to the back of the fabric before cutting.) Usually, the grain line of this fabric should match that of the background. Cut slightly bigger than the template if it is going on top of padding.

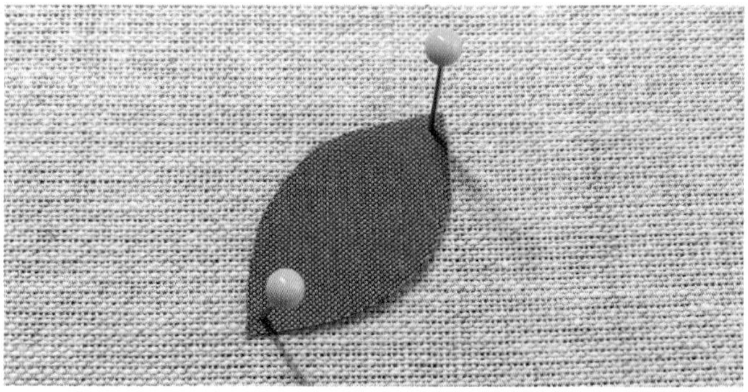

2 Position the piece of fabric on to the background fabric, and use pins sparingly around the edge to keep it in place. If it is direct on the fabric it should be flat and smooth; if it is over padding, it should be smooth and tight on the padding. Remember that the grain line should usually match that of the background fabric.

3 With a matching sewing thread, make small stitches into the edge of the fabric in the same way that you would for felt, placing them every 5–10mm ($^1/_4$–$^3/_8$in). Bring the needle up on the design line and take it down into the edge of the fabric, making a stitch 1–2mm ($^1/_{16}$in) in length, at right angles to the edge.

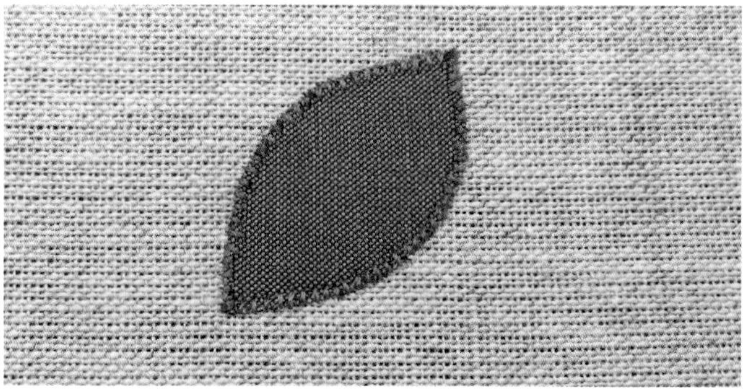

4 Go round the shape again, placing stitches every 1–2mm ($^1/_{16}$in) to fully secure the fabric.

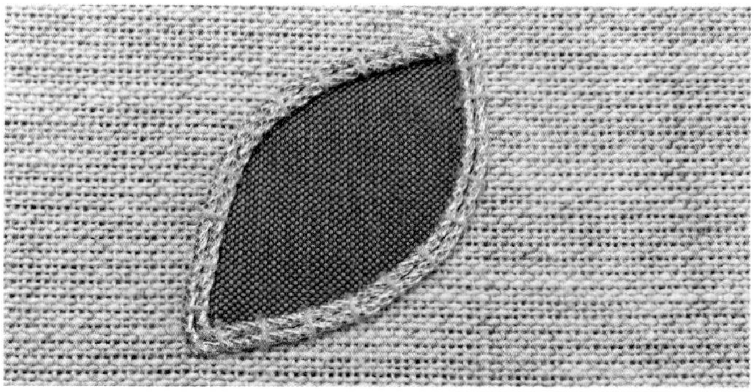

5 Stitch an edging to cover the securing stitches.

SPLIT STITCH

Split stitch provides a foundation for either satin stitch or long and short stitch (that is, if they are not to be outlined with gold or other stitches). It gives the stitches a beautifully neat, crisp edge which cannot be achieved otherwise, and also helps prevent distortion of the fabric.

Split stitch can also be used as an outlining stitch, or as a filling stitch in its own right. In *Opus Anglicanum* you can see it used to fill the faces of the figures – worked round and round in swirls to lend depth to the cheeks, for example.

It really is a beautiful stitch, well worth spending some time practising.

1 Usually a single thread works best for split stitch. Bring the needle up at the start of the design line and make a stitch 1–2mm ($^1/_{16}$in) along the line.

2 Bring the needle up through the first stitch, piercing the thread (hence the name 'split stitch') about halfway along it.

3 Make another stitch the same length as the first, along the design line. Try not to be tempted to make the stitch longer than 1–2mm ($^1/_{16}$in).

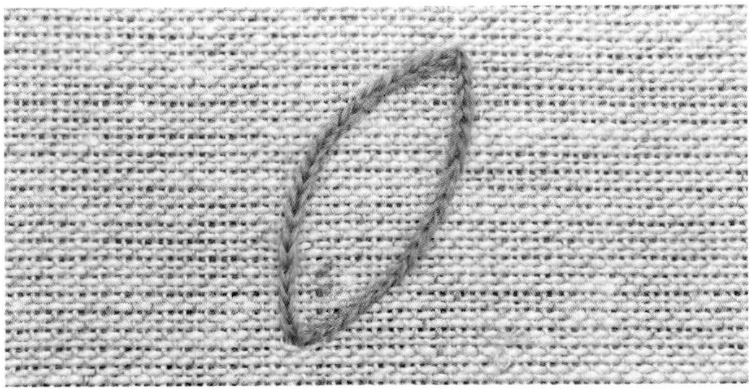

4 Continue to stitch along the line, splitting each stitch through the middle of the thread.

5 At the end of the line, bring the needle up through the last stitch and take it down at the very end of the line (a half stitch).

SATIN STITCH

This stitch can be a lovely addition to any design. It is a simple way to achieve a little pop of colour, and is simple to work in many types of thread. Usually satin stitch is worked with just one colour of thread.

If there is to be an outline (of gold, or other stitches) then it can be worked without the split stitch, but if it is to sit alone, then split stitch underneath will give a lovely finish to the work.

Traditionally satin stitch is worked on a slant – it is important with satin stitch always to stitch towards the acute angle to preserve the tension and stitch angle. If worked straight across a shape you can stitch in either direction.

1 Bring the needle up partway along one side of the shape, outside but as close as possible to the split stitch (the widest point is a good place to start so you can get the best possible stitch angle). Decide on the angle by holding the thread across the shape, and take the needle down on the other side, angling slightly towards the split stitch.

2 Bring the needle up next to the start of the first stitch, in the obtuse (wide) angle. Leave a little breathing room between the stitches (a thread's width). Take the needle down next to the first stitch, angling the needle towards the previous stitch and the split stitch.

3 Repeat the process to the end of the shape. Then start again in the middle, bringing the needle up next to the end of the first stitch (in the obtuse angle). Take the needle down next to the first stitch, angling it towards that stitch and the split stitch.

4 Repeat the process again all the way to the end to complete the shape.

If you did not work split stitch, outline the shape with gold.

SILK SHADING (LONG AND SHORT)

Silk shading is one of the most traditional forms of embroidery. It allows you to fill a space with varied colour, and to change the flow of the stitches to enhance the shape. In some situations you may choose to shade in a naturalistic way, but as an enhancement for goldwork you may simply choose an attractive combination of colours.

Long and short stitch is simple in principle, but can be challenging. Remember that with this stitch, practice makes perfect. It is easier to achieve a smooth blend of colours with ones that match fairly closely, but it is a good idea to practise with ones that have quite a big difference so that you can see the technique better – as shown in this example. Use one or two strands of cotton or silk thread.

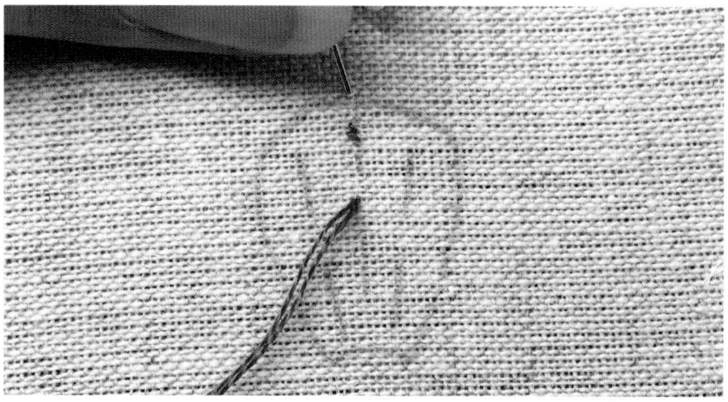

1 Draw the desired stitch angles on the fabric with short pencil lines. Begin stitching partway along the edge of the shape, in a place where it is very clear what the angle is to be. Bring the needle up in the middle of the shape and take it down on the edge (tucking around the split stitch if there is one) to make a long stitch – about 10mm (3/8in).

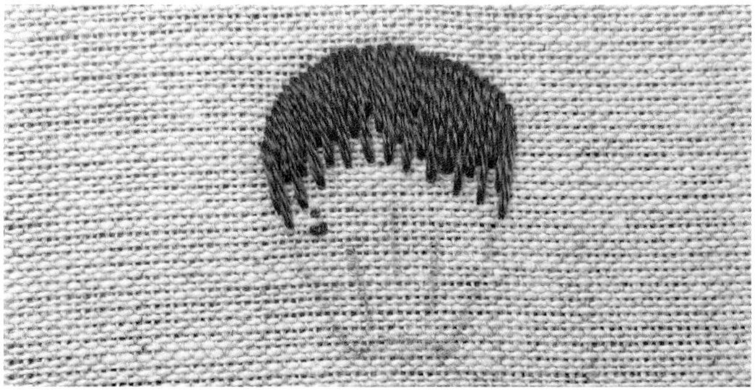

2 Make another stitch right next to the first one, this time 5–8mm (3/16–5/16in). Make another stitch next to that, a different length to the first two, and so on. The stitches should be varied in length between 5–10mm (3/16–3/8in), with more long than short. If the angle changes, gradually adjust the stitches accordingly – a short stitch between two long ones can help get things going.

3 For the second row, bring the needle up through the middle stitch of the first row. The needle should ideally split the thread, piercing through it angled in the same direction the stitch is travelling (which is opposite to that of the first row). Make a stitch about 10mm (3/8in) long. This stitch may be at exactly the same angle as the one it splits, or very subtly altered if the stitches need to flow along a curve.

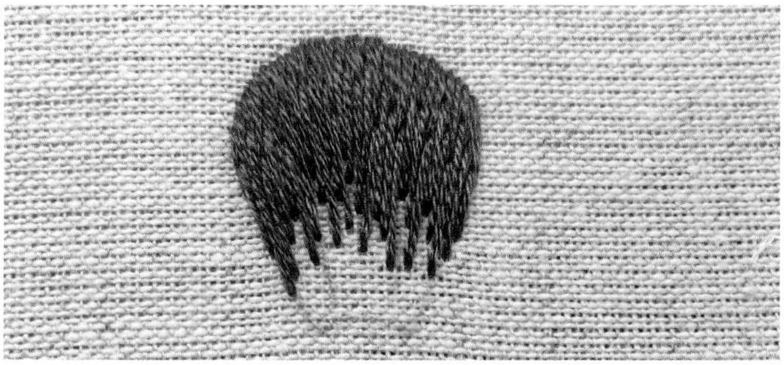

4 Repeat this for all (or most) of the stitches in the first row, starting in varying positions, depending on the length of the original stitch.

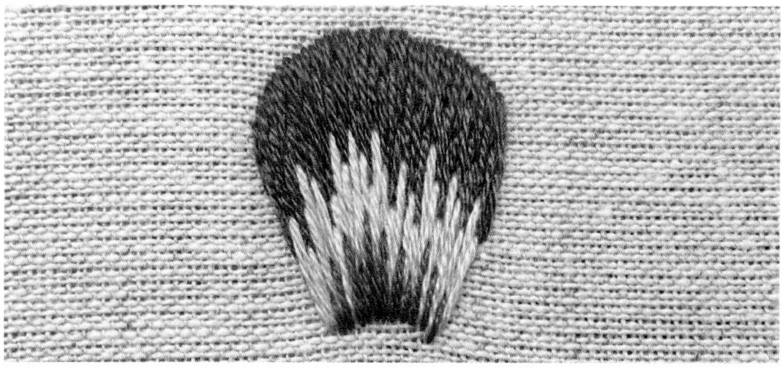

5 Do the same for the subsequent rows until the shape is filled with long and short stitches. Once complete, it is ready to be outlined with gold.

STEM STITCH

Stem stitch can complement goldwork very well. It is useful to run alongside couching, either for a pop of colour or to disguise design lines that haven't been quite covered.

Stem stitch works well in any thread, and flows beautifully around curves. As the name suggests, it makes good stems – but there is so much more to this handy stitch.

This stitch may be worked with a single thread, or multiple threads to alter its width. It can also be stitched in rows to fill a shape, and gives a beautiful flowing directional line for the eye to follow.

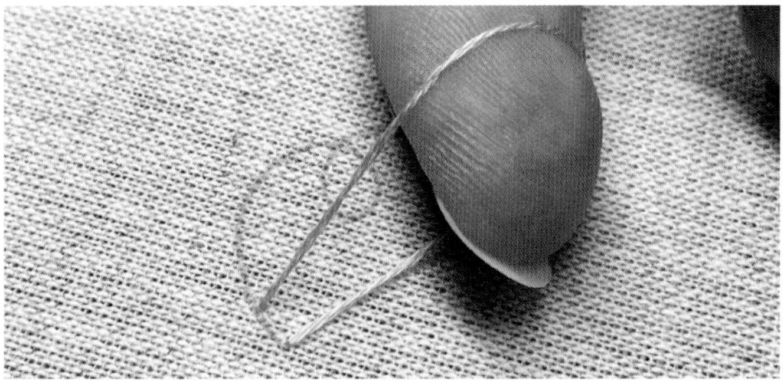

1 Bring the needle up at the start of the design line and make a stitch 3–4mm (1/8in) along the line. Hold the loop of thread. If working left to right, hold it to the bottom; if working bottom to top, hold it to the right (and vice versa).

2 Bring the needle up halfway along the first stitch, on the design line.

3 On the back, pull the thread so that the loop closes against the needle, and pull the needle all the way through.

4 Make another stitch the same length as the first (try not to be tempted to make it longer). Hold the loop in the same direction as before, and bring the needle up at the end of the first stitch.

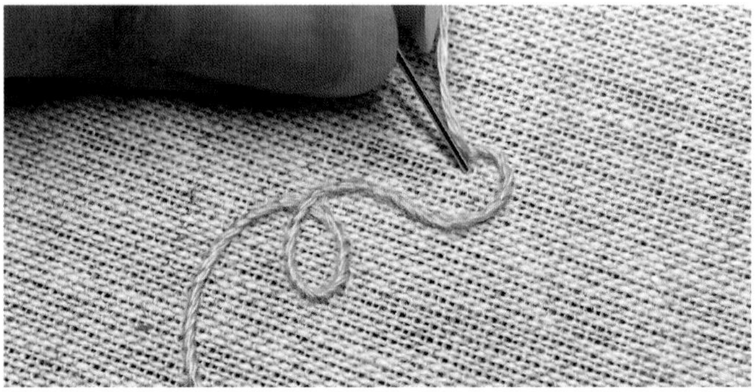

5 Repeat the process to the end of the design line. Hold the last loop and make a short stitch to complete the line.

FRENCH KNOTS

French knots are lovely things, and can be a good addition to all sorts of embroidery projects to add a different texture. They are often worked incorrectly, and so many people believe they are difficult or complicated, when in fact if they are worked correctly they are simple and attractive.

French knots are a lovely way to incorporate a bit of colour into a design, and they can also be worked in metallic machine threads to blend in with an all-metal design. They can be useful in places where a chip of bright check would be either too sparkly or likely to catch, as they are more resilient.

To increase the size of the knot, use thicker thread (or more strands) rather than wrapping round more than once.

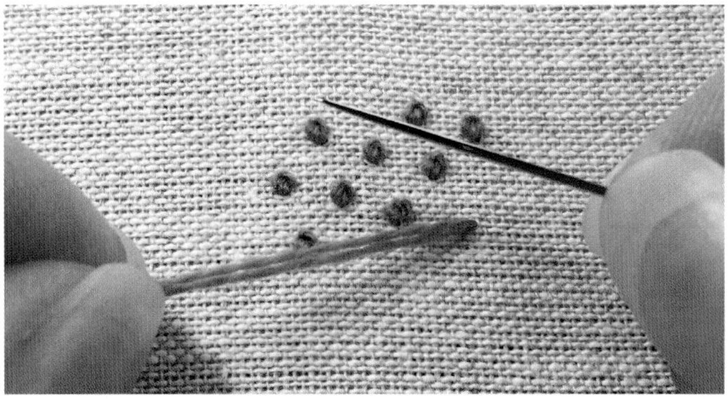

1 Begin by bringing the needle up in the spot where the knot will sit, and pull the thread all the way through. Hold the needle in one hand and the thread in the other.

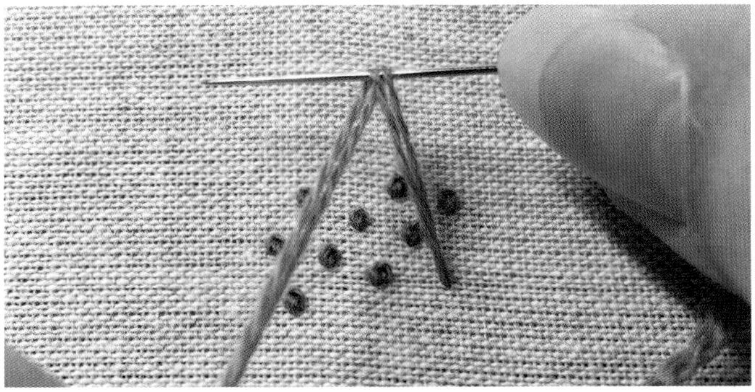

2 Wrap the thread (the part between the fabric and your fingers) around the needle just once. When you are making multiple knots, it is a good idea to wrap each one in the same direction to make them look consistent.

3 Place the tip of the needle into the fabric, a tiny distance from the starting point (one thread of the fabric is enough in most cases). Do not take the needle through at this stage.

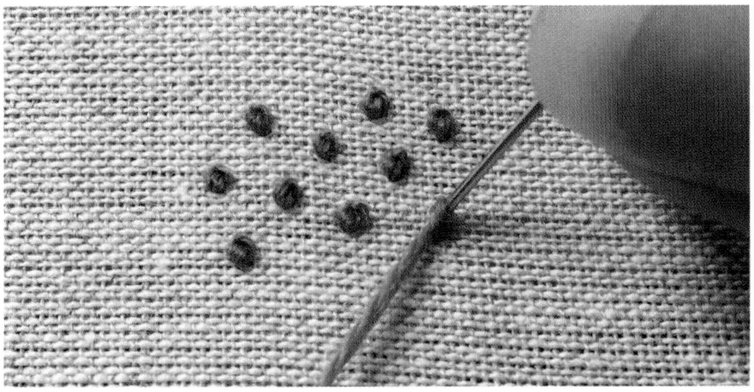

4 Pull the thread so that the wrap (which will be the knot) closes around the needle and rests against the fabric.

5 Pull the needle through the fabric, then slowly and gently guide the thread through until the finished knot rests neatly on the fabric.

CHAPTER 9

PROJECTS

This chapter contains a selection of projects to inspire you to practise the skills you have learned throughout this book. It begins with the simpler projects, and progresses to more complex designs with more challenging techniques. With each project you will find a full-size template and a list of what you will need to complete it.

The finished All that Glitters project.

PROJECT 1

ALL THAT GLITTERS

Butterflies of all kinds make wonderful subjects for embroidery, especially goldwork. This design includes a little of the most fundamental techniques – couching and chipping – with some of the more unusual components for a bit of added glamour.

This design is a good example of 'white space', where the background fabric shows through to enhance the design. Sometimes less really is more.

What you will need:

Materials

- Normandy linen: at least 20cm (8in) square
- Calico: at least 20cm (8in) square
- Felt: 5cm (2in) square
- Gold kid leather: 5cm (2in) square
- Gutermann Sew-all sewing thread No. 968 (dark gold)
- Gilt smooth passing No. 6: 100cm (39in)
- Gilt pearl purl No. 2: 30cm (12in)
- Gilt pearl purl No. 1: 20cm (8in)
- Gilt rococco, very fine: 80cm (32in)
- Gilt bright check No. 6: 20cm (8in)

Equipment

- Hoop frame: at least 15cm (6in)
- Embroidery scissors
- Goldwork scissors
- Beeswax
- Mellor
- Embroidery needles (9–12)
- Chenille needle (20–22)
- Paint, pen or pencil

Design Template

1 Transfer the design with your preferred method: tracing or prick and pounce.

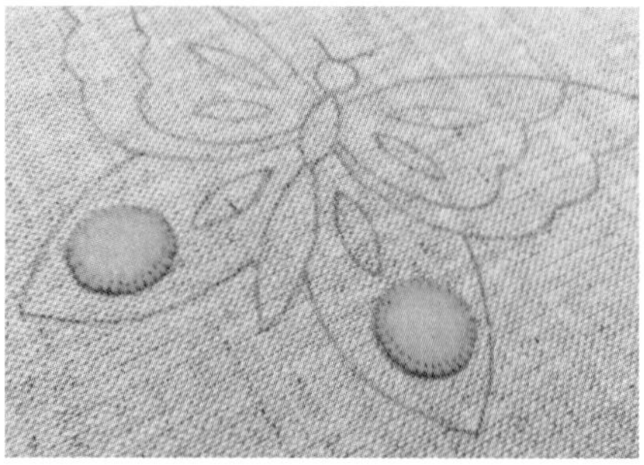

2 Using the template provided, cut two circles of felt. Cast on a single sewing thread. Match the felt to the lines on the fabric, and secure them first with four stitches: top, bottom, left and right. Come up in the fabric and down in the felt with a stitch 1–2mm ($^1/_{16}$in) in length. Then go round the felt circle making a stitch every 1–2mm ($^1/_{16}$in).

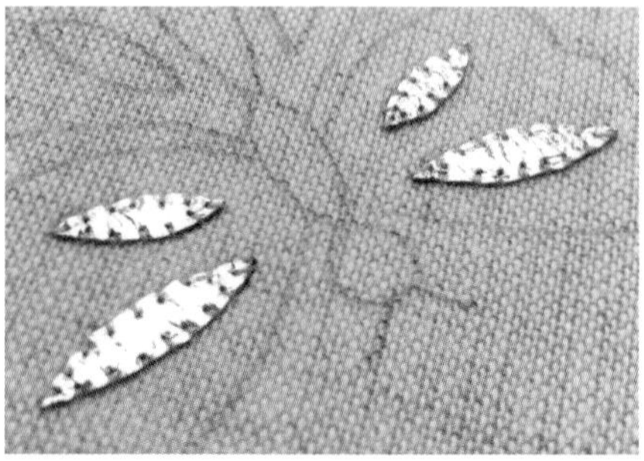

3 Using the template provided, cut the tiny pieces of kid leather. Remember to mark the leather on the back with a permanent fine-tipped pen. Cut the shapes very carefully with sharp scissors, match them to the lines on the fabric, and begin to secure them. These shapes are small and quite simple, so you can begin with a stitch at each end and one or two on each side, then fill between with stitches spaced 2mm ($^1/_{16}$in) apart.

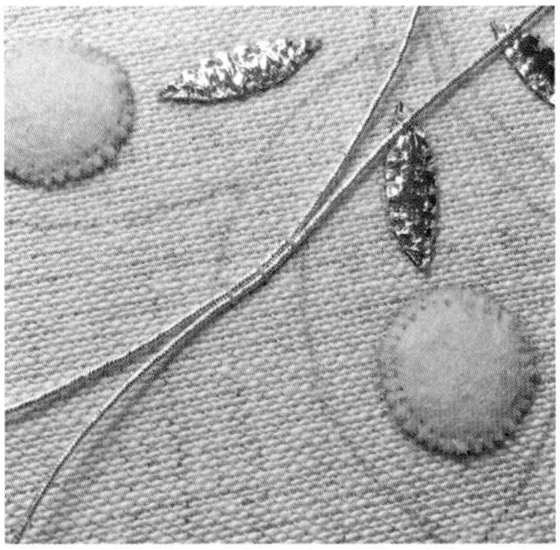

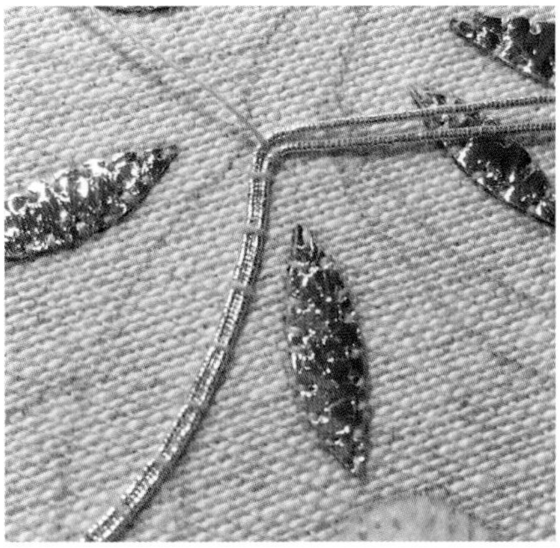

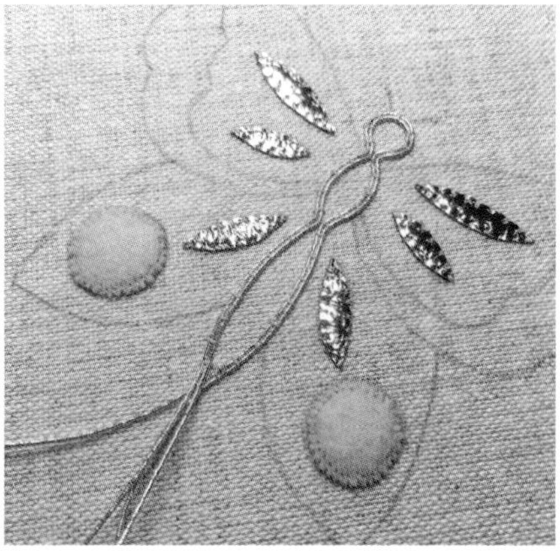

4 Stitch the body and head with paired smooth passing threads, using a single waxed thread. Begin at the tip of the abdomen and work up the body. Leave a tail of at least 25mm (1in). Bring the needle up on one side of the line and down over the two threads, keeping the stitches snug but not too tight, and placing stitches every 3–4mm ($^1/_8$in). Remember to adjust the angle of the stitch to match the curve, keeping the stitch at right angles to the gold threads.

5 When you reach the join of the abdomen to the torso, turn the gold threads individually. Begin with the outer thread, bringing the needle up in the corner. Bend the smooth passing tightly against the sewing thread, and secure with a tiny stitch. Then do the same again for the second gold thread.

6 Continue to stitch around the body and head, keeping the stitches evenly spaced and turning the corners neatly. When you get to the end, trim the smooth passing so that there is an inch or two to spare.

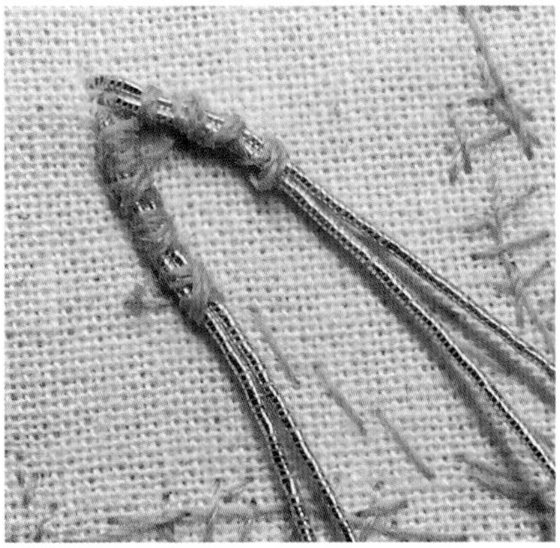

7 Plunge the smooth passing threads on alternate sides so that they create as subtle a join as possible. Use a large chenille needle to take each one through individually. If necessary, add an extra stitch near the end to secure them fully.

8 On the reverse, use a curved needle to bind the smooth passing in pairs. With a double thread, scoop underneath the back of the stitches and catch a little calico, and trap the gold threads; repeat until you have bound about 10mm ($^3/_8$in), then go back a few stitches and cut off all the ends neatly.

9 Begin the pearl purl wing outlines up against the body, using No. 2 pearl purl and a single waxed thread. Remember to stretch the pearl purl just enough to allow the sewing thread to pass between the coils, and trim the end neatly with sharp goldwork scissors. Make the first stitch close to the start of the line, and twirl the pearl purl in your fingers so that it sits neatly right up against the neighbouring threads.

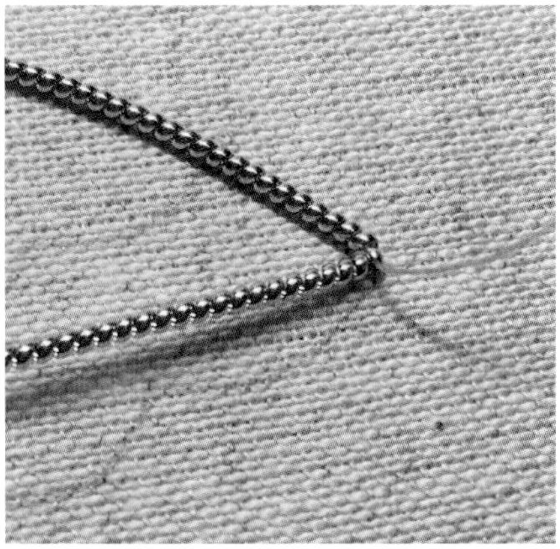

10 Stitch the pearl purl every two or three coils, making sure that the stitches are small enough to be invisible, until you get to the corner. To turn the corner neatly and get a really good shape, bend the pearl purl with your fingers, slightly more than is necessary for the design. Then ease it back into place and make a tiny stitch to secure the corner. Place the next stitch very close to the corner, and carry on as before.

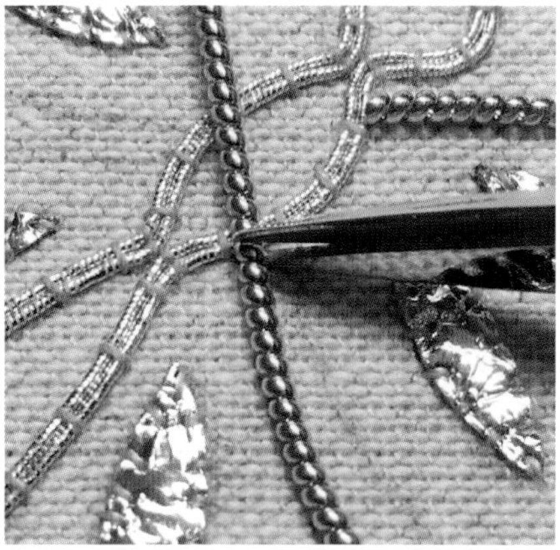

11 Finish the pearl purl carefully up against the smooth passing of the body. Stop stitching three or four coils before the end of the line, but don't finish off the sewing thread. Choose where to cut, and make one decisive cut with sharp goldwork scissors. Make sure that it fits well, and then secure with a last stitch or two before casting off.

12 Repeat the same process for both wings of the butterfly, taking special care over the corners and joins.

13 Stitch the wing details with No. 1 pearl purl. Again, be very careful about the joins. Stretch and cut the pearl purl neatly, and twirl it in your fingers so that it meets the existing pearl purl line as neatly as possible.

14 Repeat the pearl purl stitching so that all the upper wing outlines and details are complete.

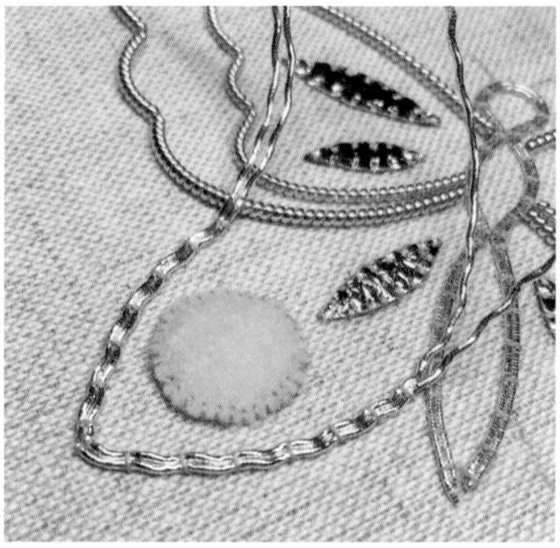

15 Using a single waxed thread, couch a pair of very fine rococco threads around the lower wing outlines. Begin at one end, bringing the two gold threads together so that the wiggles match reasonably neatly. Stitch every 3–4mm (1/8in), adjusting the angle of the stitch to stay at right angles to the gold threads.

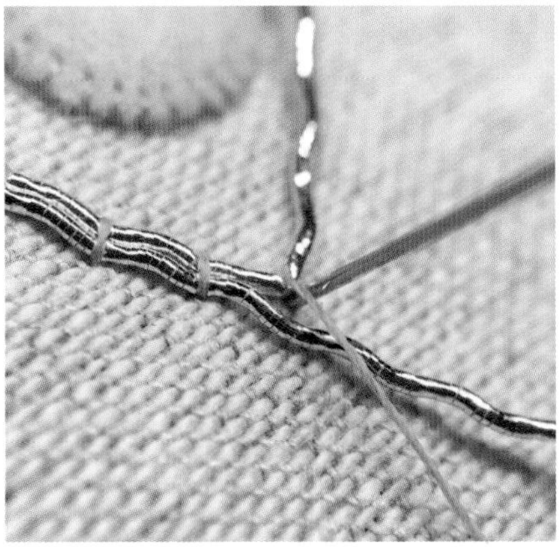

16 At the corner, turn the rococco threads individually, making sure that they sit either side of the design line so that it doesn't show. Bring the needle up in the corner and use it to bend the rococco sharply round, then secure it with a tiny stitch. Make a holding stitch further along the design line.

17 Bring the needle up between the two threads and repeat the same process, bending the rococco and securing with a tiny stitch. This is a little more difficult with rococco than it would be with smooth threads, because the wiggles can be deceiving. As you work the next stitch or two, check that the corner looks neat and tidy.

18 Once the couching is complete, plunge the rococco threads with a large chenille needle. Because they are plunged up against existing stitching it is important to be careful with the needle so as not to damage anything. Angle the needle slightly towards (underneath) the existing stitching, and carefully pull the needle through on its own before taking the gold through. Aim to make it so that no gap shows in between.

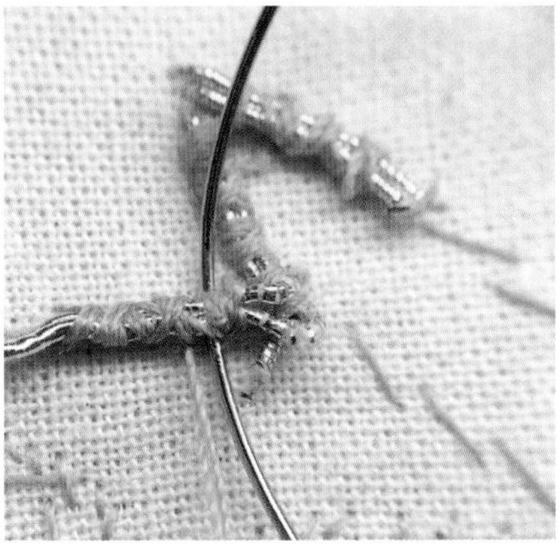

19 Once all the threads are plunged, bind them on the reverse with a curved needle and trim all the ends neatly.

20 Now all the outlines are complete and finished off neatly on the back.

21 Begin the border of the left-hand felt circle opposite the kid leather shape, using a single waxed thread over a pair of smooth passing threads. Bring the needle up on the outline and down into the felt, and work anticlockwise. Place the stitches 3mm ($^1/_8$in) apart, or a little closer if you find that holds more comfortably. As you start the second row, bring the needle up on the inside and tuck it under the first row, creating a brick pattern with the stitches.

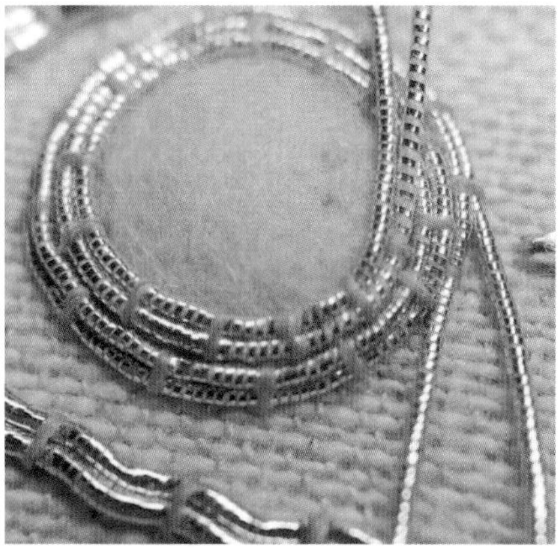

22 When you have completed two rows, add an extra tiny stitch on each end, over just one of the passing threads, so that they can be plunged in a staggered pattern.

23 Plunge the smooth passing threads with a large chenille needle, staggering the ends to create as smooth a finish as possible.

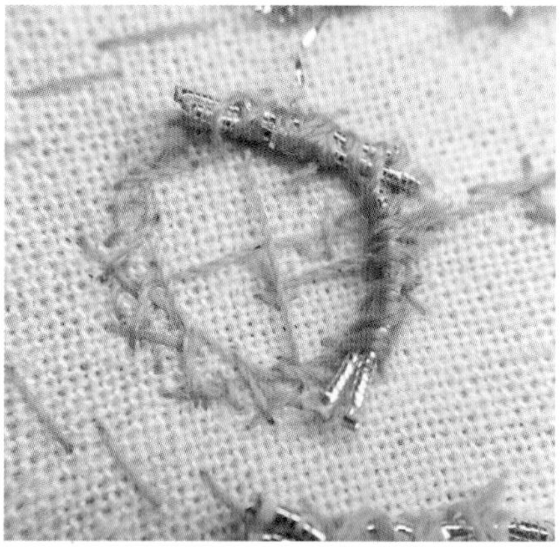

24 Bind the ends of the smooth passing on the reverse using a double waxed thread in a curved needle. Make sure to keep to the back of the couching, as you will need to stitch through the centre of the circle in the next step.

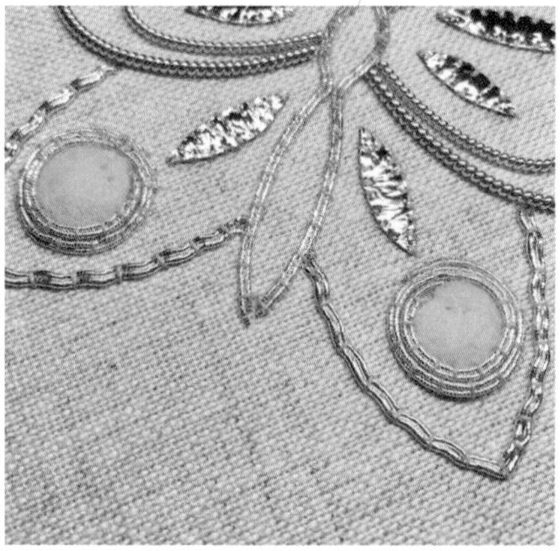

25 Stitch the right-hand circle as a mirror image, working clockwise round the circle and staggering the finish as before. Finish off the threads on the back ready for the next stage.

26 Cut a few chips of bright check, making sure that they are all small and square. Cast on a double waxed thread in the centre of one of the felt circles, ready to start chipping.

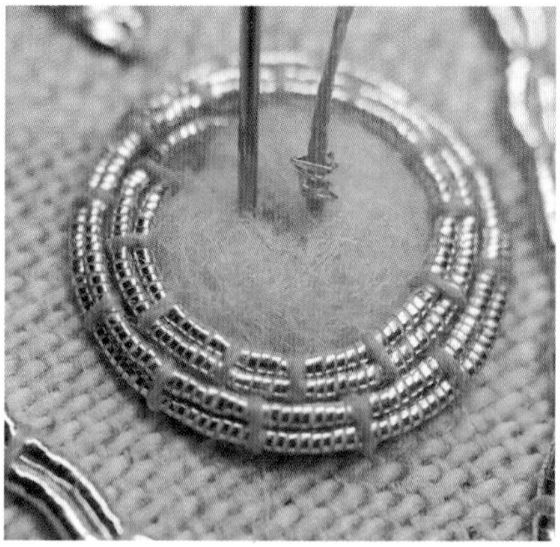

27 Bring the needle up and thread on a single chip, then slide the chip down to the surface of the felt. Take the needle down through the felt, making a stitch the same length as the chip.

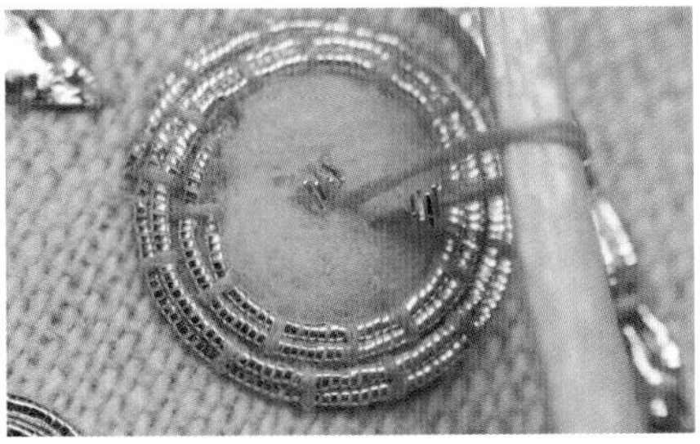

28 For each subsequent chip, bring the needle up a chip's length away from the existing chip(s) and down towards them at a slight angle. Use a mellor to hold the thread out of the way while tightening the stitch.

29 Work gradually out from the centre towards the edge of the shape, always taking the stitches back towards the existing chips at a slight angle.

30 Try to make the stitches at as many varied angles as possible to achieve the most sparkle. Continue chipping until the shape is completely filled and no felt is showing. If necessary you can cut some smaller chips to fill gaps around the edge.

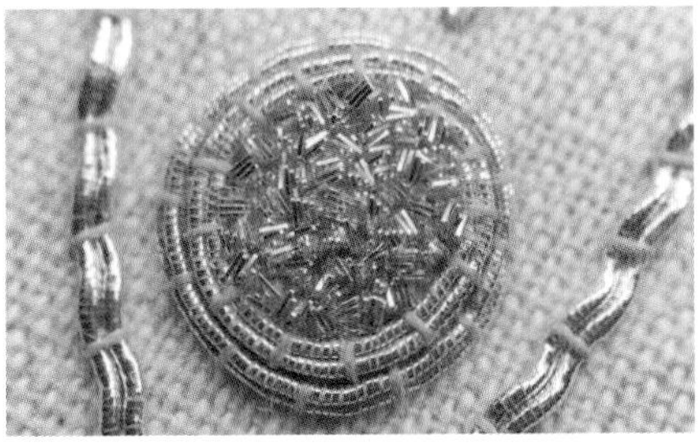

31 Fill the other felt circle with chipping in the same way.

32 Prepare to stitch the antennae by casting on very carefully on the line with two tiny stitches. Cut two chips of bright check the same length as the antennae.

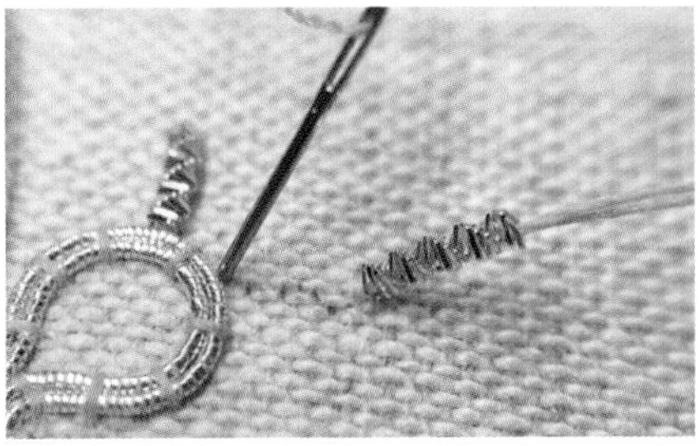

33 Bring the needle up at the tip of one antenna, thread on one long chip and take the needle down at the base of the antenna, tucking the needle towards the smooth passing thread at a slight angle. Repeat for the second antenna.

34 Prepare to stitch the spangle details on the wings by casting on very carefully in the spot where you will place the largest spangle. The spangle placement is not marked on the diagram – you can position them as you wish, just try to make them about the same on both sides.

35 Bring the needle up and thread on a 6mm spangle. Cut a chip of bright check that is slightly longer than normal, and thread this on too. Position the spangle so that the dent sits in the same place as you want the stitch to be, and take the needle down.

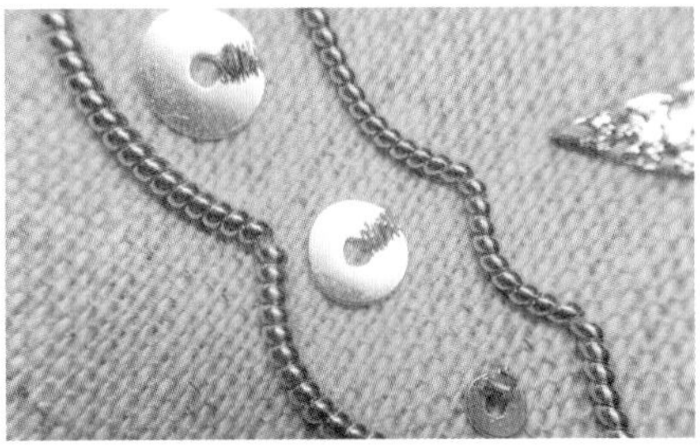

36 Carefully position and stitch the remaining spangles, using chips of bright check to secure them and disguise their dents.

PROJECT 2

THE HOLLY AND THE IVY

Christmas is the perfect time for goldwork, as all the glitter and sparkle cheers up those cold winter days.

This design is based on the old carol 'The Holly and the Ivy' – intertwining branches of those beautiful leaves that epitomize the season.

It includes gorgeous coloured metal threads, but would be equally as lovely worked in a combination of gold and silver or copper.

The finished The Holly and the Ivy project.

What you will need:

Materials

- White Normandy linen: at least 20cm (8in) square
- White calico: at least 20cm (8in) square
- Red felt: 10cm (4in) square
- Gutermann Sew-all sewing thread No. 488 (gold)
- Gutermann Sew-all sewing thread No. 156 (red)
- Gutermann Sew-all sewing thread No. 402 (dark green)
- Gutermann Sew-all sewing thread No. 919 (light green)
- Gutermann Sew-all sewing thread No. 800 (white)
- Cedar Green $1^1/_2$ twist: 2.5m (8ft)
- Grass Green $1^1/_2$ twist: 2.5m (8ft)
- Gilt pearl purl No. 1: 50cm (20in)
- Vivid Red wire check No. 6: 100cm (39in)
- Gilt bright check No. 6: 20cm (8in)
- 2mm spangles × 20–30
- 4mm spangles × 10

Equipment

- Hoop frame at least 15cm (6in)
- Embroidery scissors
- Goldwork scissors
- Beeswax
- Mellor
- Tweezers
- Embroidery needles (9–12)
- Chenille needle (20–22)
- Paint, pen or pencil

Design Templates

- Design template
- Felt template

1 Frame up the linen and calico. Transfer the design with your preferred method: tracing (before framing up) or prick and pounce (after framing up). Stab stitch with white sewing thread every 5–10mm ($^3/_{16}$–$^3/_8$in) on the design lines. Keep the stitches very small so that they don't show.

2 Use the template provided to mark the berries on the red felt. They are very similar, so cut each one as you come to stitch it to save confusion.

3 Cast on a single red sewing thread inside one of the berry shapes on the fabric. Match the felt to the lines on the fabric. Secure it first with four stitches: top, bottom, left and right. Come up in the fabric and down in the felt with a stitch 1–2mm ($^{1}/_{16}$in) in length. Then go round the felt circle making a stitch every 1–2mm ($^{1}/_{16}$in). Repeat this for each berry.

4 Bring together two ends of cedar green twist. Use a single length of waxed dark green sewing thread to make the first couching stitch close to the end of the design line, leaving a 5cm (2in) tail. Continue to couch along the line, holding the metal threads under a little tension and manipulating them along the curved line. The couching stitches should turn slightly as you stitch, so that they stay at right angles to the metal thread.

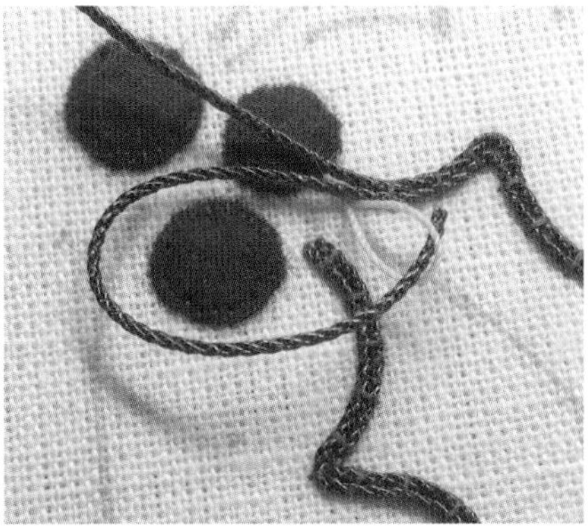

5 At the corner, you will need to make a sharp turn with each metal thread. Bring the needle up in between the two metal threads, right at the corner. Pull the outer metal thread tightly against the sewing thread, and make a tiny stitch over the bend. Bring the needle up inside the inner metal thread and pull the metal thread tightly against the sewing thread, then make a tiny stitch to meet up with the previous one. Do the same for each corner along the side of the leaf.

6 At the tip of the leaf, the corner is slightly sharper and so needs different treatment. Bring the needle up right in the corner, on the design line, between the two metal threads. Pull the outer metal thread tightly against the sewing thread, and make a tiny stitch over the bend. Pinch the outer thread to keep the corner sharp, and make a stitch over the pinched threads to hold them together. Turn the inner thread as before, and then continue to couch along the line.

7 Once the couching is complete, plunge the metal threads individually with a large chenille needle and a lasso of extra strong thread. Make sure to cover the end of the design line.

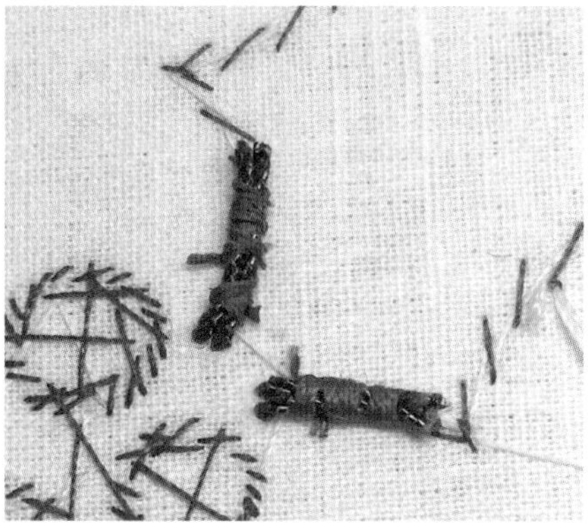

8 Tie back the metal threads on the back with a double waxed thread in a curved needle. Overcast the threads back behind the couching so that it won't show on the front. Stitch for about 10mm (5/8in) to keep the threads secure.

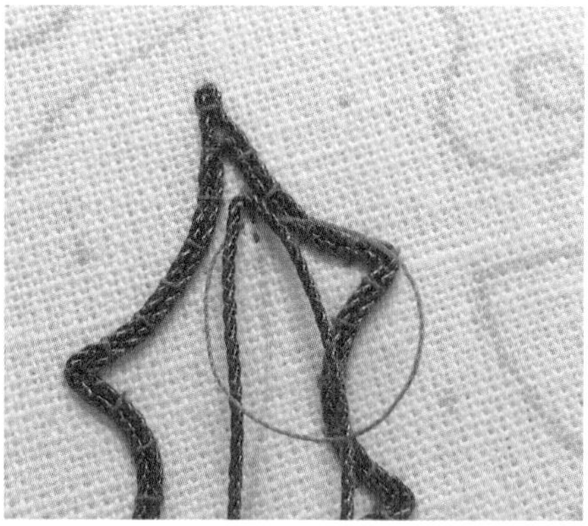

9 Couch cedar green twist on the holly leaf veins and stems. For the veins, start with a fold in the metal thread. Bring the needle up at the end of the design line and make a tiny stitch, catching the folded metal thread. Pinch the fold with fingers or tweezers, and make a couching stitch close to the fold, catching both lengths of metal thread. This stitch should keep the fold tight with no fabric showing between the threads.

10 Continue to stitch the holly leaves, veins and stems. Plunge all the ends neatly and tie them back.

11 Couch the ivy leaf and stem in the same way as the holly but with grass green twist – starting with a fold for the stem.

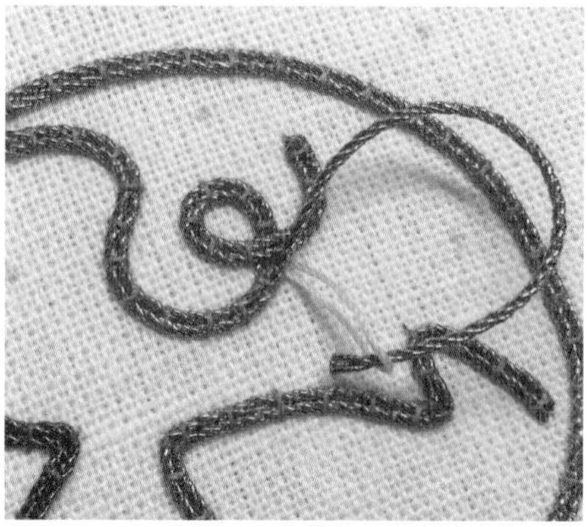

12 Stitch the tendrils, beginning each one at the tip with a fold. For the one that loops over itself, start at the tip and work round the loop. Cut the metal threads leaving the usual 5cm (2in) tail, and begin a new line of couching on the other side of the loop. Plunge the tails on either side of the loop, and tie back the threads with a waxed double thread on the back.

13 Surround each berry with a ring of pearl purl No. 1. Remember to stretch the pearl purl and trim the end neatly before you begin. Start at any point on the edge of the circle with a single waxed gold sewing thread. Bring the needle up on the edge of the felt, and take it down into the felt to make a tiny stitch, catching the pearl purl. The thread should slip between the coils.

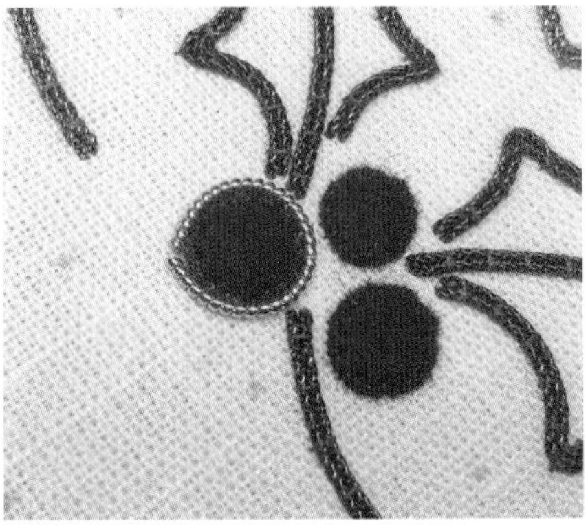

14 Spin the pearl purl so that the stitch falls between the first two coils. Continue to stitch round the circle, making a tiny stitch every two coils and shaping the pearl purl with your fingers. When you reach the start again, trim the pearl purl neatly so that it will fit up against the other end of the pearl purl. Make a stitch between the last two coils to complete the circle (it won't look perfect).

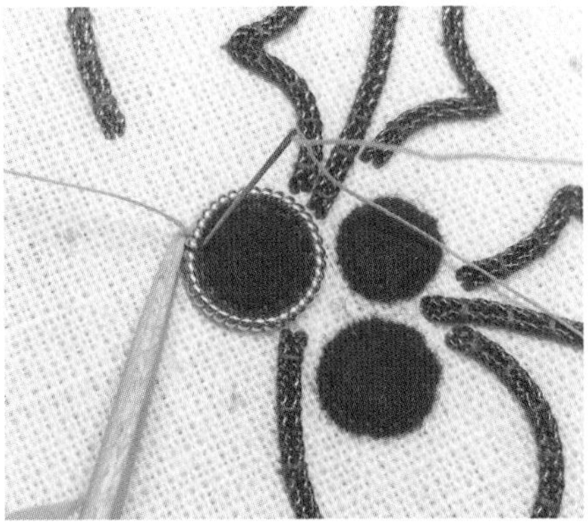

15 Make a stitch between the first two coils, bringing the needle up angled out from underneath the pearl purl, and then back towards the felt. Pull this stitch firmly to tuck in the end of the pearl purl, and use a mellor to tweak the pearl purl into shape. Make another stitch like this in the last two coils as well if necessary to make the join nearly invisible. Repeat this for all the berries.

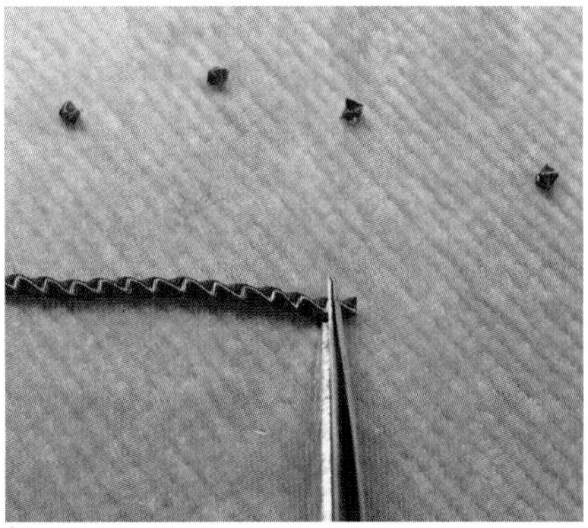

16 Cut a few chips of red wire check (they should be about as long as they are wide). Make sure to cut with the blade straight so that the end of the chip is free from tags and doesn't get crushed.

17 Begin chipping in the centre of one of the berries with a double waxed red sewing thread. Bring the needle up, thread on a chip, and slide it down to the surface of the felt. Make a stitch the same length as the chip so that the chip sits neatly on its side, and use a mellor to control the sewing thread as you pull it through to prevent tangling.

18 Continue to fill the berries with chips of red wire check. Make the stitches at varying angles so that they reflect light well and look sparkly. Always bring the needle up a chip-length away from the existing chipping and then angle the needle towards the chipping. If need be when the shape is nearly full, cut a few shorter chips to fill small spaces.

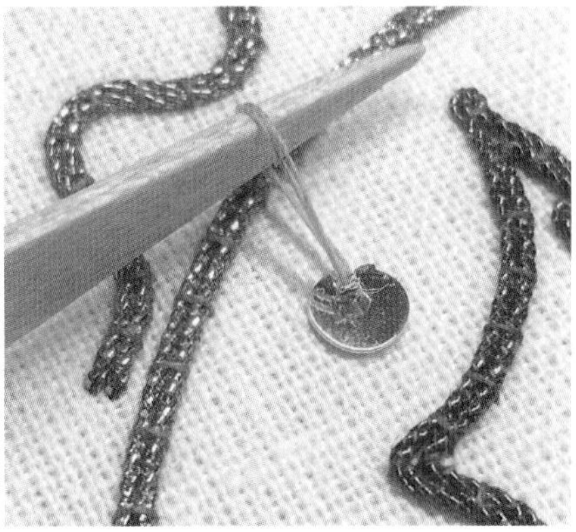

19 Scatter a mix of 4mm and 2mm spangles on to the background fabric, each one attached with a chip of gilt bright check No. 6. Using a double waxed gold thread, bring the needle up and thread on a spangle and a chip, taking both down to the surface of the fabric. Take the needle down through the hole in the spangle until the chip sits flat on its side. Repeat for each spangle.

PROJECT 3

ROSES

Roses are a beautiful subject in art, with their intertwining petals creating twists and curves. This design was refined from a simple drawing of a bunch of roses; each flower has a slightly different character.

This project is a great introduction to layered felt padding, which is used to create depth in the flowers. Each rose has areas of couching worked to add to the flow and dimensions of the design.

What you will need:

Materials

- Pink silk dupion: at least 35cm (14in) square
- Calico: at least 35cm (14in) square
- Yellow felt: 20cm (8in) square
- Gutermann Sew-all sewing thread No. 968
- K4 Japanese thread: 35m (38yd)
- Gilt pearl purl No. 1: 30cm (12in)
- Gilt pearl purl super: 30cm (12in)
- Gilt twist No. 3: 50cm (20in)
- Gilt bright check No. 6: 10cm (4in)

Diagrams

- Order of Work
- Stitch Diagram

Equipment

- Frame at least 25cm (10in)
- Embroidery scissors
- Goldwork scissors
- Beeswax
- Mellor
- Tweezers
- Embroidery needles (9–12)
- Chenille needle (20–22)
- Extra-strong thread for plunging lasso
- Prick-and-pounce kit (optional)
- Paint or pencil

Design Templates

- Design template
- Felt template

The finished Roses project.

1 Frame up the linen and silk. Transfer the design with your preferred method: tracing (before framing up) or prick and pounce (after framing up). Stab stitch with matching pink sewing thread every 5–10mm ($^3/_{16}$–$^3/_8$in) on the design lines or just inside them where they will be covered. Keep the stitches very small so that they don't show.

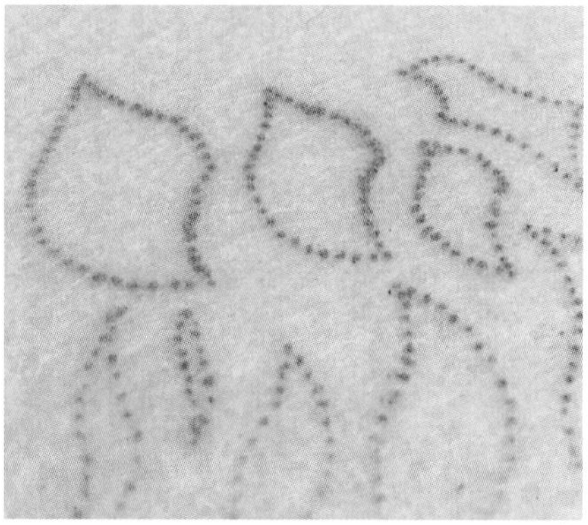

2 Use the felt templates provided to create the felt shapes – the easiest way to get these accurate is by using the prick-and-pounce method. Cut out each one as you need it, rather than all at once. When you cut, do so just inside the line (this is particularly important because there are so many overlapping shapes in this design).

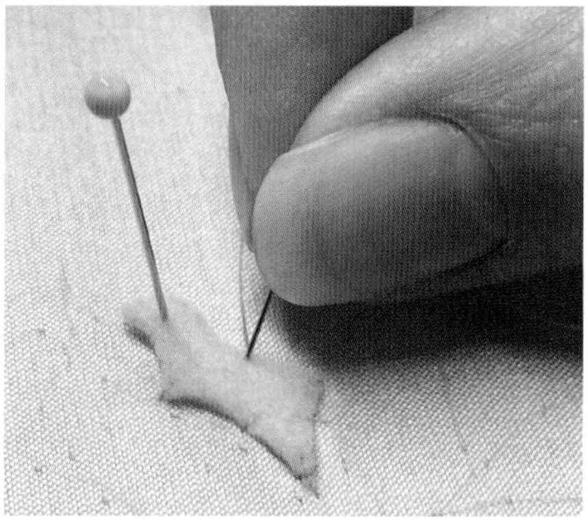

3 Cast on a single sewing thread inside one of the felt shapes on the fabric (it doesn't matter which one you do first, the numbers are simply a reference). Match the felt to the lines on the fabric, or place it inside the lines if it is a lower layer. Use pins to hold it in place. Bring the needle up in the fabric and down in the felt with a stitch 1–2mm ($^1/_{16}$in) in length. Place a stitch every 5–10mm ($^3/_{16}$–$^3/_8$in) to secure it.

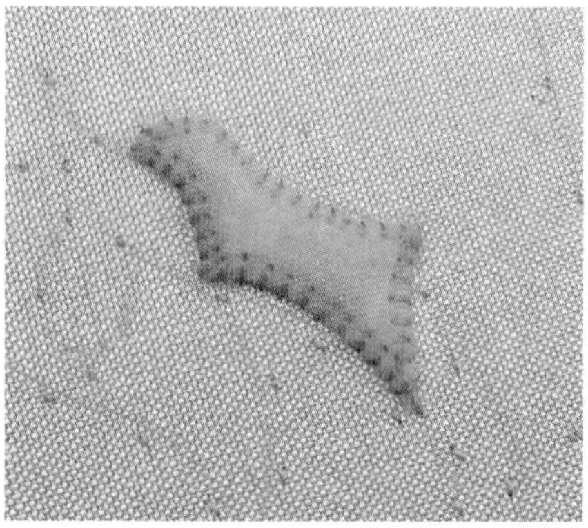

4 Go round the felt shape again, making a stitch every 1–2mm ($^1/_{16}$in); this fully secures the felt.

5 Repeat the last two steps for each felt area – for those with multiple layers, do the same method for each layer, and make sure that the top layer matches up to the design lines (so that you can just barely see the lines).

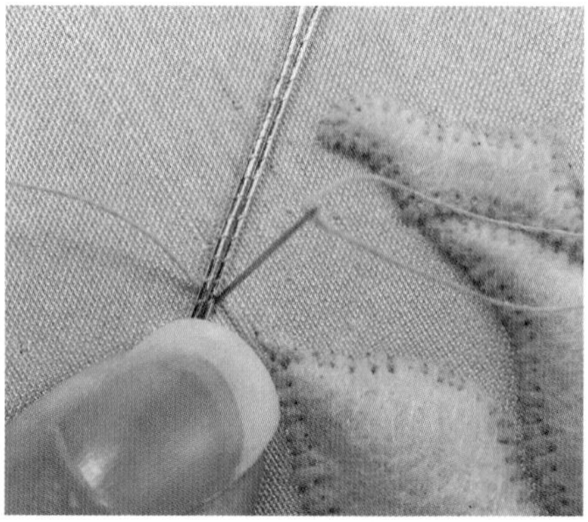

6 Most of the rose petals will be filled with couched Japanese thread. Each area has its own direction lines and specific starting point. Follow the numbers on the diagram for the order of work so that the overlapping sections work well together. Begin with number 1 on the left-hand rose, starting at the top of the section on the outline. Use a single waxed sewing thread. Bring the needle up on the outside of the design line, and make a stitch over a pair of Japanese threads leaving a 5cm (2in) tail.

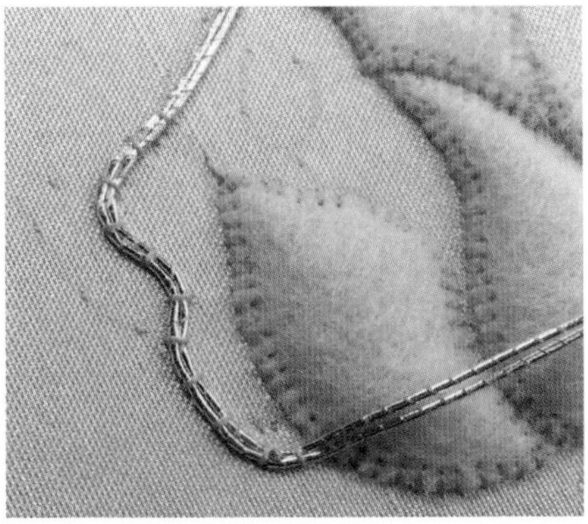

7 Stitch round the petal, bringing the needle up on the outside of the design line and carrying the stitch over the Japanese thread every 3mm ($^1/_8$in). Make sure that as you stitch you manipulate the metal threads into position before you stitch them down, so that they follow a nice line. The stitches should all sit at right angles to the gold at that point on the curve, so they will naturally change direction along the way.

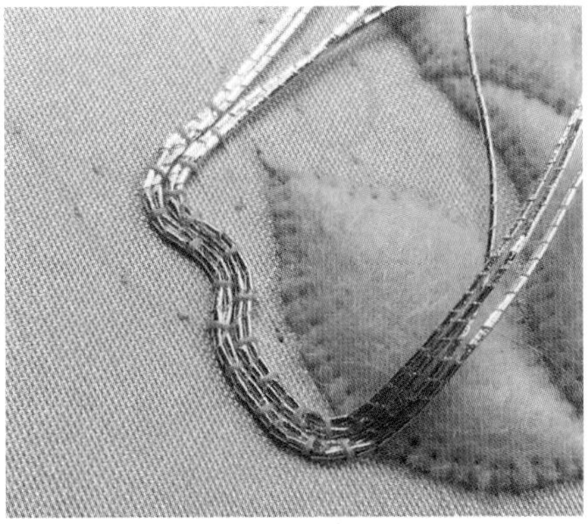

8 For the next row, bring the needle up with enough space between it and the previous row for the pair of metal threads to sit neatly parallel. Place the stitches between those of the previous row to create a brick pattern. Because of the curves, the stitches will not stay the same distance apart. When they get to a point where the gold doesn't show through or it isn't securely attached, they can be spaced further apart or closer together, breaking the brick pattern.

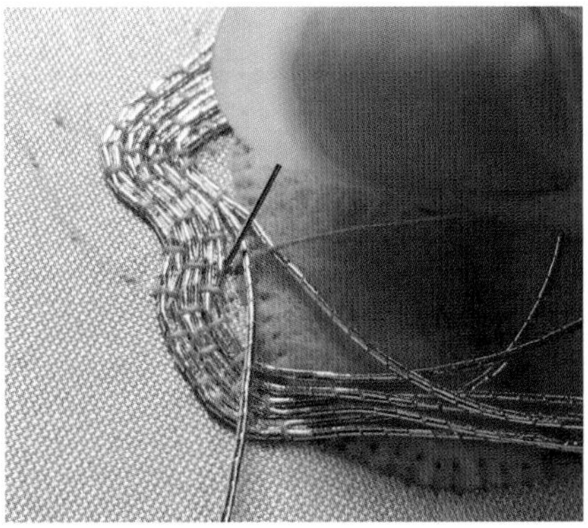

9 Continue to stitch rows of couching to continue the shape, keeping to the brick pattern as far as is reasonable. When you bump into the edge of the shape you may need to stitch over just one thread to fill the space – cut the other one with a tail, and join a new one in if the space widens again.

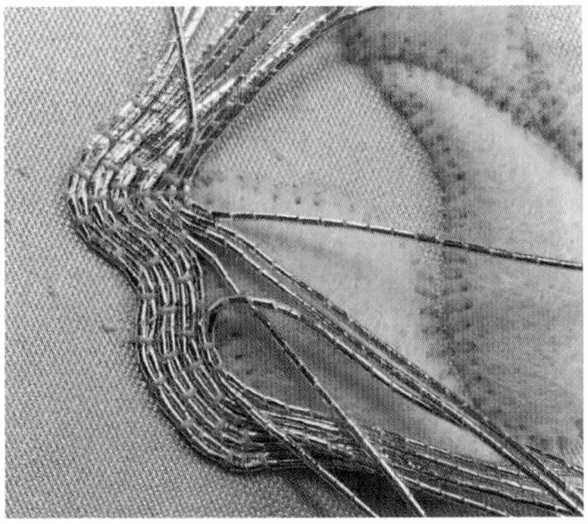

10 As you work towards the centre of the rose the corners will tighten, so you may need to turn the Japanese threads individually. Bring the needle up in the corner and fold the first Japanese thread back on itself to create a tight bend, then make a tiny stitch over the corner. Then do the same for the second one. The last few pieces of Japanese thread will be very short to fill the top right-hand corner – make sure to still cut with long enough tails for plunging.

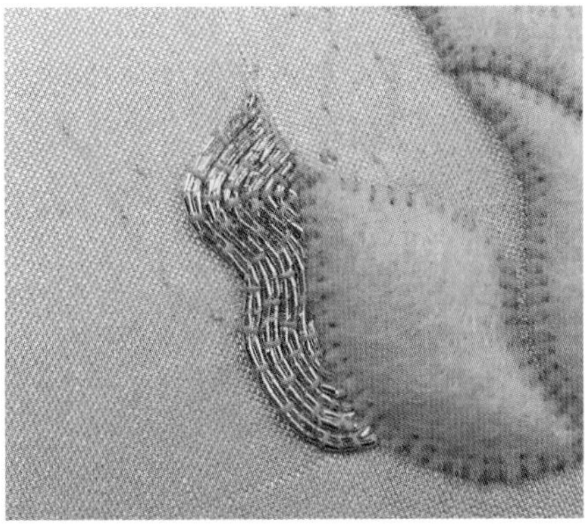

11 Plunge all the metal threads. Start on the outside edge at one end and work towards the middle, and then start again on the other outside edge and work towards the middle again. This should preserve the outer shape to give a good finish.

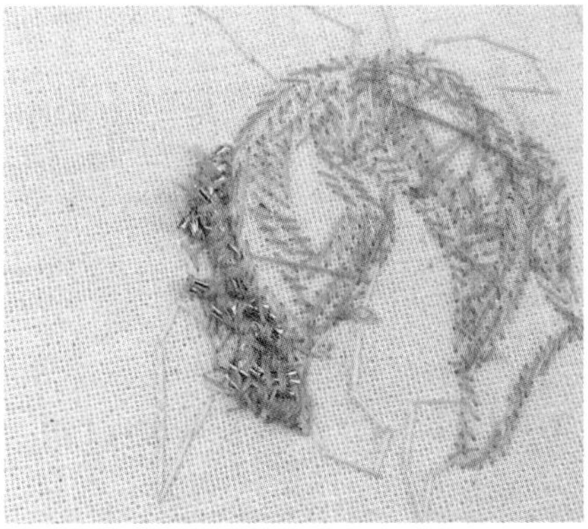

12 Tie back the metal threads on the reverse with a double waxed thread in a curved needle. Try to tie back fewer than four threads at a time, and remember to fold them back under themselves so that they won't be in the way of the next section of embroidery.

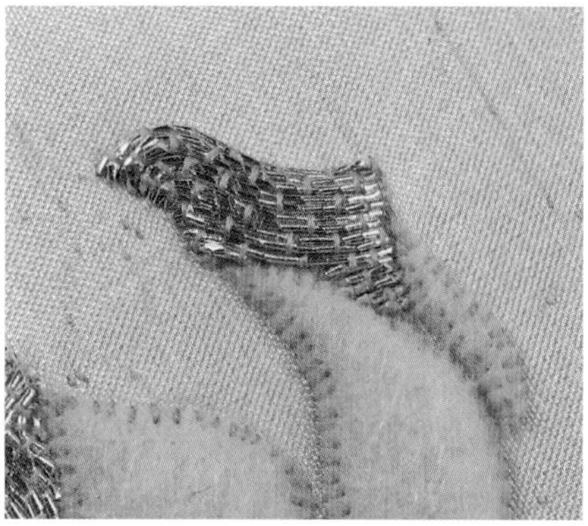

13 Couch petal 2 in the same way, beginning on the outside edge (top right). Be careful to follow the curve with each row so that the couching fills the space. As you work towards the middle of the rose the rows of couching get very short – one stitch will hold them if need be. If you are unsure if another row is needed, leave it for now as a tiny bit can be placed in later. Plunge and tie back the Japanese thread, leaving the design line showing for the next petal.

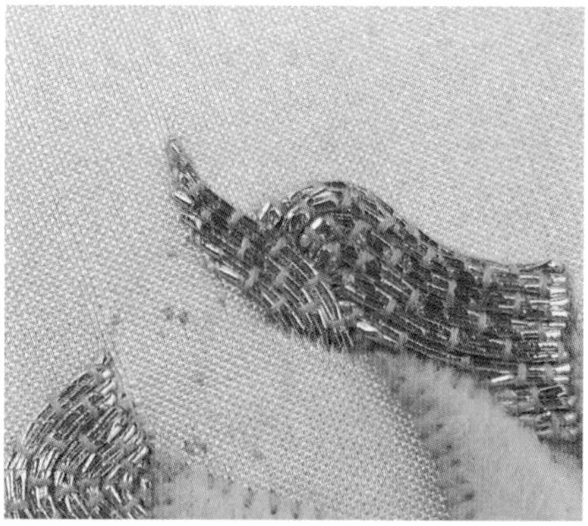

14 Couch petal 3, starting on the right-hand edge. On the first row when stitching next to the existing couching take the stitch towards it, whereas when you are stitching against blank fabric you should stitch in towards the middle as usual. Subsequent rows should be stitched towards the previous row as usual. Plunge and tie back the metal threads, covering the design lines.

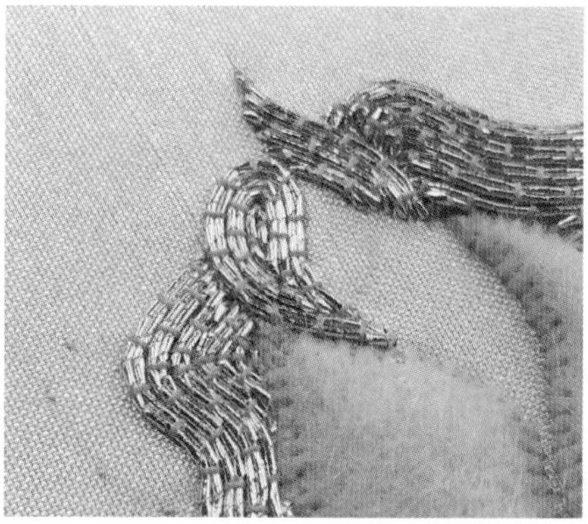

15 Couch petal 4, starting in the bottom corner and working clockwise round the shape back to the start. Use a single metal thread in the centre if needed. Plunge and tie back the metal threads.

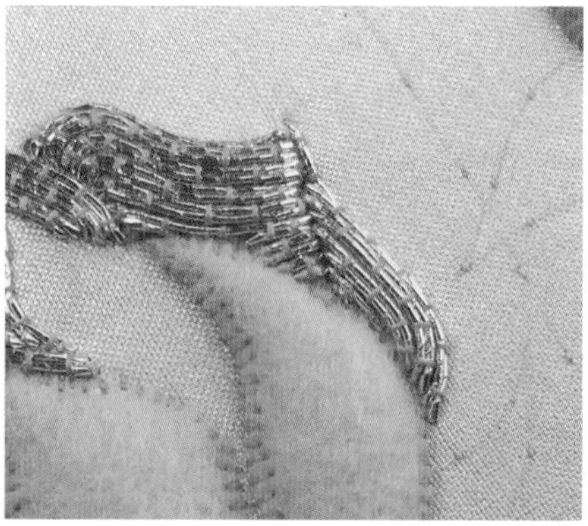

16 Couch petal 5, starting on the outer edge and working towards the middle. Plunge and tie back the metal threads, leaving the design lines showing for the next petal.

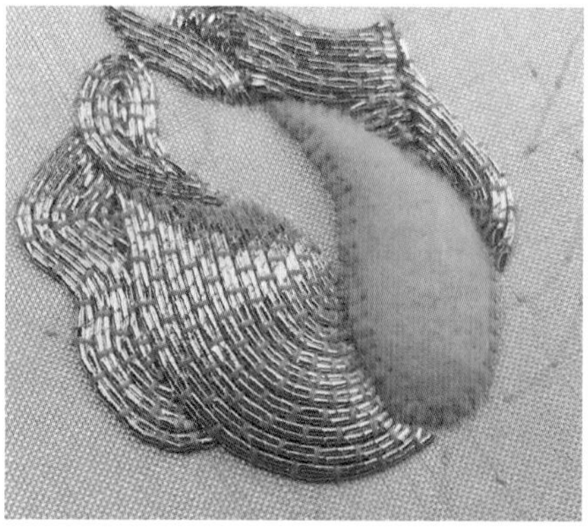

17 Couch petal 6, beginning on the outer edge (left-hand side) and working towards the centre of the rose. Be extra careful to keep the tension even throughout the couching as the padding is high. Once finished, the rounded shape should still be evident. Carefully plunge the threads to preserve the shape, and tie back the threads on the reverse.

18 Couch petal 7, beginning on the outer edge (right-hand side) at the very bottom point of the petal, and working up to the tip of the petal. Continue to couch towards the centre of the rose. The curve will gradually become tighter until you need to make a sharp turn on the last few rows. Carefully plunge the threads to preserve the smooth edge, and tie back the threads on the reverse.

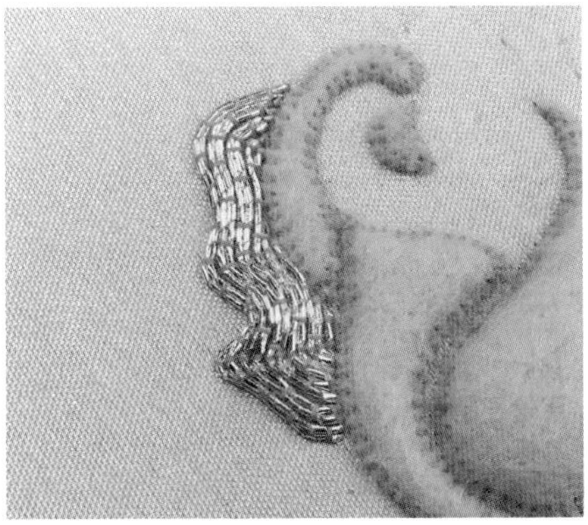

19 Couch petal 8 on the middle flower. Begin on the outer edge, stitching from the outline inwards for the first row. For the corner, turn each metal thread individually to achieve a sharp point. As you continue to couch towards the centre of the rose, repeat the sharp turn. Carefully plunge the threads, leaving the design lines showing for the next petals. Tie back the metal threads on the reverse.

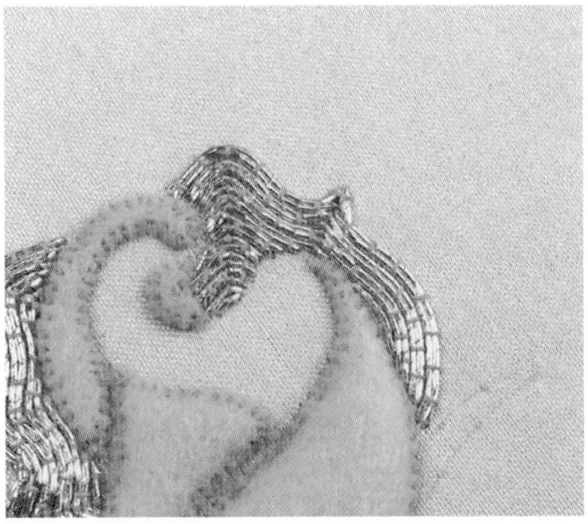

20 Couch petal 9, beginning on the outer edge. To achieve a good point at the sharp corner you will need to turn the outer metal thread and plunge the inner one. It is a good idea to plunge and tie back the inner thread straightaway so that you can see the shape clearly for the next row, which will probably not need plunging. Continue to couch to fill the shape, and then plunge the threads and tie them back on the reverse.

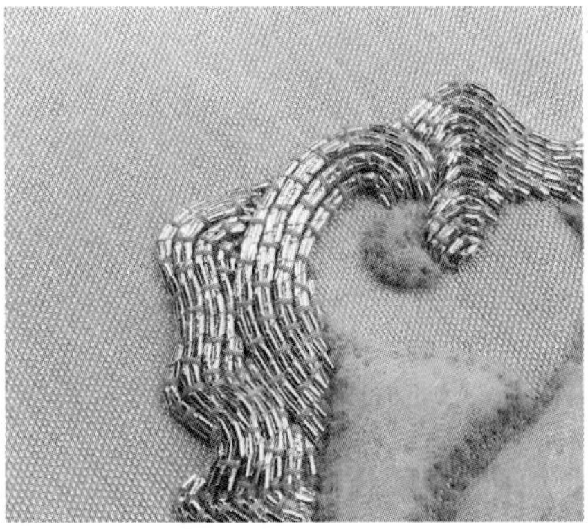

21 Couch petal 10, beginning on the outer edge. On the first row when stitching next to the existing couching, take the stitch towards it, whereas when you are stitching against blank fabric you should stitch in towards the middle as usual. Subsequent rows should be stitched towards the previous row as usual. Plunge and tie back the metal threads.

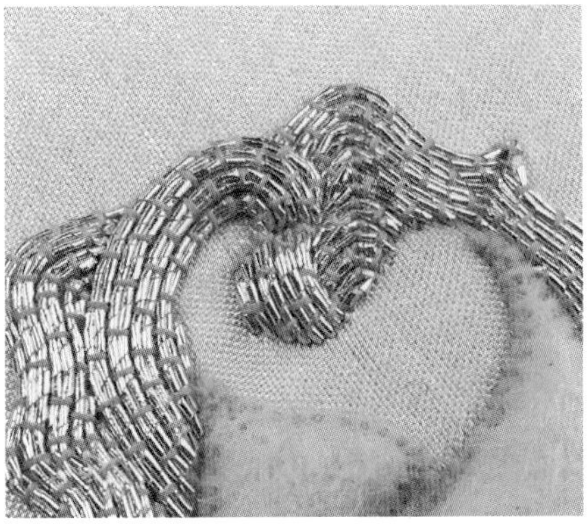

22 Couch petal 11, beginning on the right-hand side. The lengths required are very short, but it is important to continue to cut with plenty of excess, as the metal thread is more likely to pull through further than intended with so few stitches to secure it. Continue to couch across the shape, then plunge to cover the design lines and tie back the threads on the reverse.

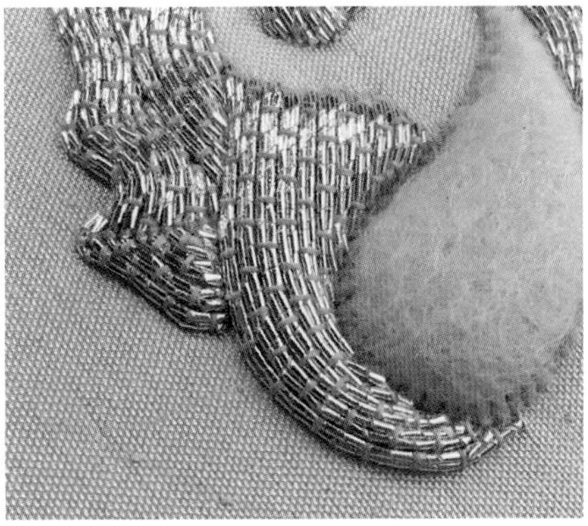

23 Couch petal 12, beginning on the outer edge (left-hand side). Work across the petal to the right-hand side, where the lengths will get very short to fill the space. Plunge the metal threads very carefully on the top right edge to preserve the shape, and leave the outline showing for the next petal on the lower right. Tie back the threads on the reverse.

24 Couch petal 13, beginning on the outer edge (right-hand side) and working from the tip to the base where it meets the previous petal. Continue to couch towards the centre of the rose. The curve will gradually become tighter until you may need to make a sharp turn on the last few rows. Carefully plunge the threads to preserve the smooth edge, and tie back the threads on the reverse.

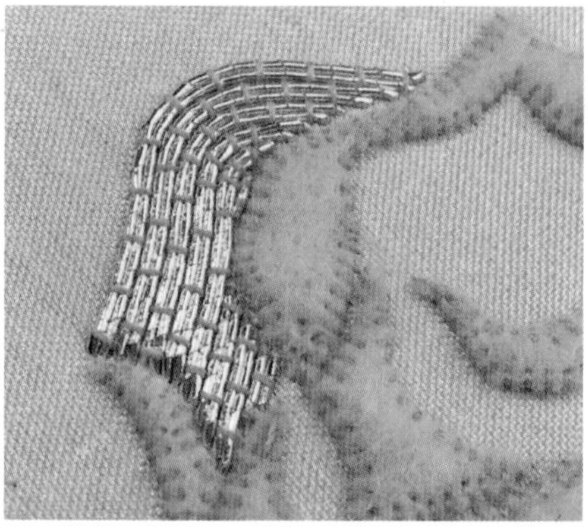

25 Couch petal 14, beginning on the outer edge with the needle coming up on the outer edge of the design line so that it will be covered. Continue to couch towards the centre of the rose. Plunge the threads so that you can see the outlines of the next petals, and then tie back on the reverse.

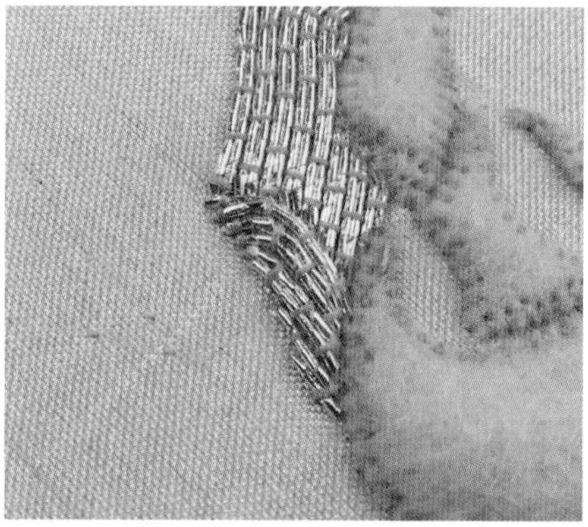

26 Couch petal 15, beginning on the inner edge (right-hand side). On the first row when stitching next to the existing couching, take the stitch towards it. Subsequent rows should be stitched towards the previous row as usual. Plunge and tie back the metal threads, covering the design lines.

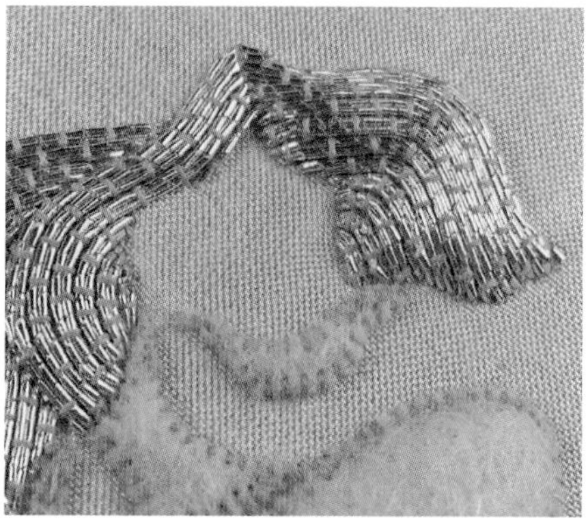

27 Couch petal 16, beginning on the outer edge. On the first row when stitching next to the existing couching, take the stitch towards it, whereas when you are stitching against blank fabric you should stitch in towards the middle as usual. Subsequent rows should be stitched towards the previous row as usual. Plunge and tie back the metal threads to preserve the shape, covering the design lines except where they are overlapped by petals.

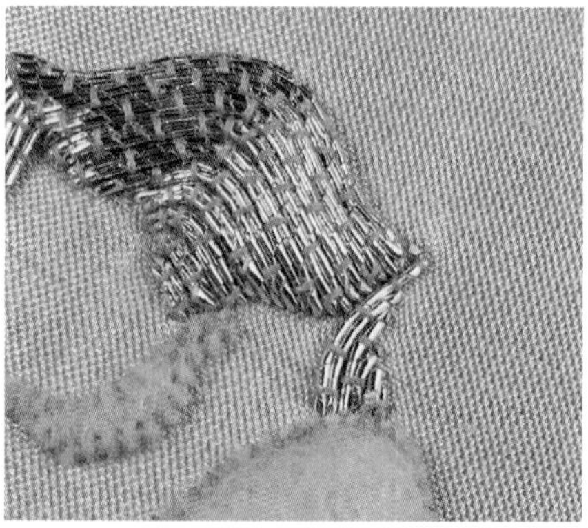

28 Couch petal 17, beginning on the inner edge (left-hand side) and working across the petal. Take extra care with the tiny pieces of Japanese thread, especially when plunging and tying back – it is easy to expose the core when pulling such short lengths.

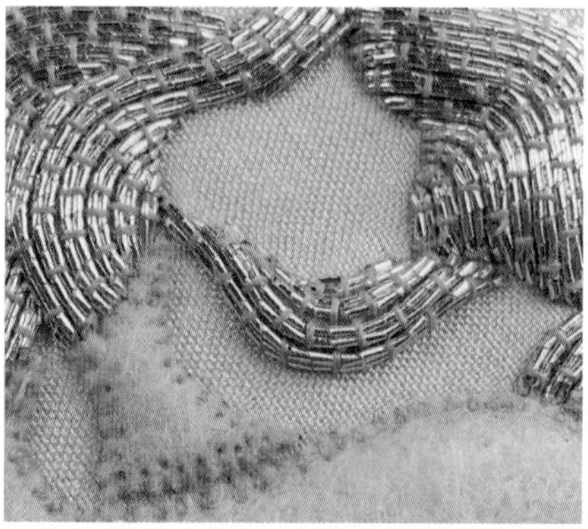

29 Couch petal 18, beginning on the outer (bottom) edge and working upwards. Plunge the threads, taking extra care where the ends meet the plunged ends of the previous petal on the right-hand side. Tie back the threads on the reverse.

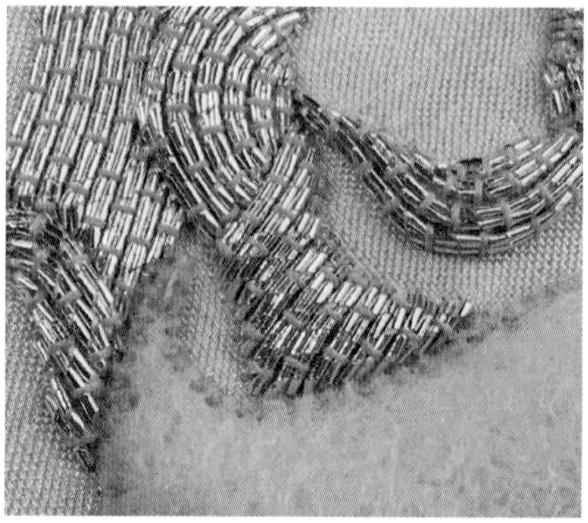

30 Couch petal 19, beginning on the outer (top) edge and working downwards. Plunge the metal threads, taking extra care to pull them through gently because the lengths are quite short. Cover the design line on the right-hand side of the shape nearest the centre of the rose, and leave it showing against the next petals.

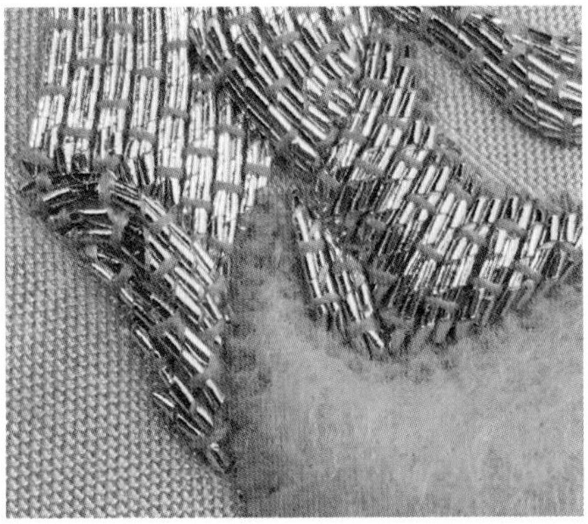

31 Couch petal 20, filling the tiny space at an angle similar to that of petal 14 so that it is distinctly different from petal 19. It will only take a few short lengths to fill the tiny space. Plunge the metal threads and tie them back on the reverse.

32 Couch petal 21, beginning on the outer edge, working from the pointed end on the left-hand side to where it meets the previous petal on the right-hand side. Continue to couch towards the centre of the rose. In the centre of the petal you may end up needing to couch round and round to fill a little space – do so with a pair of Japanese threads until they don't fit comfortably, then go down to one thread. Plunge the threads to cover the design lines, and tie them back on the reverse.

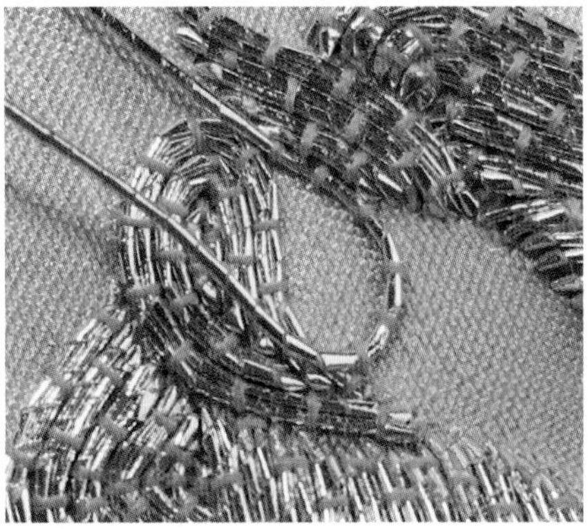

33 On the left-hand rose, couch a single Japanese thread along the left-hand side of petal 2, and then continue along the design line to join up with petal 5. Take care to cover the design line – if one Japanese thread isn't enough, add another one next to it.

34 Plunge and tie back the ends of the Japanese thread.

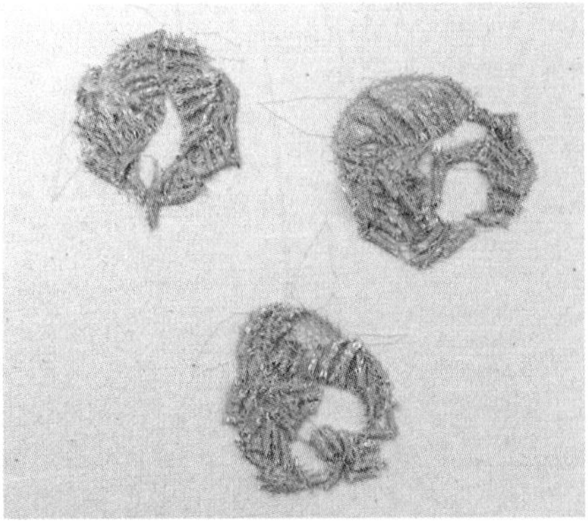

35 Once the Japanese threads are all tied back, the reverse of the embroidery should still look neat and tidy, but will be quite lumpy because the thread ends will cover a large amount of the stitched surface.

36 Begin to stitch No. 3 twist for the rose stems, using the invisible couching method with a single sewing thread. Take care to keep the stitches very small, and cover the design lines (bring the needle up on one side of the line and down the other side to ensure the size is kept to a minimum). To get started, make the first stitch 2–3mm ($^{1}/_{8}$in) from the start of the line, passing the thread through the twist, catching one of the three threads to the fabric. Allow a tail of about 5cm (2in) for plunging.

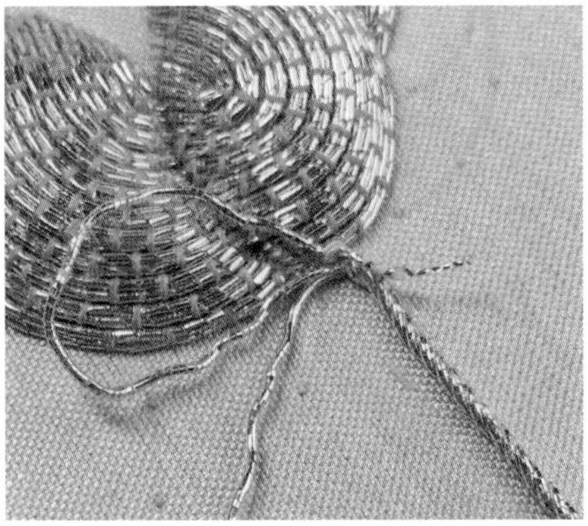

37 Unravel the twist to the plunge point (up against the rose petals or at the end of the design line). Plunge the twist, one ply at a time, retwisting if necessary to preserve the appearance right to the end of the line. Tie back the twist on the back with a curved needle and double sewing thread, taking care to keep the stitches hidden behind the couching so that they don't show or cause unsightly lumps.

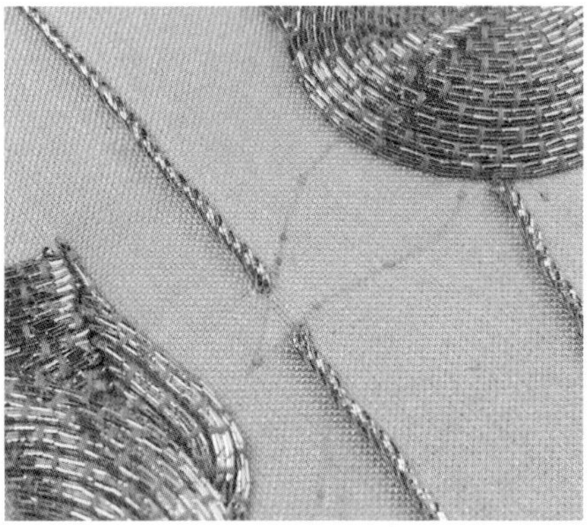

38 On the centre stem, finish the twist on either side of the leaf which crosses it. Take care to leave the design line of the leaf showing.

39 Stitch the leaves with pearl purl. Refer to the diagram for the size of the pearl purl – No. 1 or super. Begin the line of pearl purl up against the rose petals, working outwards to the tip. Cut the pearl purl at the tip, and restart with a new piece slightly offset to create the sharpest possible point.

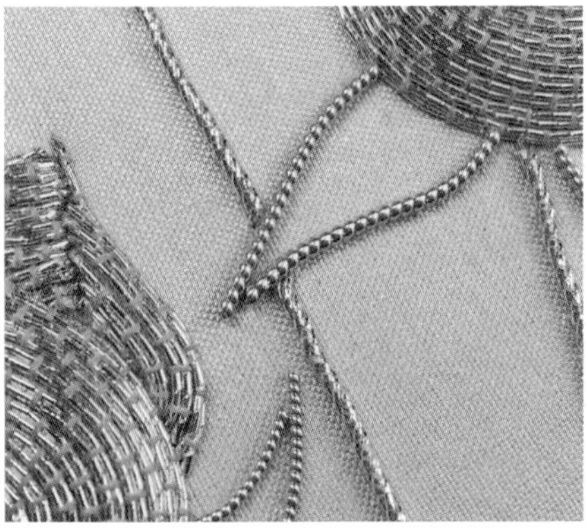

40 Take extra care with the leaf crossing the centre stem that the pearl purl follows a smooth line where it sits against the twist (this shouldn't be a problem if you left the outline showing clearly when you plunged the twist).

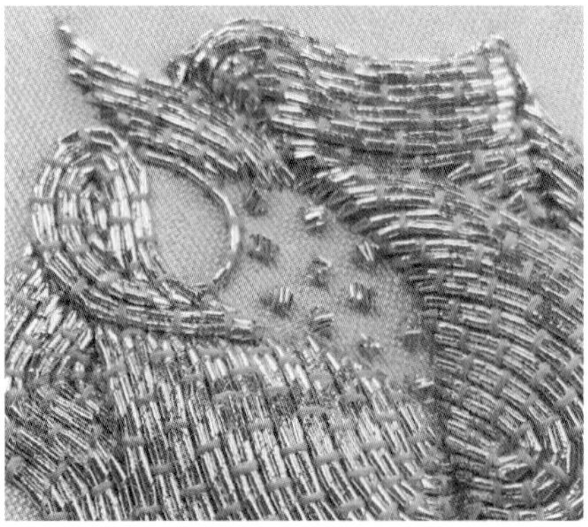

41 Scatter chips of bright check in the blank spaces of each rose, using a double waxed thread in a small needle. Try to keep the spacing even, but the chips at random angles as much as possible so that they reflect the most light. Use a mellor to guide the thread to avoid tangling with the chips.

42 Scatter the chips as closely or as far apart as you prefer in order to fill the spaces. Once complete, you may wish to cast off the final threads by oversewing on the back with a curved needle.

Design template.

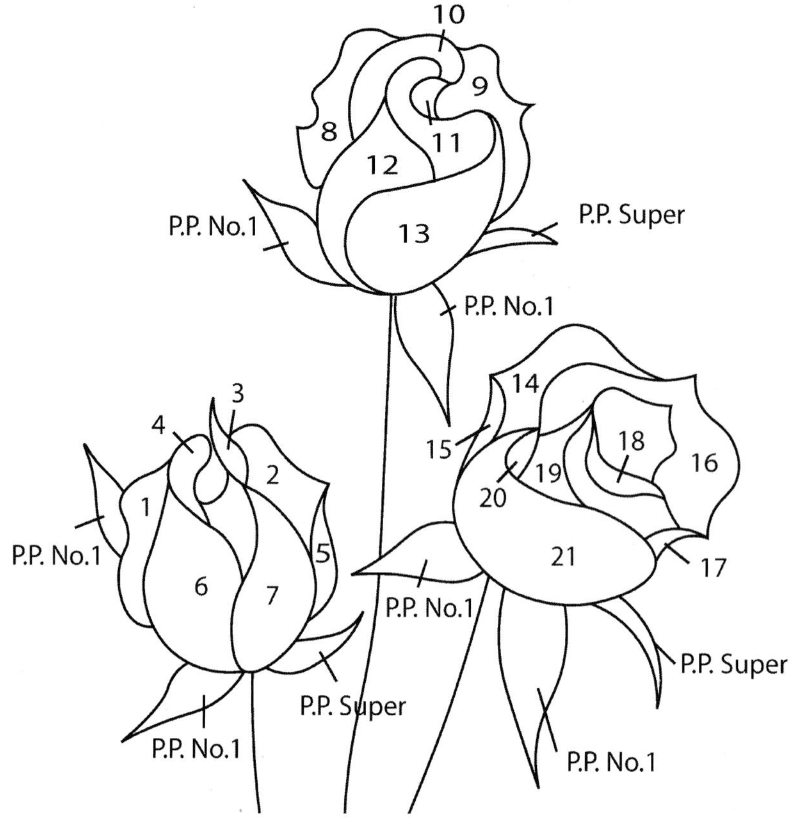

Order of work for couching Japanese thread, to be followed by stems stitched with twist, then leaves stitched with pearl purl, then scattered chips in the remaining rose petals. These numbers also apply to the felt pieces.

Diagram to show the positioning of the felt pieces.

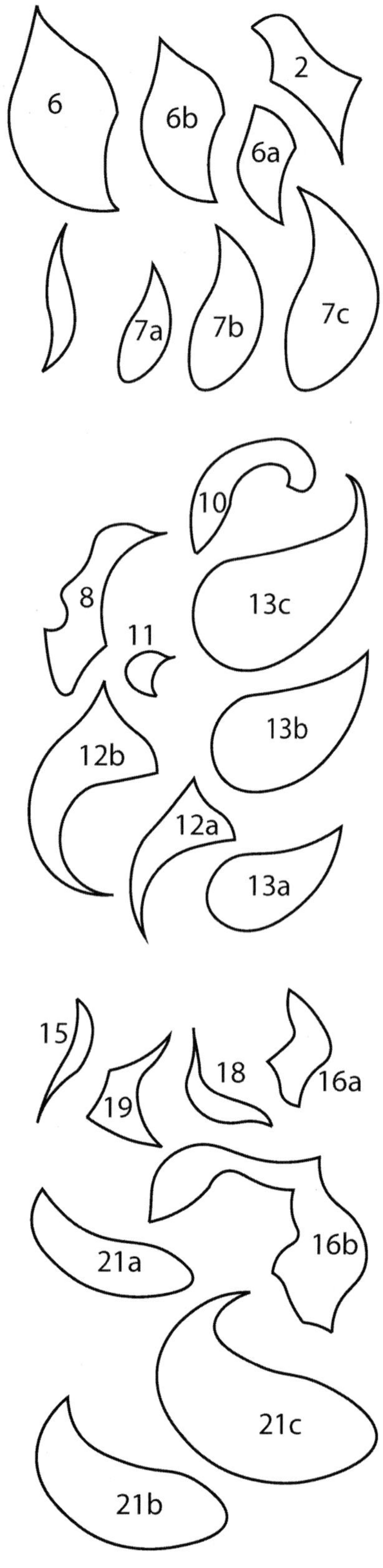

Felt templates.

PROJECT 4

SILK AND GOLD BUTTERFLY

Butterflies are a fantastic source of inspiration. This design features a good mix of techniques with felt padding, leather, couching, chipping and cutwork, and additional techniques of silk shading and French knots.

This butterfly project involves techniques that are a good step up from basic techniques, and is a lovely way to introduce some extra elements to your goldwork.

The finished Silk and Gold Butterfly project.

What you will need:

Materials

- Normandy linen: at least 25cm (10in) square
- Calico: at least 25cm (10in) square
- Felt: 20cm (8in) square
- Gold kid leather: 5cm (2in) square
- Gutermann Sew-all sewing thread No. 488 (gold)
- DMC stranded cotton in 3808, 3809, 3810, 352, 350 and 777 (or your preferred colours)
- Gilt smooth passing No. 7: 5m (5$^1/_2$yd)
- Gilt pearl purl No. 2: 50cm (20in)
- Gilt pearl purl No. 1: 50cm (20in)
- Gilt bright check No. 8: 1m (39in)
- Gilt rough purl No. 8: 50cm (20in)
- Gilt wire check No. 8: 50cm (20in)

Equipment

- Hoop frame: at least 20cm (8in)
- Embroidery scissors
- Goldwork scissors
- Beeswax
- Mellor
- Embroidery needles (10–12)
- Chenille needle (20)
- Extra-strong thread for plunging lasso
- Prick-and-pounce kit
- Paint or pencil

Design Templates

- Design template
- Felt template

1 Frame up the linen with calico behind. Transfer the design with your preferred method, tracing or prick and pounce – for this design it is well worth using prick and pounce, because it can then be used to make sure the felt matches up perfectly. Make tiny stab stitches in thread that matches the background fabric to secure the two layers of fabric.

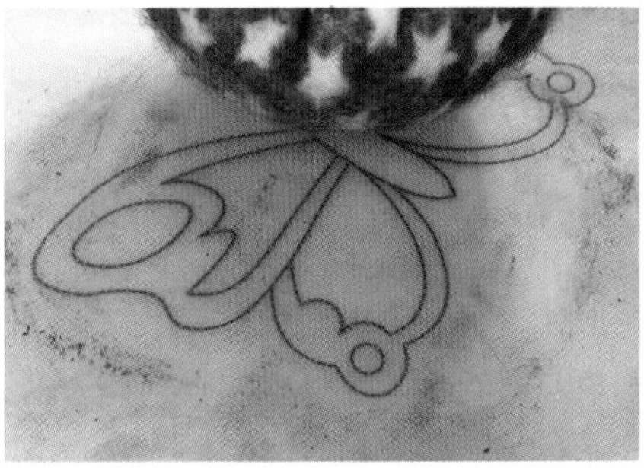

2 Use the pricking you made for the main design transfer to pounce on to the felt. Draw over the lines if you wish, or cut out the shapes straightaway if the dots are clear enough.

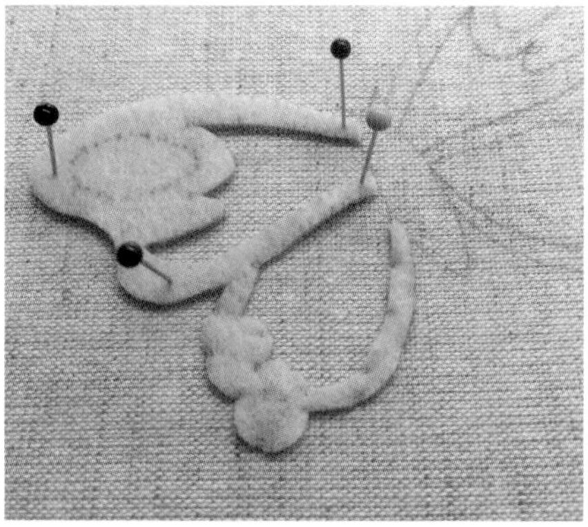

3 Cast on a single sewing thread. Match the felt to the lines on the fabric and secure the first shape with a few pins. Then make some securing stitches about 8mm ($^{5}/_{16}$in) apart and at each corner. Bring the needle up in the fabric and down in the felt with a stitch 1–2mm ($^{1}/_{16}$in) in length. As you stitch round, make sure that the shape still fits well, and trim if necessary, particularly where it meets the body.

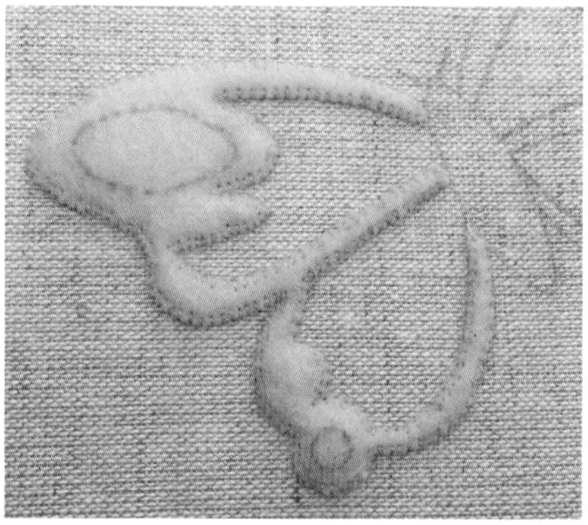

4 Work round the shape again, making the stitches 1–2mm ($^{1}/_{16}$in) apart, bringing the needle up in the fabric and down in the felt. Do the same for the second felt shape.

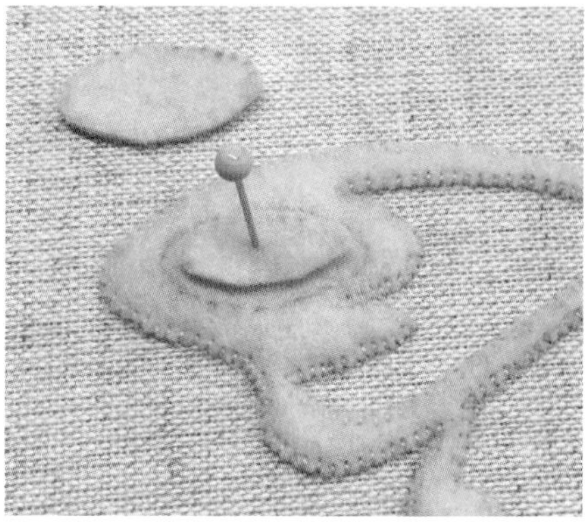

5 Use the extra felt template to create a pricking for the second layer on the butterfly's 'eye'. Pounce this on to the felt alongside the same part of the main template, and cut out the pieces.

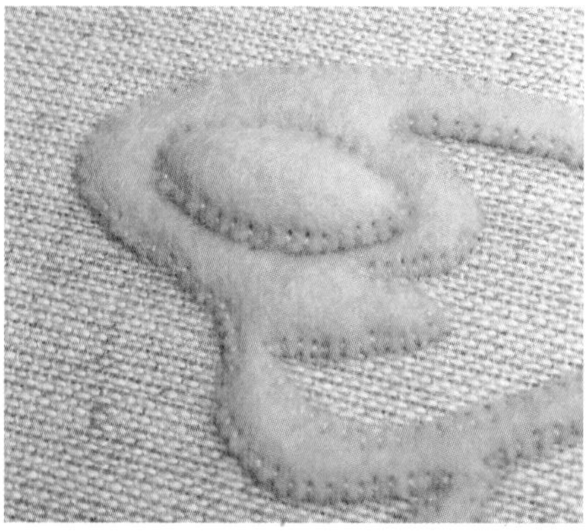

6 Align the smaller piece inside the design line. Bring the needle up in the background felt and down into the new piece of felt to make small stitches 1–2mm ($^{1}/_{16}$in) in length. Place a stitch at each end of the shape and each side to secure it initially, and then stitch round again with a 1–2mm ($^{1}/_{16}$in) gap between the stitches. Do the same for the larger piece, aligning it with the design line.

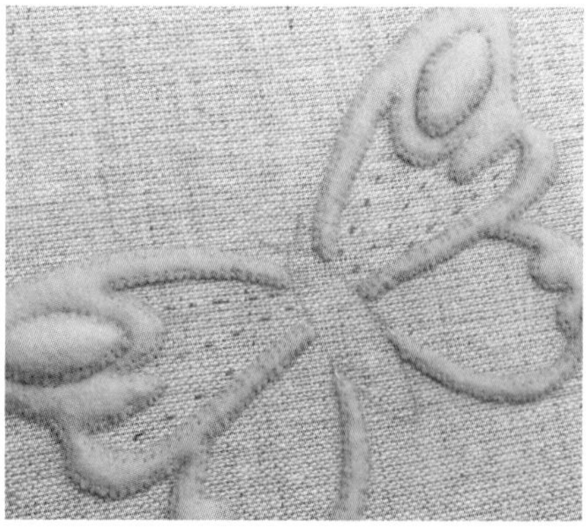

7 Before beginning the silk shading in the top wings, mark lines on the design roughly where the colour transitions will be. Add lines (in a different colour if you prefer) to indicate the angle of the stitches – slightly angled towards the centre. These are not set in stone, but serve as a reminder.

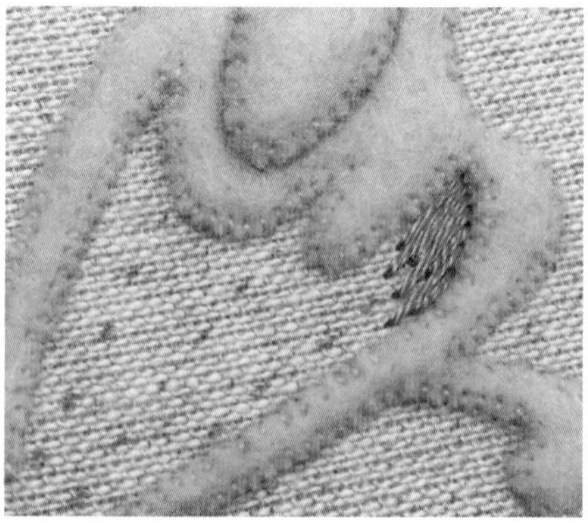

8 Begin the silk shading with the lightest turquoise, and use two threads in the needle. Because the shape is uneven, it needs to be started in the bottom corner (where it is longest). Bring the needle up in the centre and down at the edge of the felt. Make sure that the stitches are between 6mm ($^{1}/_{4}$in) and 10mm ($^{3}/_{8}$in) in length – any shorter than this and there will be no opportunity to split them well in the next row.

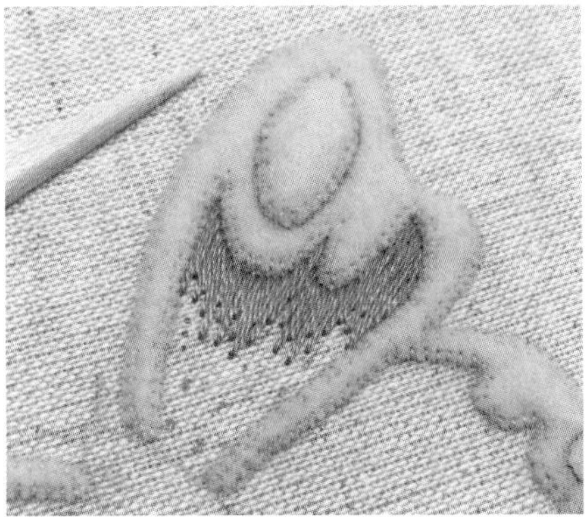

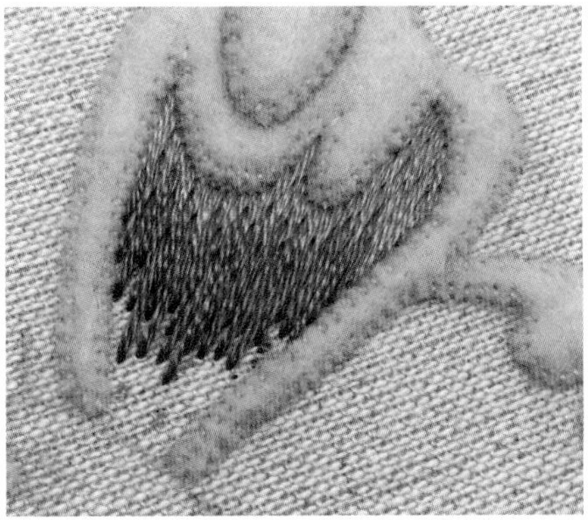

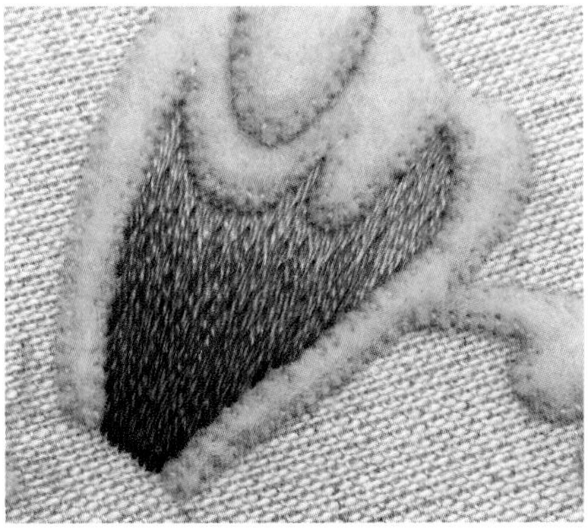

9 Begin the second row in the bottom corner, splitting the stitches of the first row by bringing the needle up through them. Make all the stitches about 10mm (3/8in) in length. Once those stitches have all been split, work to the side, bringing the needle up in the centre and down at the edge of the felt, like the first row. Make the stitches long and short like the first row, echoing the curved outline.

10 For the third row, pick up the medium turquoise as well as the light. Bring the needle up through the stitches in the second row, varying the starting point as much as possible to create a smooth blend of the two colours. Use a few stitches of the light turquoise where necessary to blend the colours better (particularly the bottom corner where the stitches will fall shorter). All the stitches should be about 10mm (3/8in) in length, which means the end points will vary to maintain the 'long and short' effect.

11 For the fourth row, pick up the dark turquoise as well as the medium. As before, bring the needle up through the previous stitches. Use the medium turquoise for just a few stitches to help the blending. This time some (or all) of them will reach the end of the shape and should be finished so that the outline can still just be seen. Fill in any gaps with another part row of stitches in the dark turquoise. Repeat the shading on the opposite wing.

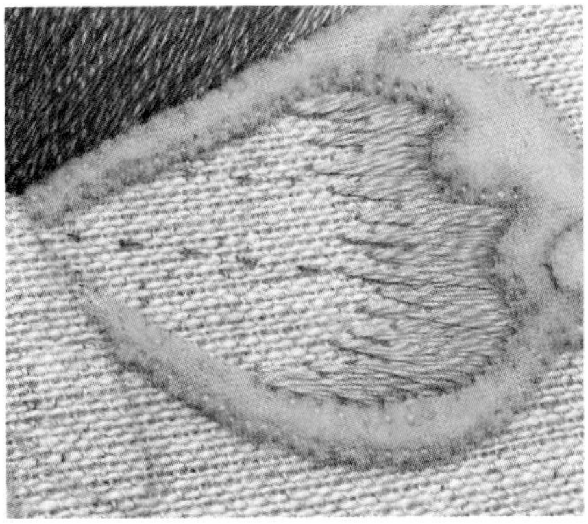

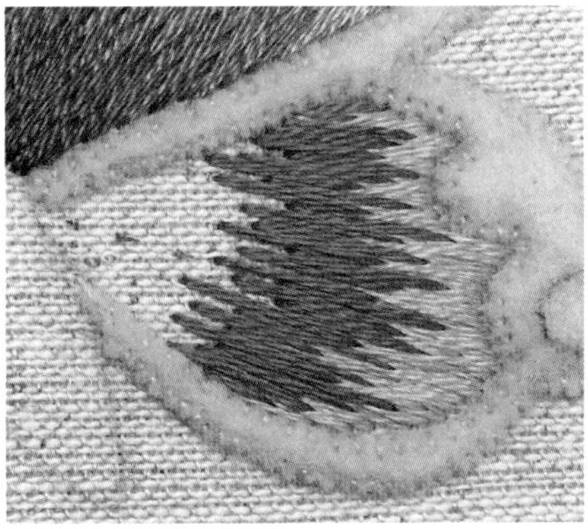

12 Before beginning the silk shading in the bottom wings, mark lines on the design roughly where the colour transitions will be. Add lines (in a different colour if you prefer) to indicate the angle of the stitches – slightly angled towards the centre. These are not set in stone, but serve as a reminder.

13 Begin the silk shading with the light peach, using two threads in the needle. Start in the middle of the outer edge. Bring the needle up in the centre and down at the edge of the felt. Make sure that the stitches are between 6mm (1/4in) and 10mm (3/8in) – any shorter than this and there will be no opportunity to split them well in the next row. The long and short should echo the shape of the curved outline.

14 Stitch the second row with coral thread and a few light peach stitches if needed. Begin in the middle, splitting the stitches of the first row by bringing the needle up through them. Make all the stitches about 10mm (3/8in) in length.

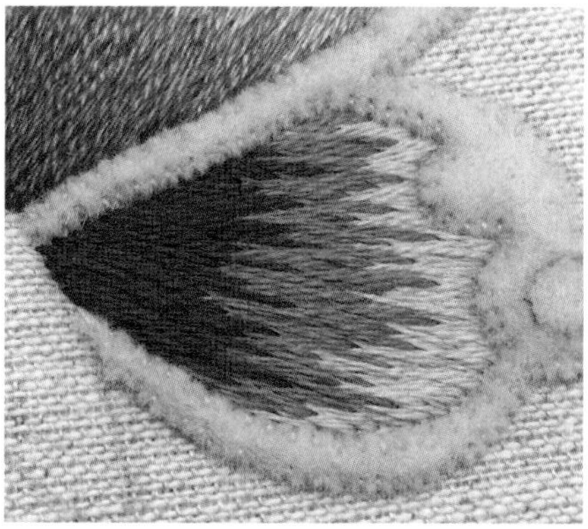

15 Stitch the third row with plum thread and a few stitches of coral to ease the blend. Begin in the middle, splitting the stitches of the second row by bringing the needle up through them. Make all the stitches about 10mm ($^{3}/_{8}$in) in length. Some (or all) of the stitches will reach the outline. Fill in any gaps with a part row of stitches in the same colour. Repeat for the opposite wing.

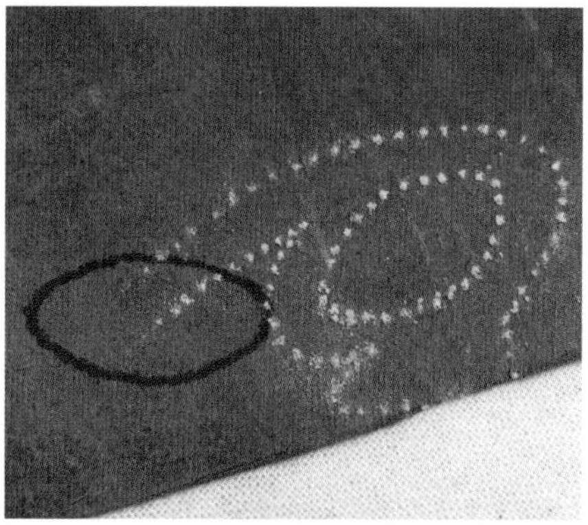

16 To transfer the design on to the kid leather, turn the leather over so the suede side is facing up. Pounce one eye shape on to the leather from the main template. Draw over it with a fine permanent marker, and brush off the pounce. Do the same for the second one close by so as not to waste too much leather. Cut out the shapes carefully and position one on the design (do not use pins).

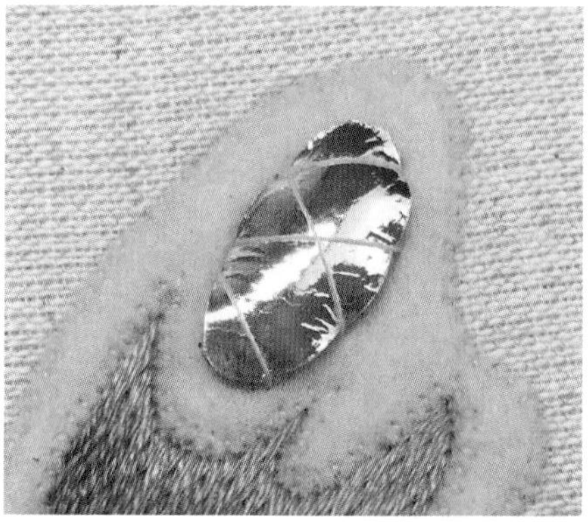

17 To hold the leather in place while stitching, make a few long stitches criss-crossing the whole shape. These do not need to be too tight, just enough to keep the leather in place.

18 Work round the edge of the leather, placing stitches at each end, the middle of each side, and one between each of those. Bring the needle up in the felt and down into the leather. The stitches should be 1–2mm ($^{1}/_{16}$in) in length, at right angles to the edge. This secures the leather in the perfect position so you can remove the criss-cross stitches.

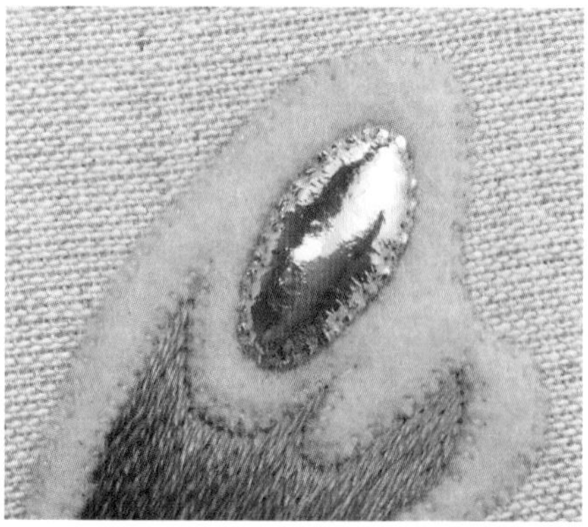

19 Work round the leather again, placing three more stitches between each of the securing stitches. Repeat for the opposite wing.

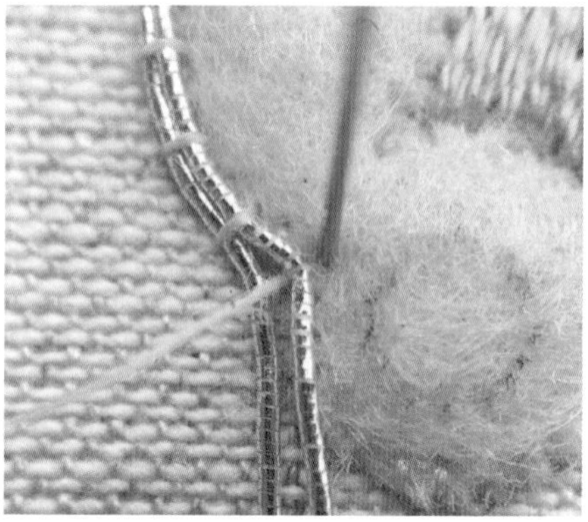

20 Begin the couching on the lower wings by bringing together two ends of smooth passing at one end of the shape (whichever direction you prefer to work is fine) on the outer edge. Couch the smooth passing with small, neat stitches at right angles to the line, 3–4mm ($^{1}/_{8}$in) apart. When you get to the corners, turn the inner one first and then the outer.

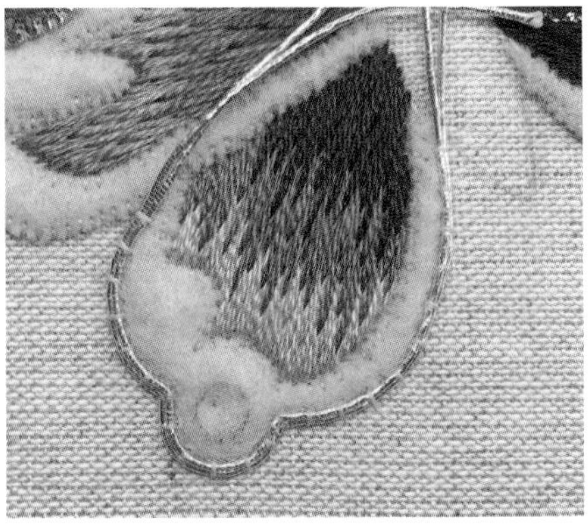

21 Continue couching to the end of the outline, and cut the smooth passing threads with enough excess to plunge.

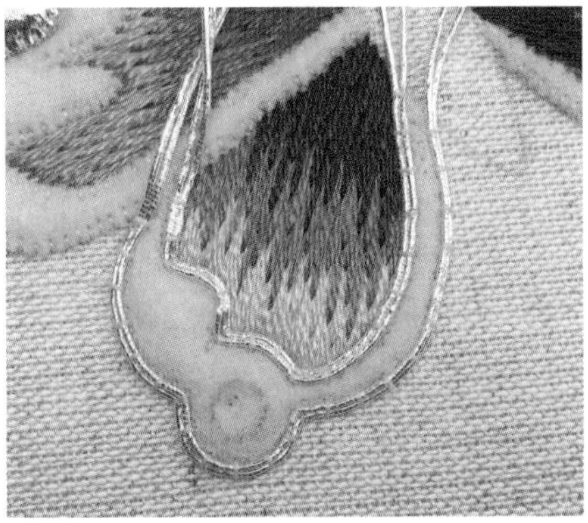

22 Couch in the same way along the inner edge of the lower wing, turning each corner carefully to maintain the shape.

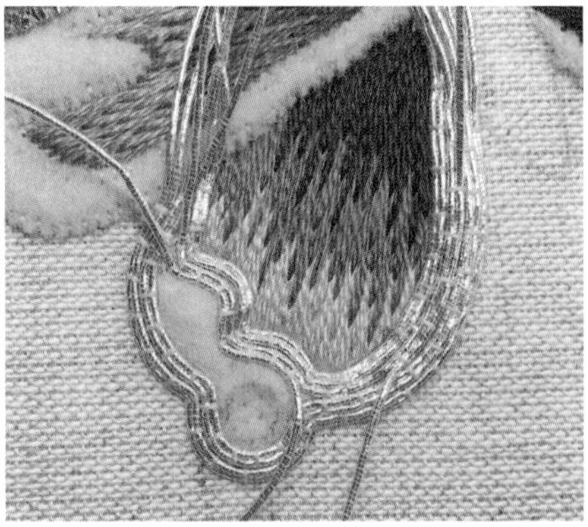

23 Stitch another row of couching on the outer edge, placing the stitches in a brick pattern and tucking it neatly against the first row. Take extra care with the corners: turn the thread nearest the first row, and then the second thread. Do the same on the inner edge – starting at the top of the wing is easier this time. The row will be shorter, and it is likely that you will need to drop one of the threads as you work into the lower part of the wing.

24 Begin a new row on the outer edge, keeping to the brick pattern. This time the row should loop round to the inner edge, turning neatly where necessary to cover the felt. Once back at the start, keep just one of the gold threads and loop it round until the space is filled.

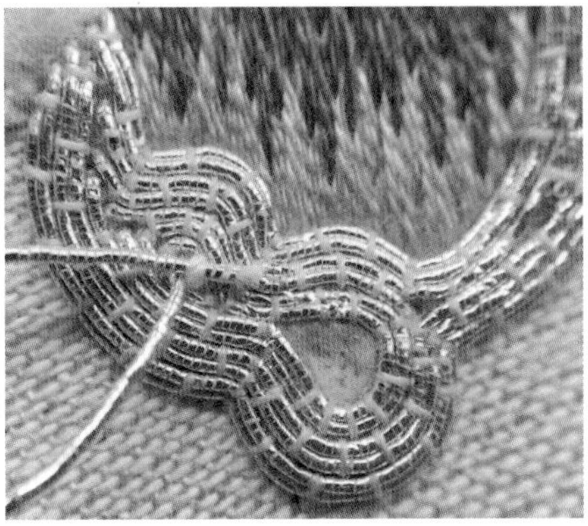

25 Plunge all the gold threads one at a time, taking care to preserve the shape.

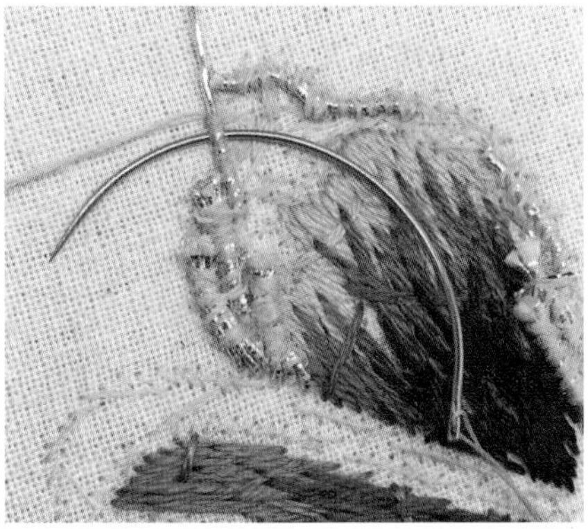

26 Tie back the gold threads on the back with a double thread in a curved needle. Tie them back in bundles of a maximum of four threads. Repeat the couching and tying back on the opposite wing.

27 Outline the body with No. 1 pearl purl, starting at the head, using a single thread. Make sure to relax the pearl purl first, and start with a clean cut. Make tiny stitches over the pearl purl at least every three coils to control the line. Pull the thread so that it slips down into the pearl purl and becomes invisible.

28 Work round the shape, turning tightly at the tail end, and finish the pearl purl so that the two ends meet. Cut the pearl purl cleanly with a sharp pair of scissors before making the last one or two stitches.

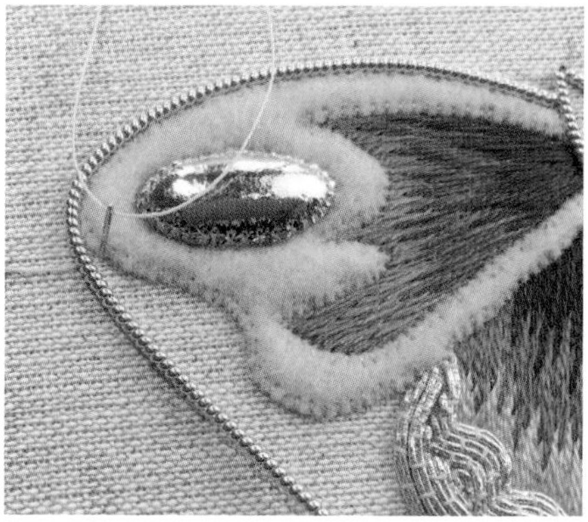

29 Stitch No. 2 pearl purl round one top wing outline, beginning at the head end. Butt the new pearl purl up to the existing pearl purl, and make the first stitch accurately between the first two coils to get a very neat join. Continue to stitch around the wing, making the stitches from the outside inwards, at least every three coils. Where the shape bends sharply on the outer edge, make the stitches at least every two coils to maintain the curves.

30 Once you reach one or two stitches from the end, cut the pearl purl cleanly against the existing pearl purl and complete the stitches to secure the end. Repeat for the opposite wing.

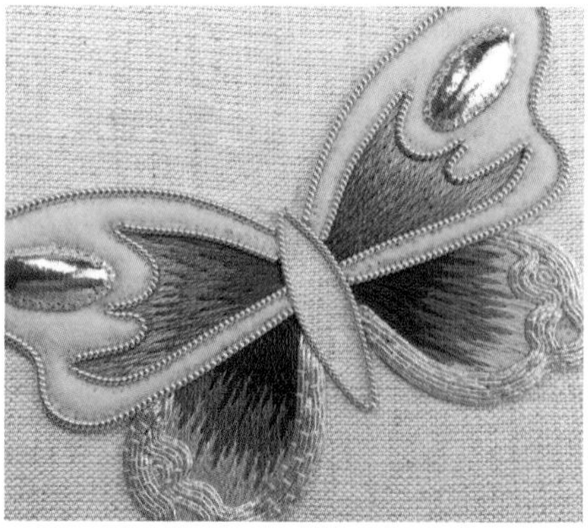

31 Stitch No. 1 pearl purl around the blue shading in the upper wing. Be sure to pinch the pearl purl firmly at each corner so that it turns tightly and neatly. Take care at the joins to cut the pearl purl cleanly, and secure it between the last two coils. Repeat for the opposite wing.

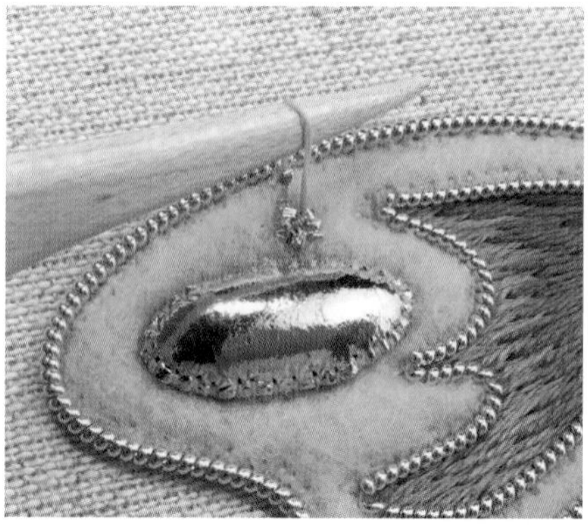

32 Fill the remaining space in the upper wings with chipping using bright check No. 8. Make sure that all the felt padding is covered. Use a double thread in a size 12 needle to slip easily through the gold. Begin in one of the larger spaces near the butterfly's 'eye', and work outwards from there. Bring the needle up away from the existing chips, and down angled towards them, working at random angles as much as possible.

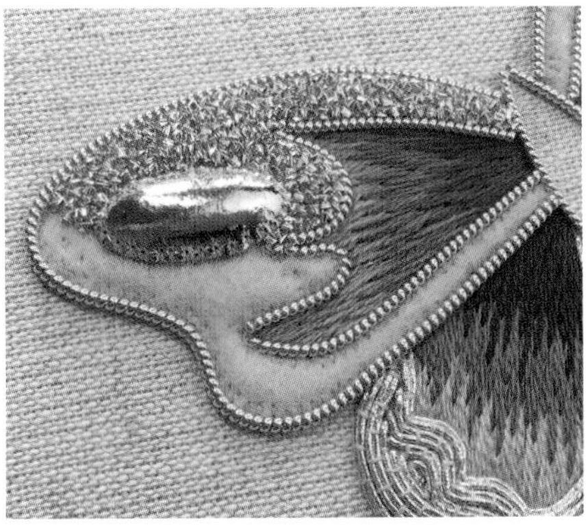

33 Gradually work around the shape, keeping the angles as varied as possible. In tight spaces this is more difficult to achieve, but with a bit more concentration it can be done – try to make sure that the chips don't line up in rows.

34 Round the edges, tuck in the chips close to the pearl purl. Be careful not to bring the needle up through the leather, as this could scar. Repeat for the opposite wing.

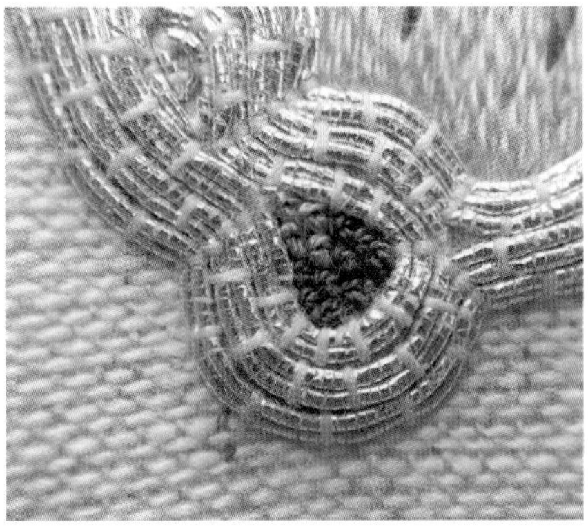

35 Work French knots to fill the eye in the bottom wing. Use two strands of cotton – dark blue at the bottom and light blue at the top. Bring the needle up through the felt and wind the thread round the needle, then position the needle a short distance away. With the needle resting in the fabric, tighten the knot round the needle. Then gently pull through to complete the knot. Repeat to fill the space.

36 Fill the centre of the butterfly's body with flat cutwork with alternating No. 8 wire check and No. 8 rough purl. Use a double thread in a No. 12 needle to allow it to pass through the gold wires easily. Start at the widest point to determine the angle – straight across the body. Bring the needle up just inside the pearl purl, and cut a length of purl wire to fit the shape. Take the needle down just inside the pearl purl.

37 Continue to fill the shape with chips of alternating purl wires, getting progressively shorter until you reach the end of the shape. If necessary, break the alternating pattern at the end so that the chips fill the shape as best they can. Repeat in the opposite direction.

38 Once the body is all stitched, use the same thread to make the antennae with No. 8 rough purl. Bring the needle up at the tip of each antenna, thread on a chip of rough purl, and take the needle down angled towards the pearl purl.

Design template.

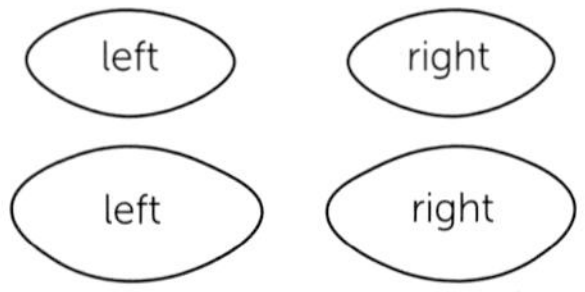

Felt template.

Project 5

Exuberant Spirit

The design for this project has been around for years and has been through various iterations in terms of the content. I considered having a pattern of cutwork blocks for the central shape, filling the petal shapes with couching and Or Nué and all sorts of other ideas.

This design would work really well with a different combination of colours, perhaps with silver or copper as the metal base. Why not make it your own by tweaking the combinations to suit your own preferences?

This project explores some of the more challenging couching techniques – Elizabethan twist, basket-weave and Italian couching. These methods take some time, and it is worth setting aside a good while to sit and concentrate – the repeated couching of Elizabethan twist in particular can be quite therapeutic and should be enjoyed at leisure.

Once complete, this project will need suitable protection, a frame for example, because it includes delicate looped purl petals which could be easily damaged. If you need it to be more robust, you could replace the loops with couched pearl purl filled with brightly coloured chipping, so that it still gives the same pop of colour.

The finished Exuberant Spirit project.

What you will need:

Materials

- Silk dupion: at least 35cm (14in) square
- Calico: at least 35cm (14in) square
- Gutermann Sew-all sewing thread No. 488
- Gutermann Sew-all sewing thread No. 663
- DMC stranded cotton No. 991, 922
- Parcel string
- Gilt smooth passing No. 7: 8m ($8^3/_4$yd)
- Gilt Elizabethan twist: 8m ($8^3/_4$yd)
- Gilt pearl purl No. 2: 20cm (8in)
- Gilt pearl purl No. 1: 30cm (12in)
- Gilt pearl purl very fine: 50cm (20in)
- Baby Pink rough purl No. 6: 1m (39in)
- Gilt 2mm spangles: 22

Equipment

- Frame: at least 25cm (10in), preferably slate
- Embroidery scissors
- Goldwork scissors
- Tweezers
- Beeswax
- Mellor
- Embroidery needles (9–12)
- Chenille needle (20–22)
- Curved needle
- Extra-strong thread for plunging lasso
- Prick-and-pounce kit (optional)
- Paint or pencil

Design Template

1 Transfer the design with your preferred method. Because the silk dupion is dark, it is easiest to frame up first and transfer with prick and pounce. Pencil or paint are the more suitable choices as pens tend to run on silk. Stab stitch throughout the design to secure the two layers of fabric.

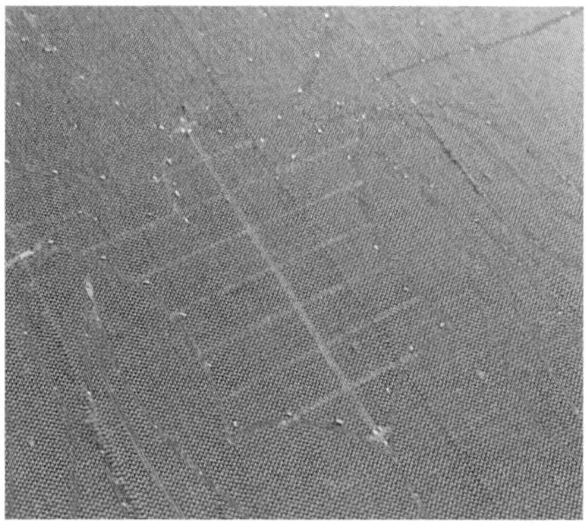

2 Mark parallel horizontal lines on the central section – place the first one near the top of the shape, just underneath the two side points. The lines should be about 6mm (1/4in) apart, assuming that your string is about 3mm (1/8in) wide – if it is narrower, place the lines a little more closely together; if it is wider, place them further apart. Mark another line from top to bottom of the shape, through the centre.

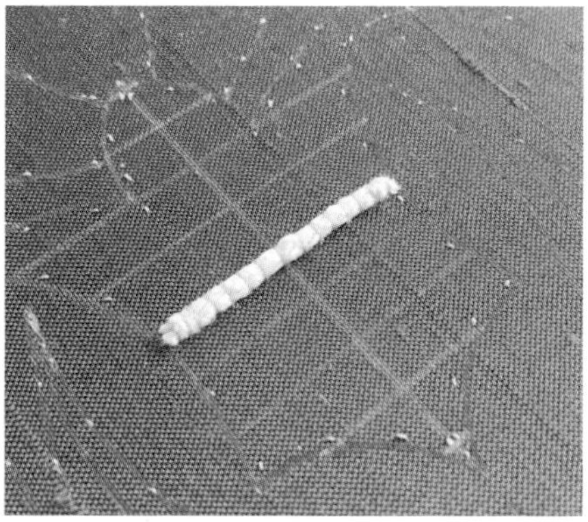

3 Coat some parcel string with beeswax and cast on a single length of waxed sewing thread near the middle, on a horizontal line. Lay the string along the middle horizontal line and couch over it, keeping to the bottom of the drawn line. Couch to each end of the line, and finish off by chamfering the string at 45 degrees just inside the end of the line, tapering it towards the fabric, and place a stitch or two into the end of the string.

4 Couch each horizontal line in the same way, chamfering the ends neatly each time. Make sure that you can still see the outline clearly all the way round the shape.

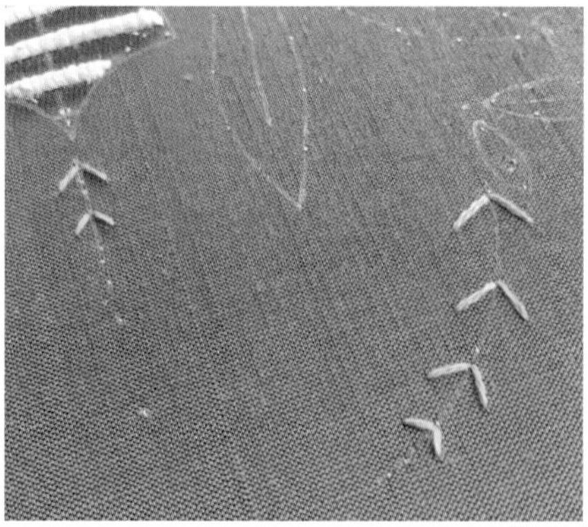

5 Use two strands of light blue stranded cotton to create straight stitches where they are marked on the design. Try to make them approximately symmetrical on either side, but use your creativity in their placement. Simply bring the needle up at one end and down at the other to create the length of stitch that you want.

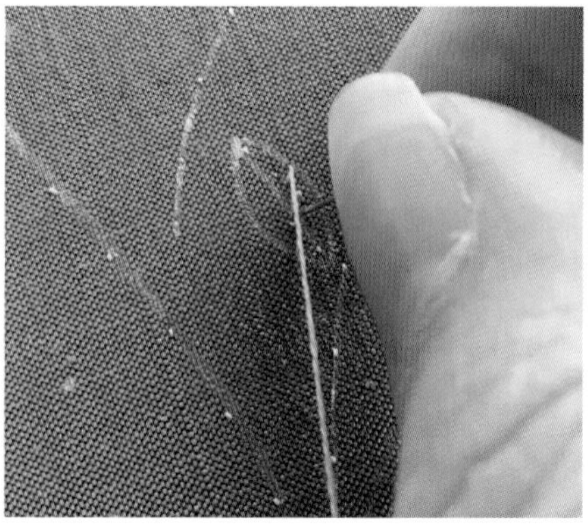

6 Fill all the veined leaf shapes with satin stitch, using single strands of stranded cotton. No split stitch is needed because they will all be outlined with gold later. Follow the colour placement shown on the diagram. Start each half leaf partway along the shape, and make the first stitch angled towards the central vein, as shown in the diagram. Make sure to stitch into the acute angle, so that the tension remains even. Work all the way to one end of the shape.

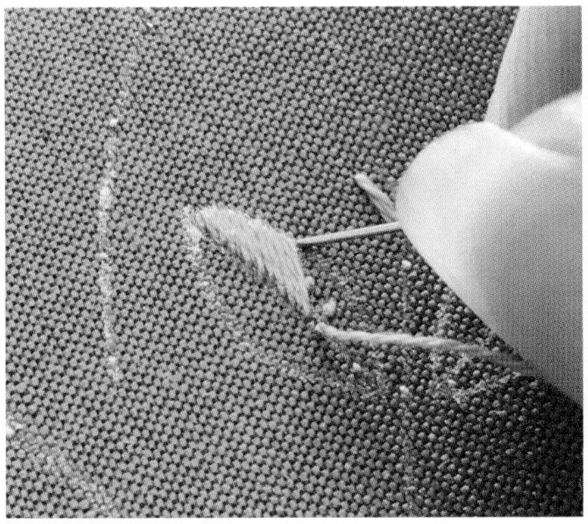

7 Once the first half is complete, start again in the middle, making the stitch in the opposite direction so that it is still facing into the acute angle. Repeat all the way to the end of the shape.

8 Stitch the other side of the leaf, mirroring the angle to give a 'V' shape, emphasizing the shape of the leaf. Do the same for each veined leaf on the design.

9 Work satin stitch on the non-veined leaves following the colour placement on the diagram. Use single strands of stranded cotton, without split-stitch outlines. Make the first stitch partway along each leaf, following the angles on the diagram. Ensure that each subsequent stitch points into the acute angle to keep the tension even.

10 Begin to cover the long leaf shapes with Elizabethan twist, couching with the colour indicated on the diagram. Measure out 2m (6.5ft) of twist: fold it in half so that it makes a pair, and then in half again to find the middle. Position the middle of the pair of threads about halfway along the leaf, at the angle indicated on the diagram. Couch down the pair of threads using a single thread of stranded cotton coated with beeswax. Place a stitch on each design line across the leaf.

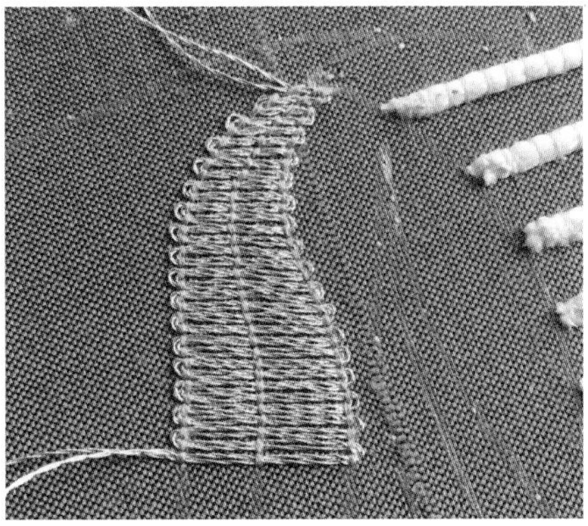

11 At one side of the shape, turn the threads tightly and make a tiny stitch on the design line, coming up outside the new threads and down into the same hole as the previous stitch, so that the threads lie right next to the previous row. Hold the pair of twist threads at tension across the leaf so that it sits alongside the previous row. Make a tiny stitch on the central vein, coming up outside the new twist threads and down towards the previous row. Make another stitch on the line on the other side, and turn the threads again.

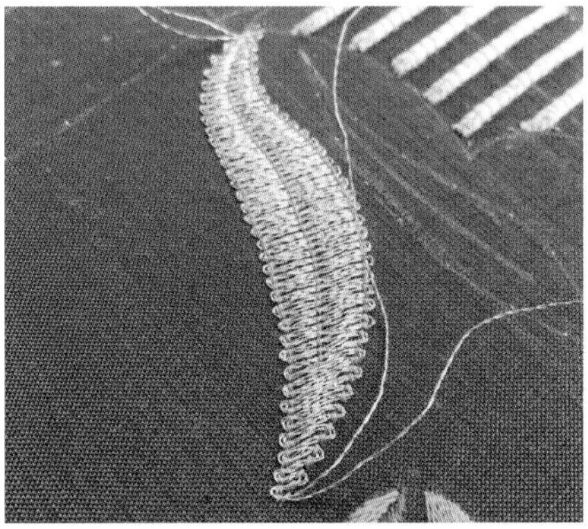

12 Repeat this process of stitching on each side and the central vein and turning the twist threads tightly at the sides. Once one end of the leaf is covered, begin again in the middle and work all the way to the other end.

13 Use a No. 8 crewel needle to plunge the ends of the Elizabethan twist through to the back – make sure that the pair of threads pass through separate holes so that they lie flat and parallel right to the end.

14 Turn the frame over. Using a double waxed sewing thread, tie back the Elizabethan twist, stitching it on to the calico with a curved needle (without catching the silk).

15 Couch the remaining leaves in the same way, using the colours marked on the diagram.

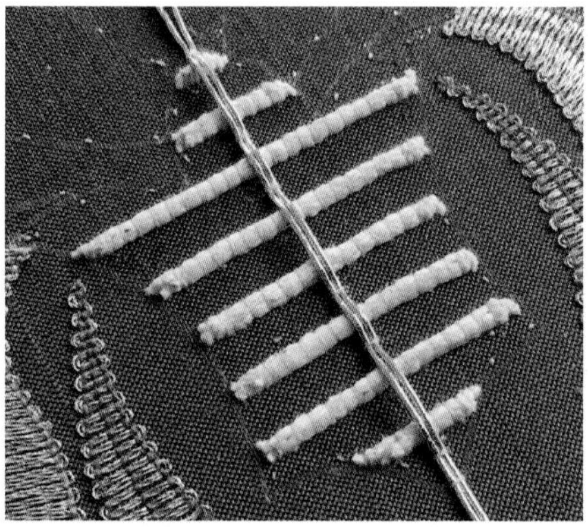

16 To begin basket-weave couching, bring the needle up on one side of the central vertical line that you marked earlier, halfway between two strings just above halfway down the shape. Make a horizontal couching stitch over a pair of smooth passing threads so that the needle goes down just on the other side of the central line. Make a holding stitch to keep the tension firm. Continue to couch down the centre line, making a pattern alternating over one and two string lines.

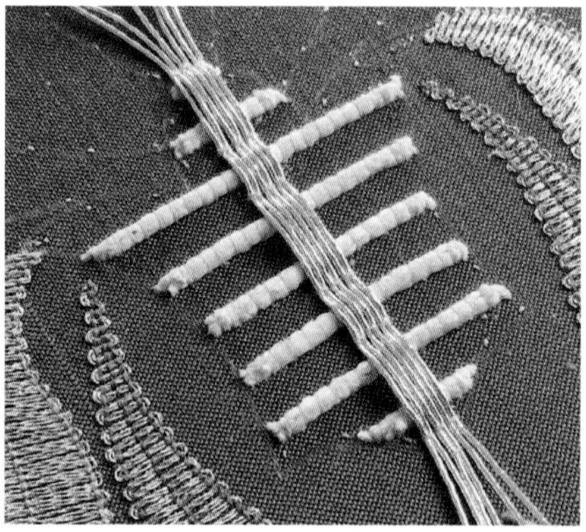

17 Place another row of couching on either side of the middle one, matching the pattern so that there are three pairs in a row.

18 Work to one side of the central line and then the other, making the same alternating pattern but shifted down one string for each three pairs of gold threads. When you get to the far right- and far left-hand side, make sure to stop the couching so that you can still see the design outline on the fabric (this will be covered later). At the top right and top left, there will be a space to fill with normal couching – there may only be space for one stitch, so keep the tension firm and use holding stitches.

19 Starting in the middle, plunge all the threads round the edge of the shape. Be very careful to keep the lines of smooth passing straight. Where the threads are quite short with only one or two couching stitches, be extra careful not to pull too hard so that the threads don't slip through and disappear.

20 Tie back the threads in sets of four or fewer with a curved needle, using a double waxed thread.

21 Begin Italian couching on the central large petal shape. Start by couching a pair of smooth passing threads with standard spacing of 4mm ($^1/_8$in) using a waxed single strand of dark blue stranded cotton. Turn the pair of threads tightly at the top, one by one. Leave tails of about 5cm (2in) at each end, and make sure that the couching stitches stop so that you can easily see the outline of the basket-weave shape – more stitches can be added later if need be.

22 To create the shading, go round the shape again adding two new stitches between each existing stitch. At the base of the petal, make both stitches in dark blue, then change to one each of dark and light blue, and then to both light blue – about one third of each. Then go back in between these stitches adding extra dark blue stitches just on the bottom quarter of the petal. At the top of this section, space out these extra stitches for about 6mm ($^1/_4$in).

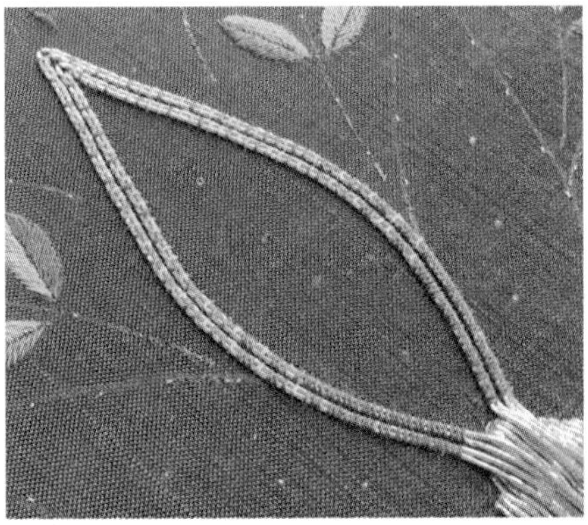

23 Add another row of couching inside the first, using the same method. Make sure to bring the needle up leaving just enough space for the new pair of smooth passing threads to sit between it and the existing row. Then tuck the needle down towards the existing row as much as possible (it isn't quite as easy as with standard 'bricking' because there is less space between the stitches). Don't worry if you can't stitch easily right up to the plunge point at this stage.

24 Stitch the remaining large petal shapes with the same method, using the shading to create shadows where the petals overlap one another. Plunge the threads so that there is a gap between these threads and the basket-weave couching – but where the petals overlap one another, the ends meet closely.

25 Tie back the gold threads in pairs or fours with a curved needle using a waxed double thread.

26 Return to the front and fill in any areas near the plunge points with stitches to match the existing pattern (that is, close stitches in dark blue thread).

27 Invisibly couch No. 3 twist round the central shape with a single waxed sewing thread, starting in one of the inward-pointing corners. Bring the needle up on the outline and pass it through the twist, catching one ply of the twist with a very small stitch. Repeat every 3mm ($^1/_8$in), making sure to twist the gold thread as you go so that it maintains its appearance. At each corner, make a stitch right on the corner, twisting the gold thread more than usual, then make another stitch immediately after the corner and continue.

28 Once the shape is fully outlined, trim the twist so that each tail is about 5cm (2in), and unravel the tails back to the plunge point. Use a chenille needle and lasso to plunge each individual gold thread separately (they may pass through the same hole in some cases as it is a very small area, but keeping them separate creates less strain on the fabric).

29 Tie back the gold threads with a double waxed sewing thread in a curved needle.

30 To finish off the central shape, check the corners carefully to see if any fabric shows through (it can be hard to fill the shape perfectly with basket-weave couching). If any is showing, fill the gaps with pieces of smooth passing. For tiny pieces, there is no need for a couching stitch – simply cut a piece of smooth passing to allow for longer tails than usual, plunge at both ends, and tie back on the reverse.

31 Stitch the stems at the top of the design with pearl purl No. 1 using a single length of waxed sewing thread. First stretch the pearl purl, and then trim the end. Make the first stitch very close to the start of the line, so that when you twist the pearl purl into position it will sit exactly at the start. Make another stitch a coil or two further along the line, and continue to stitch every two or three coils towards the other end. Be sure to keep the stitches small and neat so that they don't show.

32 Stop stitching close to the other end of the line, and trim the pearl purl to fit – use very sharp, fine-tipped scissors, and slide the blades between the coils to get a neat finish. Complete the stitching with another stitch or two, making sure that the final stitch is between the last two coils to secure the end.

33 Repeat for each stem, keeping each one neat and tidy and securing the ends well.

34 Outline all the little leaves with very fine pearl purl, starting each one at the base. Use a single length of waxed sewing thread. Stretch the pearl purl gently, and trim the end before beginning. Make each stitch from outside the pearl purl in towards the leaf with really tiny stitches to hide under the gold. At the tip of each leaf, make a tight turn by folding the pearl purl with a pair of tweezers, and make the stitch from inside the pearl purl to outside.

35 Continue to stitch down the second half of the leaf, and at the end, cut the pearl purl cleanly in line with the coils. Fasten it down with a last stitch in between the last two coils.

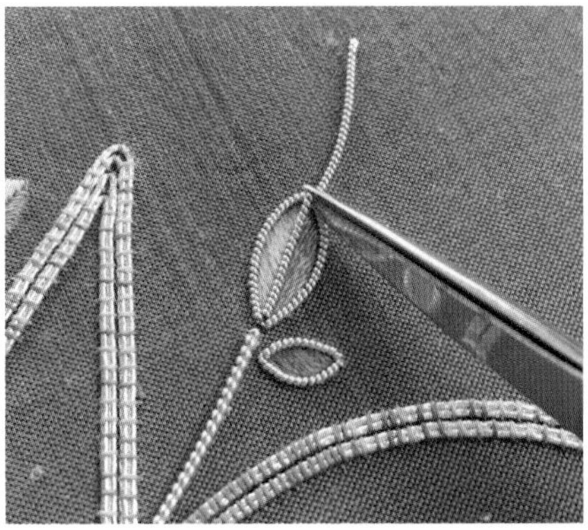

36 For the veined leaves, first stitch the outline and then take a new piece of very fine pearl purl for the vein. Make sure the cut is clean at both ends and that the vein sits comfortably inside the outline.

37 Stitch the two lower branches with pearl purl No. 2 and the central line with pearl purl No. 1, making sure to keep the stitches small and neat so they will be invisible. Cut the ends cleanly in line with the coils, using sharp, fine scissors.

38 Begin to add the flower details. For each one use a double waxed pink sewing thread, and cast on very carefully where the stitches will be covered with the loops of purl. Cut two sets of chips of pink rough purl: 10mm ($^{3}/_{8}$in) and 3mm ($^{1}/_{8}$in). Start with the top left flower. Bring the needle up slightly to the right or left of the end of the stem, and thread on a long chip. Take the needle down roughly in line with the end of the stem, and gently pull the stitch so that the chip curls over. Use a mellor to keep the chip from breaking.

39 Bring the needle up inside the loop, thread on a short chip, and take the needle down just outside the loop to create a catching stitch. Make another loop in the same way on the other side of the stem. Attach a spangle with a single stitch between the two petals, lining up the stitch with the dent in the spangle.

40 For the top centre flower, position a spangle in the middle and attach it with one stitch. Then add petals around the spangle – it is easiest to distribute them evenly by stitching the top one first, then the bottom two either side of the centre line, followed by the other two in between.

41 Next add the purl loops in the large petal shapes and at the bottom of the design, referring to the diagram for whether it should be one loop or two. The one at the very bottom is a full flower, like the one at the top. Each painted spot on the design is the position of a spangle – the stitch should sit over the dot to cover it.

42 Finally, add a spangle by the pairs of leaves towards the bottom of the design. This time use a single waxed thread, and make three stitches to secure each spangle.

Design template. Transfer only the black lines.

The finished Wyvern project.

PROJECT 6

WYVERN

I have always wanted to stitch some sort of dragon-like creature in goldwork, but haven't ever quite found the right opportunity, so here it is in all its glory. This one doesn't have legs like a typical wyvern – perhaps this is more of a winged serpent – either way, the design just sort of happened one day. It started as a little sketch with just an idea of how the head would look, where the wings would sit, and how the tail would spiral. The details evolved over time, as did the colouring. He was nearly a sea-serpent on aquamarine with silver and just a touch of copper – maybe I will stitch that version one day.

This wyvern design features a few of the more advanced techniques – plate, cutwork and shaded chipping – with a good grounding in the basics, too.

Because this design includes these more demanding techniques, it is a good idea to use a very strong frame such as a slate frame while you stitch. These techniques require you to pull very firmly on the stitches, which leads to a greater risk of puckered fabric if it is not kept drum tight throughout the project, and a slate frame will allow you to continually tighten each time you sit down to stitch.

Working on a larger frame may require you to stitch some of the design upside down; you may notice that some of the steps are shown this way. Doing this will allow you to be close enough to the work to see clearly what you are stitching.

What you will need:

Materials

- Silk dupion: at least 35cm (14in) square
- Calico: at least 35cm (14in) square
- Gutermann Polyester sewing thread No. 488 (gold)
- Gutermann Polyester sewing thread No. 847 (copper)
- Gutermann Polyester sewing thread No. 8 (silver)
- Yellow felt: 10cm (4in) square
- Brown felt: 20cm (8in) square
- Yellow tapestry cotton
- Gilt smooth passing No. 7: 2m (6.5ft)
- Copper rococco, very fine: 2m (6.5ft)
- Copper twist $1^1/_2$: 2m (6.5ft)
- Copper check thread 8 × 2: 2m (6.5ft)
- Gilt check thread 8 × 2: 2m (6.5ft)
- Gilt pearl purl No .1: 30cm (12in)
- Copper pearl purl No. 1: 50cm (20in)
- Silver-plated lizerine No. 1: 50cm (20in)
- Gilt lizerine No. 2: 30cm (12in)
- Gilt lizerine No. 1: 30cm (12in)
- Copper bright check No. 6: 20cm (8in)
- Gilt bright check No. 6: 1m (39in)
- Silver-plated bright check No. 6: 20cm (8in)
- Copper smooth purl No. 8: 50cm (20in)
- Gilt smooth purl No. 8: 50cm (20in)
- Silver plated smooth purl No. 8: 50cm (20in)
- Copper kid leather: 20cm (8in) square
- Gilt broad plate No. 6: 2m (6.5ft)
- Silver-plated 2mm spangles: 20–30

Equipment

- Square frame: at least 25cm (10in), preferably slate
- Embroidery scissors
- Goldwork scissors
- Tweezers
- Beeswax
- Mellor
- Embroidery needles (9–12)
- Chenille needle (20–22)
- Curved needle
- Extra-strong thread for plunging lasso
- Prick-and-pounce kit (optional)
- Paint or pencil

Templates

- Design template
- Felt templates
- Kid-leather template

1 Frame up the calico and attach the silk with long and short stitches. Transfer the design with your preferred method. Because the silk dupion is dark and the design is intricate, it is most accurate to frame up first and transfer with prick and pounce.

2 Paint is the best choice for this design, as pens tend to run on silk and pencil may not show up well. Take care to keep the lines thin, and err on the side of caution, painting just inside the pounce marks, especially for the horns – this is in anticipation of the design 'growing' a little when the stitches are worked.

3 Stab stitch throughout the design to secure the two layers of fabric, making the stitches in the areas that will be covered. On the wings, which will only have scattered chipping, keep the stitches on the design lines. Elsewhere you can work the stitches throughout the design area.

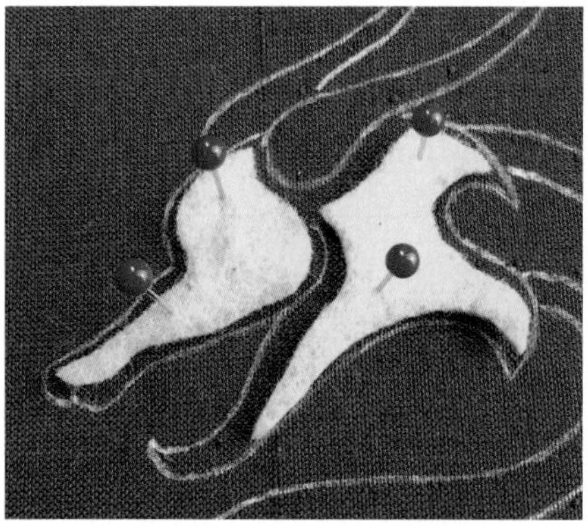

4 Begin the felt padding with the first layer of yellow felt in the head of the wyvern. Use the prick-and-pounce method to mark accurate shapes from the templates, and then cut them out with very sharp, small scissors. Hold the felt in place with a few pins while you make tiny stitches to secure it, with a single gold-coloured thread. Bring the needle up just outside the felt and down into the felt making a stitch 1–2mm ($^{1}/_{16}$in) in length, every 6mm ($^{1}/_{4}$in) round the shapes.

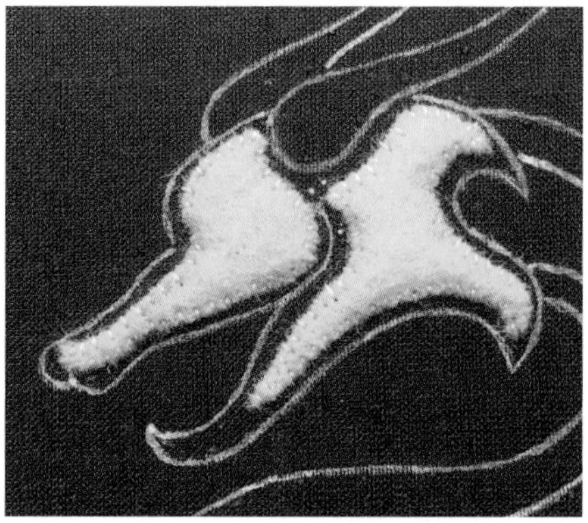

5 Work round the shapes again, making stitches 1–2mm ($^{1}/_{16}$in) in length, every 1–2mm ($^{1}/_{16}$in), so that the edge is completely held down and secure.

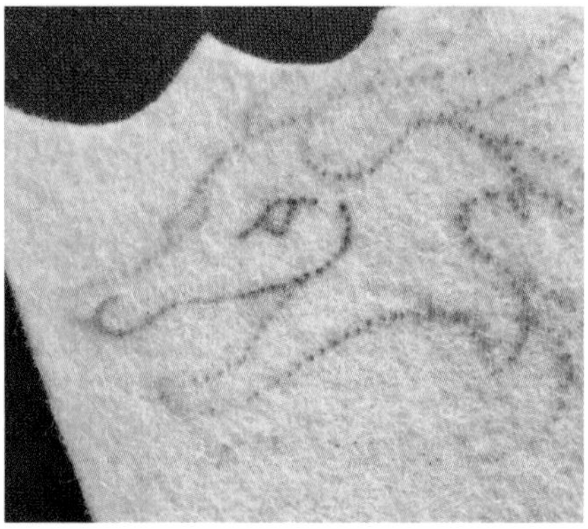

6 Pounce the main head template on to yellow felt, and draw the inner details (the nose, mouth and eye) on to the felt with a fine pen. A close colour like orange is a good choice, rather than black. You can also draw the outline if you prefer. Cut the outline as accurately as possible, and check it against the design line on the fabric. Trim if necessary, and cut a new shape if it is too small. It is worth being precise at this point to make it easier later.

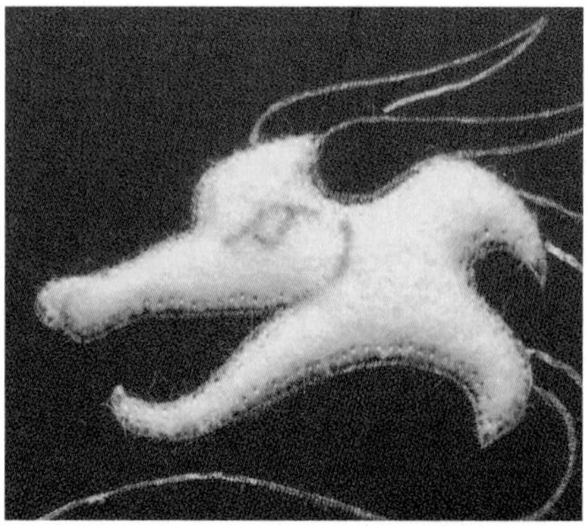

7 Hold the felt in place with a few pins while you secure it with a single gold-coloured thread. Bring the needle up on the design line (outside the felt) and down into the felt, making a stitch 1–2mm ($^{1}/_{16}$in) in length, every 6mm ($^{1}/_{4}$in) round the shapes. You should be able to see the design line. Work round the shapes again, placing stitches every 1–2mm ($^{1}/_{16}$in) so that the edge is completely held down and secure.

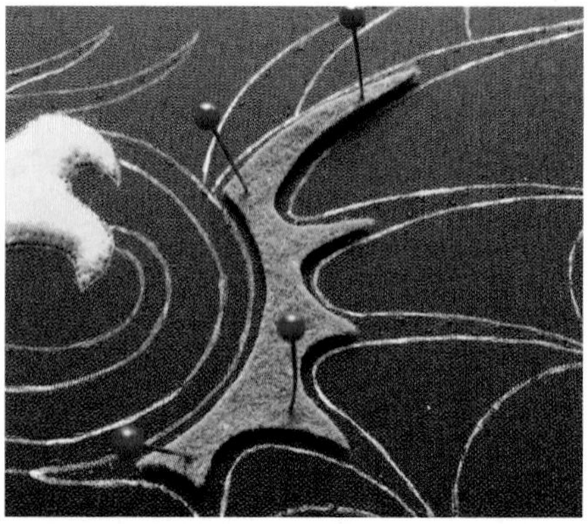

8 Pounce the smaller wing template on to brown felt, and cut out the shape accurately. Hold the felt in place with a few pins while you make tiny stitches to secure it with a single copper-coloured thread. Bring the needle up just outside the felt and down into the felt, making a stitch 1–2mm ($^{1}/_{16}$in) in length, every 6mm ($^{1}/_{4}$in) round the shapes.

9 Work round the shapes again, making stitches 1–2mm ($^{1}/_{16}$in) in length, every 1–2mm ($^{1}/_{16}$in), so that the edge is completely held down and secure.

10 Pounce the main wing template on to brown felt, and draw the shape with a fine pen. Cut out the shape accurately, taking extra care on the very thin tips of the shape. Cut to the inside of the line. Check the shape fits to the design lines, and trim if it is too big. If it is too small, cut a new piece. Hold the felt in place with a few pins while you secure it with the first few stitches.

11 Make tiny stitches to secure the felt with a single copper-coloured thread. Bring the needle up just outside the felt, and down into the felt, making a stitch 1–2mm ($^{1}/_{16}$in) in length, every 6mm ($^{1}/_{4}$in) round the shape. As you stitch the thin parts, work from side to side so that the felt sits as flat as possible.

12 Work round the shape again, making stitches 1–2mm ($^{1}/_{16}$in) in length, every 1–2mm ($^{1}/_{16}$in), so that the edge is completely held down and secure.

13 Pounce the smaller body template on to brown felt, and cut out the shape accurately. Hold the felt in place with a few pins while you make tiny stitches to secure it with a single copper-coloured thread. Bring the needle up just outside the felt, and down into the felt, making a stitch 1–2mm ($^{1}/_{16}$in) in length, every 6mm ($^{1}/_{4}$in) round the shape.

14 Work round the shape again, making stitches 1–2mm ($^{1}/_{16}$in) in length, every 1–2mm ($^{1}/_{16}$in) so that the edge is completely held down and secure.

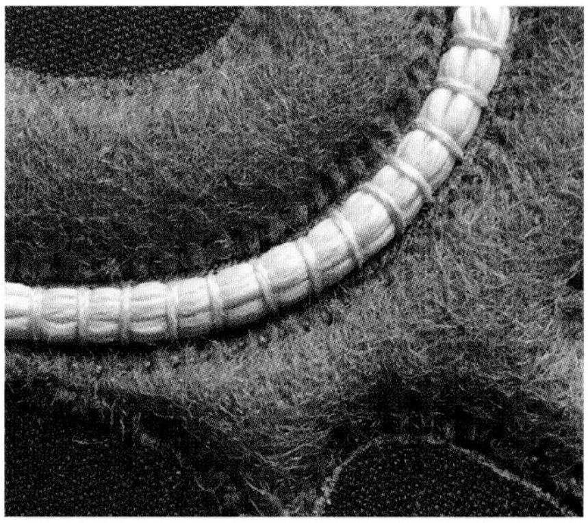

15 Pounce the main body template on to brown felt. Mark the outline and centre line with a fine pen, and cut out the shape accurately. Hold the felt in place with a few pins while you make tiny stitches to secure it with a single copper-coloured thread. Bring the needle up just outside the felt, and down into the felt, making a stitch 1–2mm (${}^{1}/_{16}$in) in length, every 6mm (${}^{1}/_{4}$in) round the shape.

16 Work round the shape again, making stitches 1–2mm (${}^{1}/_{16}$in) in length, every 1–2mm (${}^{1}/_{16}$in), so that the edge is completely held down and secure.

17 Cut six strands of tapestry cotton to a little more than the length of the spine, checking it fits the space by twisting the threads together. Wax the threads thoroughly, and bundle them together. Cast on a double waxed sewing thread about 25mm (1in) from the top of the spine, and bring the needle up inside the design line on one side. Set the waxed tapestry cotton in place and make a stitch over it, finishing inside the design line. Repeat this towards the bottom of the spine, with the stitches about 3–4mm (${}^{1}/_{8}$in) apart.

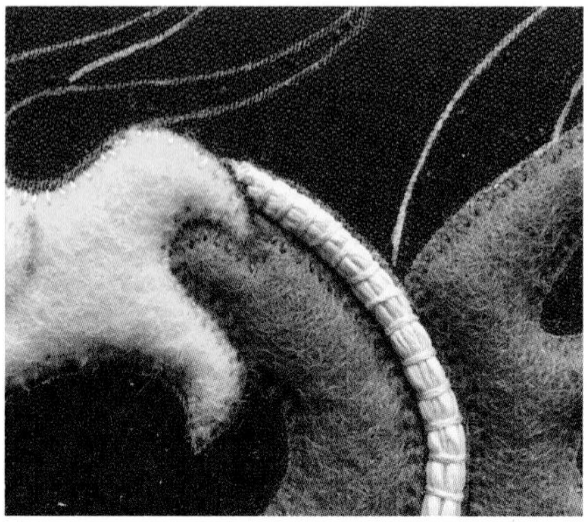

18 Begin to cut away the tapestry cotton threads from underneath the bundle as the shape narrows, which is just as it comes out of the inward curve. Remove one thread at a time, taking another two over the next 25mm (1in), before the next outward curve.

19 Keep the remaining three threads going until about an inch from the end (unless the shape appears to narrow before that). Then cut one more thread, and cut the next about 6mm (${}^{1}/_{4}$in) from the end. Cut the final one right in the tip of the shape, making sure that you can still see the design lines.

20 Begin again where you first started and work in the opposite direction, towards the wyvern's head. Keep all six threads until just before the point where the shape is overlapped by the head. Cut one thread from underneath, and then cut the threads one by one as they bump into the end of the shape, resulting in a taper to one side.

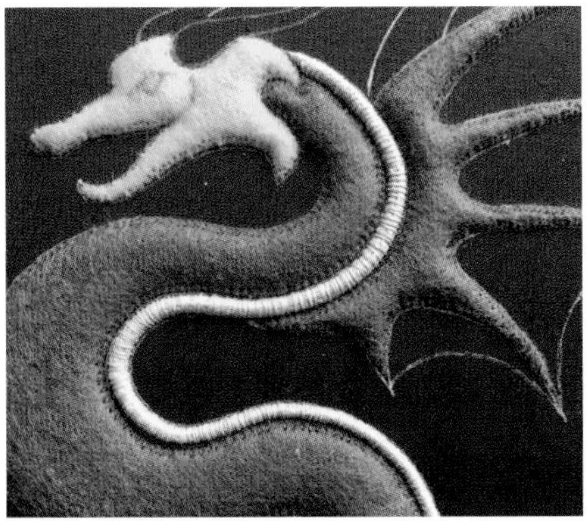

21 Work along the string padding again, placing at least one more stitch in between each existing stitch so that the padding is smooth and firm.

22 Cut about eighteen pieces of tapestry cotton a little longer than the front horn, and wax each piece thoroughly. Cast on a double waxed sewing thread in the widest part of the shape. Make two or three stitches 2mm ($^1/_{16}$in) apart to secure the threads, working towards the head. Make sure that the stitches sit comfortably inside the design lines. Then lift the bundle of threads and cut eight to ten threads from underneath, a few at a time.

23 Make another stitch, and then check how much space remains before the end of the shape. If this stitch sits very close to the end, cut all the remaining threads straightaway; if not, cut another four to five threads and repeat. At the end of the shape, make at least two stitches from the end (inside the design line) into the threads, and make another stitch or two across the threads to hold it all secure and smooth.

24 Return to the starting point and lift the bundle of threads. Cut four to five threads from underneath, and lay the threads back down to make another stitch. Repeat this twice more so that you end up with three to five threads remaining. Stitch along the narrow part of the horn until it tapers further, and then remove threads one at a time until you end up with one remaining in the tip.

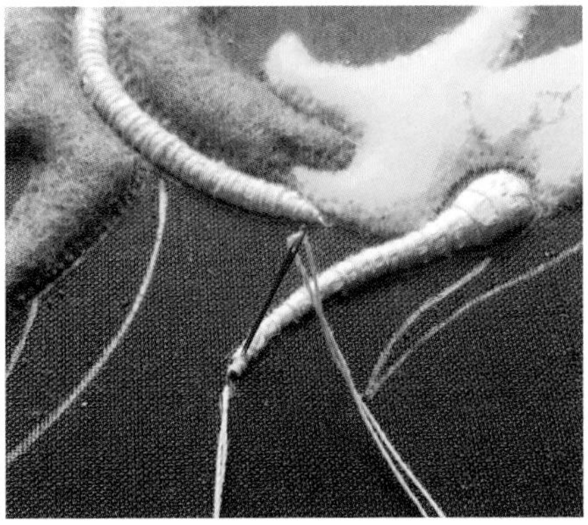

25 To secure the very tip of the padding, make one stitch from the meeting point of the design lines into the padding threads.

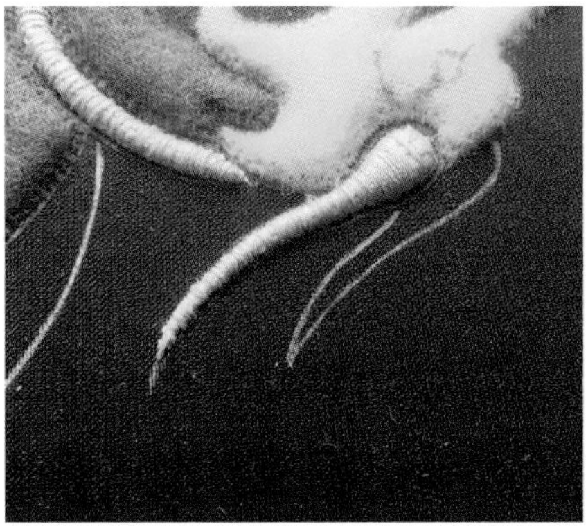

26 Work back along the shape, making at least one extra stitch between the existing ones to ensure the padding is smooth and firm.

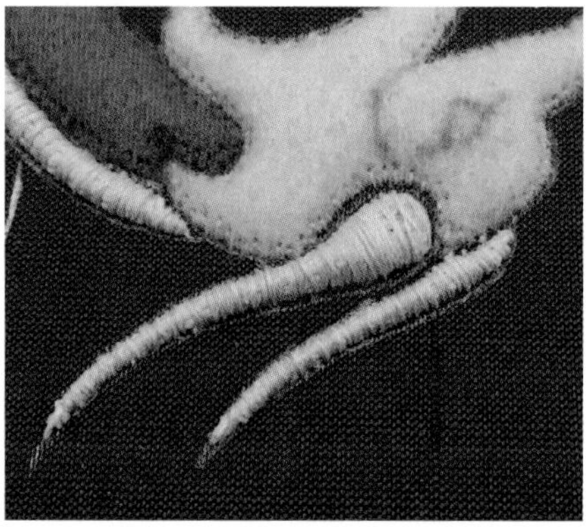

27 Repeat the process for the back horn, starting with eight threads and tapering it to one side as you did for the spine. Make sure to leave the design lines showing, and also leave a little more space between the two pieces of string padding.

28 Prick the kid-leather template, and pounce on to the back of the leather. Use a fine pen to mark the design lines. Cut the kid leather very carefully with sharp scissors, cutting to the outside of the design line and along the dividing lines. Position each piece of leather on the design, and check the shape. Trim the pieces, or cut new ones if need be. Remember that the leather will have to curve up and over the felt layers, and it should not be stretched too tightly to do so.

29 Position one piece of leather on top of the felt padding, and use a single unwaxed sewing thread (gold or silver to contrast with the copper leather) to work long, criss-crossing stitches over the leather to hold it in place. Remember that you can't use pins to hold the leather because they would leave marks. Once you move on to stitching into the leather, rather than over it, you may want to use a sturdy thimble to help the needle pass through the tough leather.

30 Work round the leather shape, making tiny stitches with a single waxed copper sewing thread to secure the edge, about 1–2mm ($^1/_{16}$in) in length, and about 6mm ($^1/_4$in) apart. Bring up the needle outside the leather on the design line, and down into the leather, pulling it down to meet the design line. As the shapes are long and narrow, it is a good idea to work from side to side of the shape so that you can remove the holding stitches as you go without disrupting the placement.

31 Work round the shape again, placing two or three stitches 1–2mm ($^1/_{16}$in) in length between the existing stitches, so that the gaps between stitches are only 1–2mm ($^1/_{16}$in), and the edge of the leather is secure. The leather should sit smoothly over the felt and not be overstretched.

32 Repeat the process of holding stitches, first securing stitches and final securing stitches with the remaining pieces of leather. Make sure that each one lies flat and smooth on the padding or silk and is not overstretched. The pieces should meet but not completely obscure the design lines (they will be outlined with pearl purl later and do not want to grow too wide in the process).

33 Begin to couch the back wing, with a single waxed gold sewing thread over pairs of smooth passing No. 7. Place the first stitch close to the base of the wing, 1–2mm (1/16in) from the start of the design line. Lay the pair of smooth-passing threads along the line, with at least a 25mm (1in) tail. Bring the needle up just outside the design line so that it will be covered, and make a stitch at right angles to the metal threads.

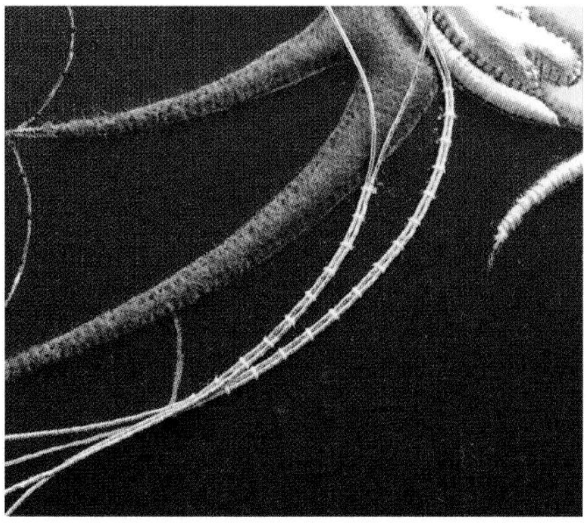

34 Continue to couch the pair of metal threads with stitches at 3–4mm (1/8in) intervals to the tip of the wing, making the last one or two stitches over just the outer of the two threads. Couch a new pair of threads on the opposite side of the wing, from the base to the tip. Again, make the last one or two stitches just over the outer of the two threads, so that the tip of the wing will come to a very narrow point to match the design line.

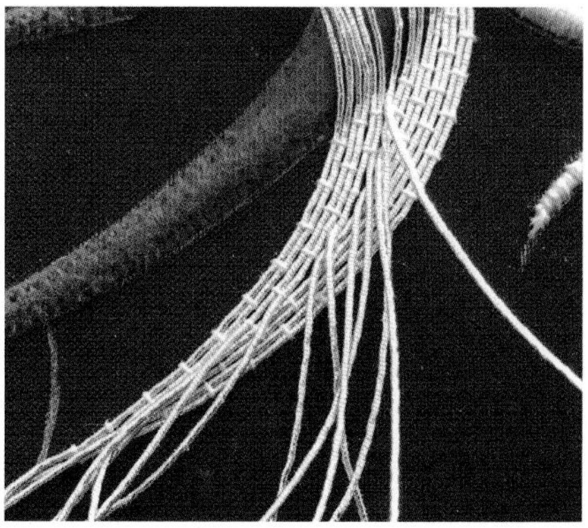

35 Continue to couch pairs of smooth passing threads, alternating sides and reducing to couching a single thread (the outer one) as the shape narrows. Bring the needle up with enough space between it and the previous row for the two metal threads, then take it down at an angle towards the previous row. Position the stitches between those of the first row, to create a brick pattern. If need be, couch a single thread down the centre of the shape.

36 Plunge all the metal threads, being very careful to preserve the shape. At the tip of the wing, plunge the outer threads first, working from the tip to the centre. At the base of the wing, begin plunging from the spine outwards, making sure that you can still clearly see the design line of the front wing so that the shape will not be interrupted.

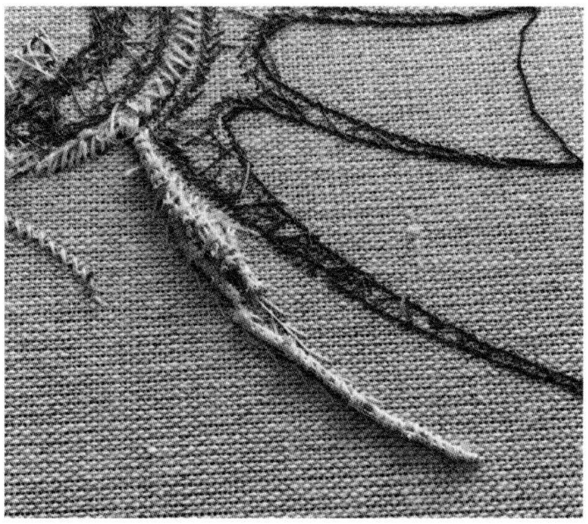

37 Tie back the metal threads in bundles of up to four at a time. Use a double waxed thread in a curved needle and make sure to catch only into the backing fabric in case the stitches might show on the front (this is more likely because there is no felt in the area).

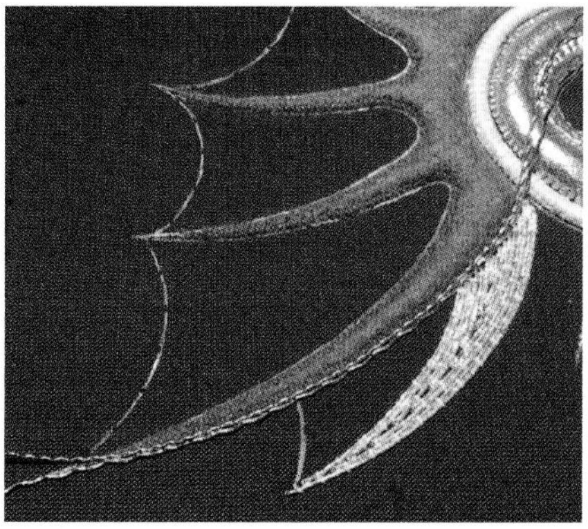

38 Begin to couch the front wing, with a single waxed copper sewing thread. For the first row use one each of copper very fine rococco with copper check thread 8 x 2, with the rococco on the outside. Place the first stitch close to the base of the wing, 1–2mm (1/16in) from the start of the design line. Lay the pair of metal threads along the line with at least a 25mm (1in) tail. Bring the needle up just outside the design line so that it will be covered, and make a stitch at right angles to the metal threads. Continue to make stitches at 3–4mm (1/8in) intervals.

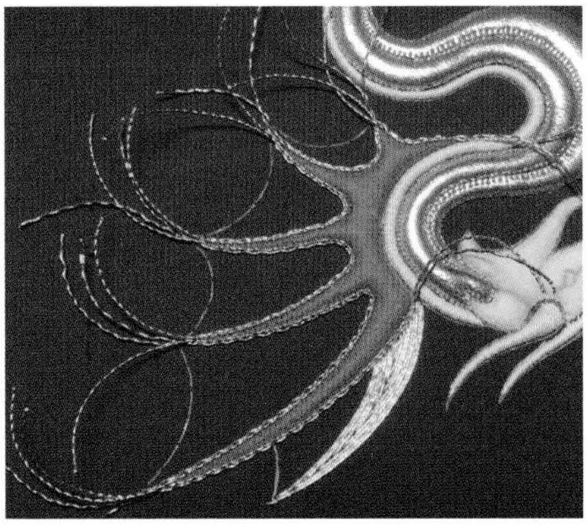

39 At the tip of the wing, make the last one or two stitches just over the outer thread (rococco). Couch a new pair of threads on the opposite side of the wing, from one tip round to the next. It is much easier to begin the couching over both threads on the straightest section, and then work to either end. Again, make the last one or two stitches just over the outer of the two threads, so that the tips of the wing will come to a very narrow point to match the design line.

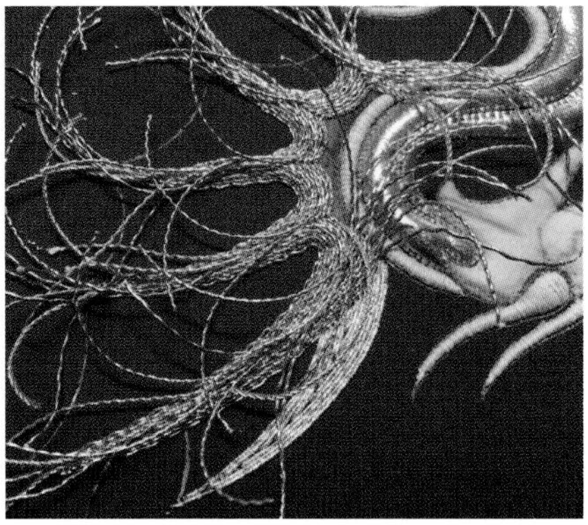

40 Continue to couch pairs of metal threads towards the centre, reducing to a single thread (the outer one) as the shape narrows. Bring the needle up with enough space between it and the previous row for the two metal threads, then take it down at an angle towards the previous row. Stitch in a brick pattern. Use threads in the following pattern: 1½ twist and rococco, gilt and copper check thread, rococco and gilt check thread, check thread and 1½ twist.

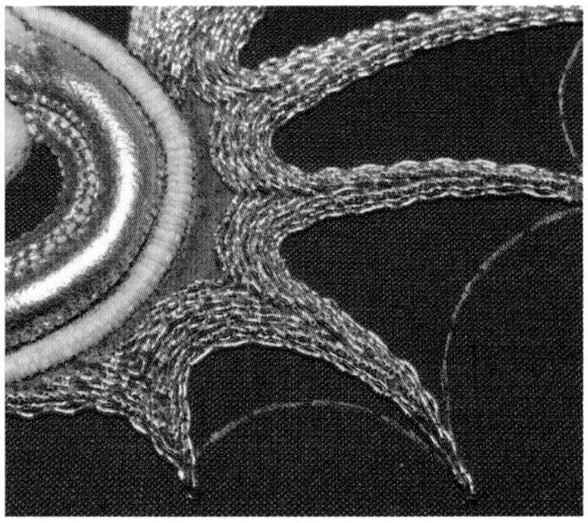

41 Plunge all the metal threads, being very careful to preserve the shape. At the tip of the wing, plunge the outer threads first, working from the tip to the centre. At the base of the wing, begin plunging from the top down, making sure that you can still clearly see the design line of the spine so that the shape will not be interrupted.

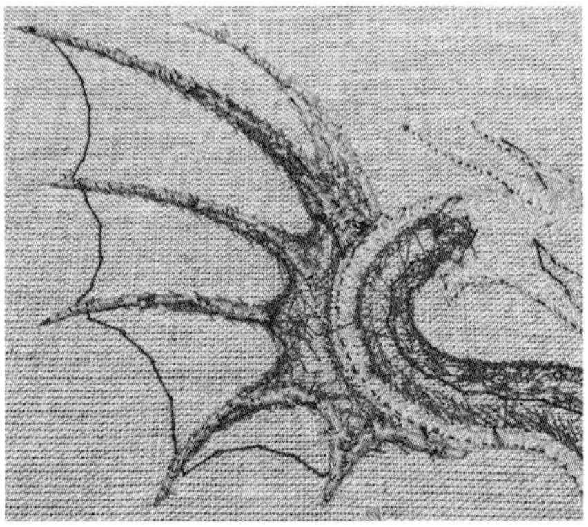

42 Tie back the metal threads in bundles of up to four at a time. Use a double waxed thread in a curved needle.

43 Couch gilt pearl purl No. 1 along one of the wing outlines, so that it sits between the wing veins that are already couched, and covers the paint lines. Remember to 'relax' the pearl purl, and trim the end neatly before starting to stitch. Begin with the first tiny stitch near the start of the line, pulling it so that it falls between the coils and then twisting the pearl purl to adjust its position against the adjacent couched threads.

44 Make another stitch between the first two coils to fully secure the end of the pearl purl, and then continue to couch along the line. Manipulate the pearl purl into shape with your fingers before securing it with stitches, making sure to keep the stitches very small so that they can't be seen on either side of the metal wire once complete. At the end of the line, trim the pearl purl so that it sits against the adjacent couching with no gap, and then make a final stitch between the last two coils to secure the end.

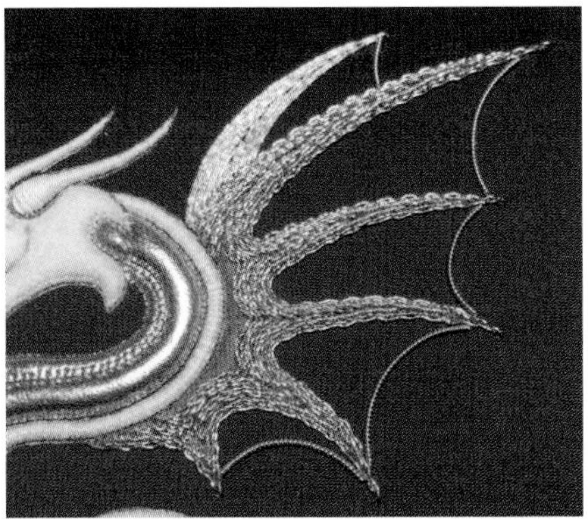

45 Repeat the couched gilt pearl purl No. 1 for the remaining wing outlines, using the same method. Be very careful to cover the paint lines completely. If they are not fully covered by the pearl purl, add a line of smaller pearl purl or smooth passing on one side of the line, or stitch a line of stem stitch in a thread similar to the background silk right next to the pearl purl.

46 Work scattered chipping to fill the front wing (leave the back wing blank). Begin by cutting chips of bright check in copper, gilt and silver. Make sure that they are small, square and neatly trimmed with no tags on the ends. Cast on a double waxed sewing thread in each of the three colours. Start chipping near the base of the wing with copper chips placed close together but not touching, at random angles. Then add one or two gilt chips into the mix.

47 Gradually switch from copper to gilt chips, and then from gilt to silver chips. At the same time, gradually leave a little more space between the chips. Work on one section at a time until all the wing sections are filled with scattered chips.

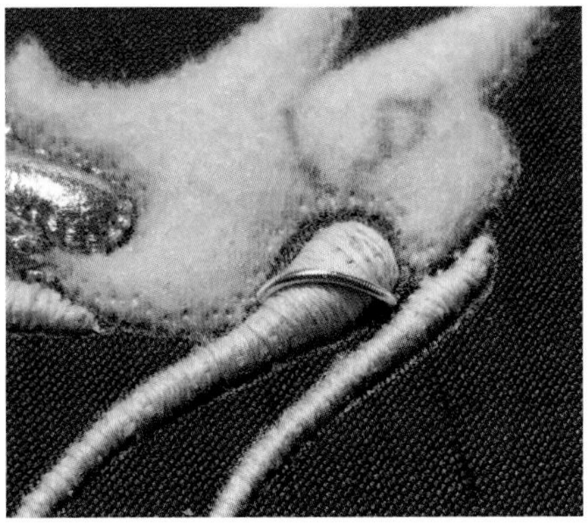

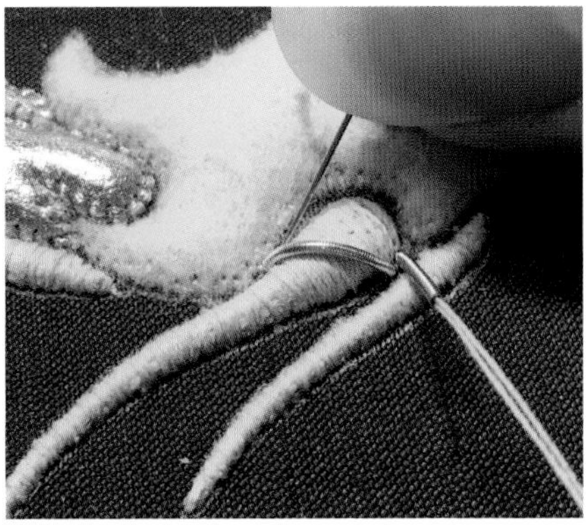

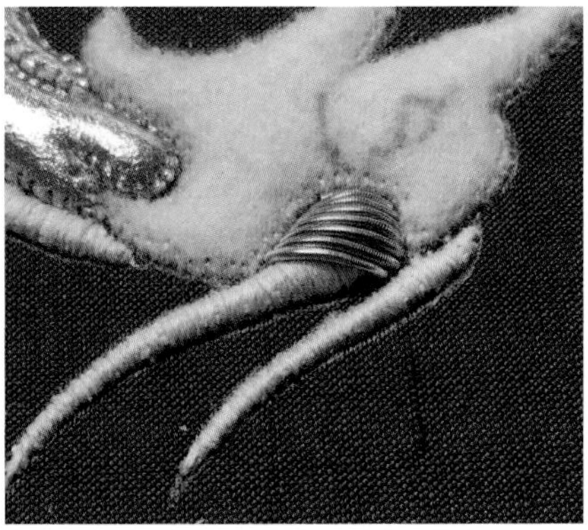

48 Stitch cutwork on the front horn at a slanted angle using a double waxed gold sewing thread. Work from the top of the design so that you can easily see both sides of the padding. Bring up the needle on the right-hand side at the widest point, and thread on a chip of gilt smooth purl, trimming to size as necessary. Take the needle down on the left to complete the stitch, checking again that the chip sits firmly on the padding.

49 Bring the needle up next to the first chip, on the far side, so that you work towards the head. Thread on a chip of copper smooth purl, trimming as necessary. Take the needle down close to the first chip, tucking the needle so that the tip disappears under the first chip slightly to bring the two stitches close together.

50 Continue to add chips of copper smooth purl towards the base of the horn, being careful to keep the angle of the chips steady and making sure they stay close together. The rounded end is challenging for this as they want to fall off the taper – hold on to the previous chips as you pull the new one down so that you can check it sits properly on the padding before continuing to the next chip.

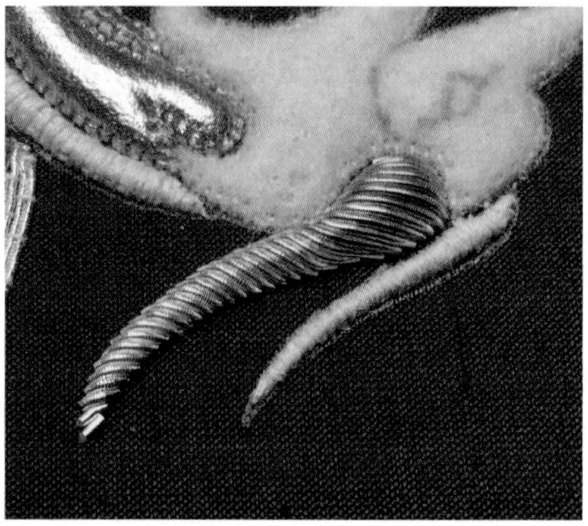

51 Once the first end is complete, return to the starting point and work in the opposite direction to fill the remaining space. Work alternating copper and gold chips, and then a few just in gold. Add a silver chip followed by two gold, and then alternating, and then silver all the way to the tip. Be careful to tuck the needle close to the previous chip with each stitch, but keep enough space on the left that the angle alters slightly – this will allow for the last couple of chips to be sufficiently long to look attractive.

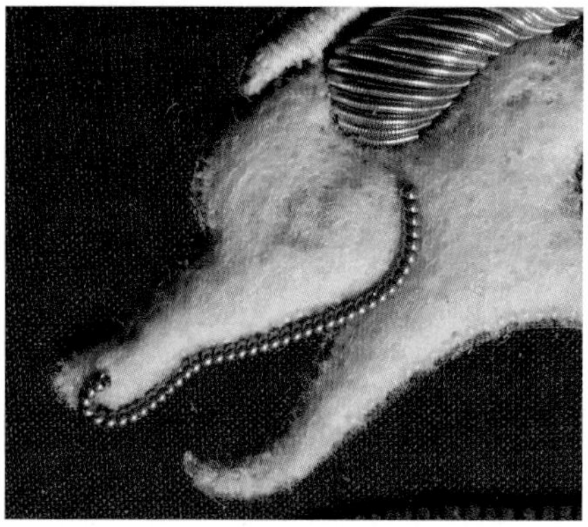

52 Stitch the outlines and details on the face with couched copper pearl purl No. 1, with a single waxed copper-coloured sewing thread. Begin with the underside of the upper jaw, working from cheek to nose. Help the pearl purl to take the curved shape by forming it with your fingers first and then stitching it down, making sure that the thread slips between the coils and disappears. On the nose, pull firmly on the pearl purl to create the tight curl of the nostril.

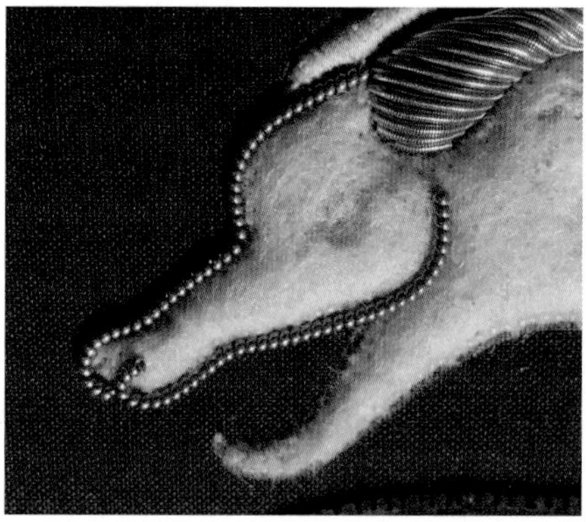

53 Next, couch pearl purl on the upper part of the face, working from forehead to nose. Be very careful with needle positioning near the cutwork – it is easy to damage the smooth purl by bringing the needle up through it. Create a neat corner at the bridge of the nose and then pull firmly on the pearl purl to create the tight curl of the nostril, cutting the purl neatly so that it sits up against the existing line.

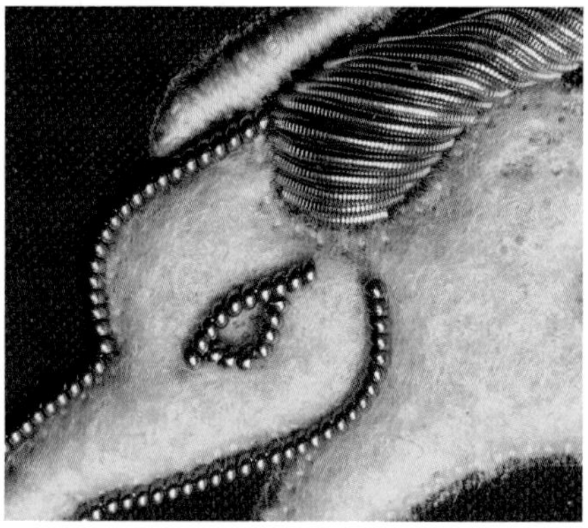

54 Couch pearl purl to create the eye with two separate pieces. Place a stitch between every coil to hold the shapes accurately. Stitch the upper eyelid first, preferably from right to left so that when you cut the end of the purl it is as far as possible from the cutwork. Then stitch the lower eyelid, creating a tight bend to give the shape, and making sure to cut the end cleanly. If the eye doesn't work out well the first time, have another go – it will be worth it.

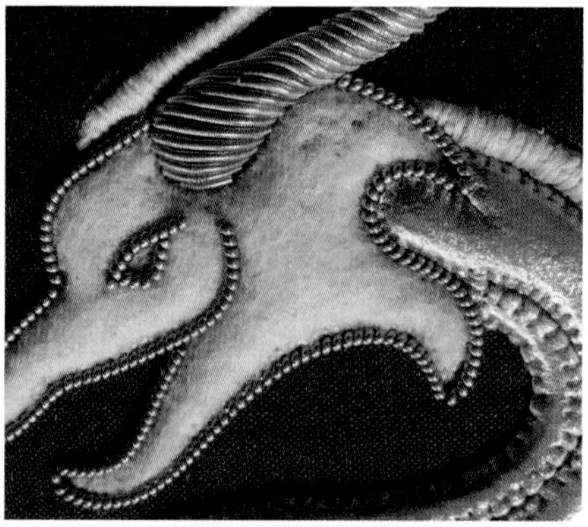

55 Finish the outline with the lower jaw and the back of the head. Begin at the jaw and work round from there. Create a tight turn for the lower lip. Be extra careful as you stitch against the leather and near the cutwork – it is easy to damage these by bringing the needle up through them. Stop stitching a short distance from the end so that you can cut the pearl purl as far as possible from the cutwork, and carefully complete the last few stitches.

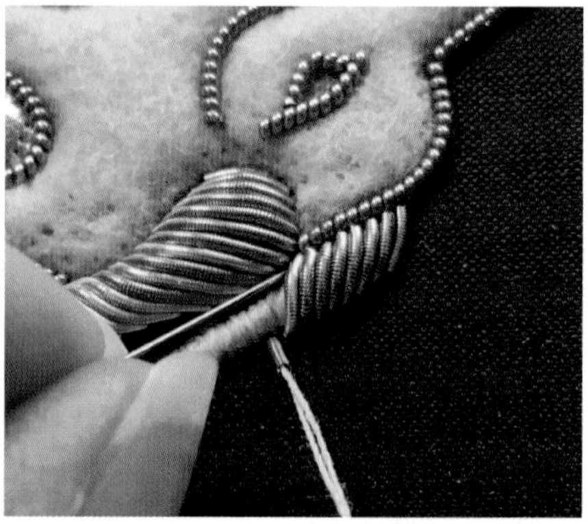

56 Stitch cutwork on the back horn, at the opposite angle to the front one. Use double waxed, gold-coloured thread. Bring up the needle at the end of the pearl purl line, between that and the padding. Make the first stitch with copper smooth purl, and then work to the base of the horn using copper purl. Once the base is covered, return to the start and bring up the needle on the upper edge. Thread on a chip of gold purl, and very carefully take the needle down between the padding and the existing cutwork.

57 Continue to stitch cutwork up to the tip of the horn, alternating the colours about the same as for the front horn, gradually changing from copper to gold and then to silver. Allow the angle to flow with the shape – it is unlikely to change so much this time.

58 Couch silver-plated lizerine No. 1 along the front of the body. Begin at the neck and work towards the tail. Use a single waxed length of silver-coloured thread. Make sure that the lizerine is adequately stretched to allow the thread to pass between the coils (it needs a little more space than pearl purl would, because the shape does not encourage the thread into place in the same way). Work all the way to where the tail curls round, cutting and securing the end neatly.

59 Couch gilt lizerine No. 2 along the void between the two pieces of leather on the body. Begin at the neck and work towards the tail, using a single waxed, gold-coloured thread. At the end of the line, cut the lizerine so that it sits as neatly as possible against the silver outline and carefully stitch it down.

60 Couch gilt lizerine No. 1 along the back of the tail. Begin at the end of the string padding of the spine, butting the neatly cut end up against the padding. Stitch round the tail and finish the lizerine neatly against the silver outline.

61 Couch gilt lizerine No. 1 on the right-hand side of the tip of the tail, taking the stitching all the way to the end of the paint line (past the end of the leather). Then stitch silver-plated lizerine No. 1 on the left-hand side, stopping just a coil or two past the end of the leather. Use single waxed threads to match the lizerine.

62 Couch copper pearl purl No. 1 round the tail flare, creating tight turns to give the pointed shapes. These can be made by folding the pearl purl tightly with fingertips or tweezers, or if desired, the pearl purl can be finished and restarted at each turn. Be very careful to keep the stitches small and placed accurately on the paint line so that it will be covered.

63 Fill the tail flare with scattered chipping in bright check No. 6, beginning with copper at the top, and working through gilt and then silver. Shade through the colours by introducing each new colour gradually amongst chips of the previous colour. Use double waxed matching sewing threads.

64 Begin to fill the head with chipping. Use a double waxed, gold-coloured sewing thread and gilt bright check No. 6. Start in the middle and work outwards, placing the chips at random angles and close together so that they fully cover the felt. Be very careful as you bring the needle up not to damage the surrounding stitching. When working up to the horns, bring the needle up a chip-length away from the cutwork and carefully take the needle down by the cutwork.

65 At the back of the head, shade into silver in the tips of the pointed shapes. Gradually introduce a few silver chips amongst the gold, ending with only silver chips right at the tips of the points. Continue chipping to completely fill the shape and cover all the felt.

66 Strap gilt broad plate No. 6 over the string padding of the spine. Use a single waxed, gold-coloured sewing thread. Begin at the tail end, making a tiny 'hook' in the plate and placing the first securing stitch so that the plate slightly overlaps the end of the lizerine. Carry the broad plate across the padding and make another stitch over it, pulling it tight against the padding.

67 Repeat the process, working from side to side. Fold the broad plate tight against the stitch on each side so that it creates a zigzag pattern, and make a holding stitch whenever necessary to hold the tension firm (even if this is between every stitch).

68 Continue to strap the broad plate along the spine. As the shape curves, the stitches will need to be placed closer together on the inside curves and further apart on the outside curves. Tuck the stitches as tightly as possible against the padding all the way along (it is normal for the broad plate to gradually work away from the padding a little, but try to rein it in as much as possible by angling the needle towards the previously laid plate).

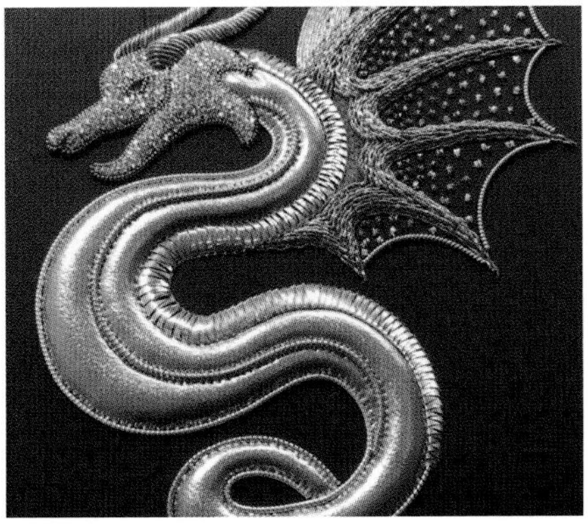

69 At the very top of the spine the shape is a little awkward because it narrows slightly and sits adjacent to the pearl purl outline of the head. It may flow naturally, in which case continue in the same way right up to the end, but if it feels very difficult, finish the existing length of plate with a fold, and add one or two small separate pieces to fill the space.

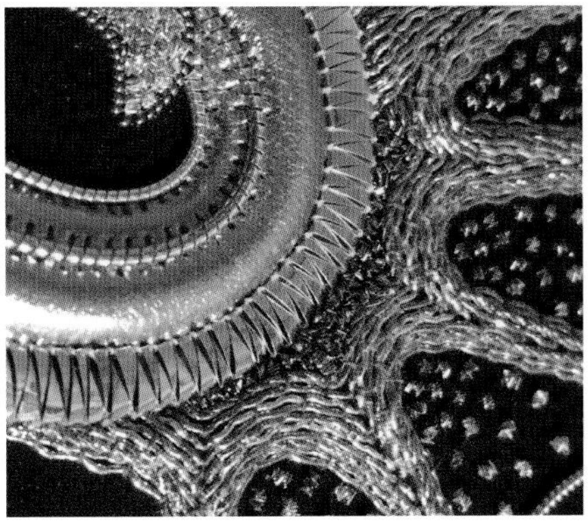

70 Fill the space in the wing with chipping using a double waxed, copper-coloured sewing thread and copper bright check No. 6. Be very careful not to pierce the broad plate as you bring the needle up. Stitch the chips close together and at varied angles so that they fully cover the remaining felt.

71 Stitch single spangles over the leather on the front part of the body using a single waxed, silver-coloured sewing thread. Begin in the widest point about halfway across the shape. Place a finger on the leather to hold it down as you bring the needle up, as the needle will encounter quite a lot of resistance and could visibly stretch the leather. Thread on a spangle and secure it with a tiny stitch over the 'dent'. Position another spangle on each side and a little above the first.

72 Repeat this pattern of three staggered spangles in the wide part of the shape, with some space between the patterns (how much space is up to personal preference). As the shape narrows, place two spangles staggered in a similar way, and then just a single spangle. Leave the very narrowest parts blank.

73 To complete the wyvern, fill the eye with a single seed bead in a dark colour (purple has been chosen here). Use a single waxed thread to match the bead. Bring the needle up just inside the pearl purl at the top of the eye, thread on the bead, and take the needle down at the bottom of the eye, so that the bead fills the space lengthways. Try to pass through the bead one more time to make it more secure. If any space should be left over, fill it with copper chips.

Design template.

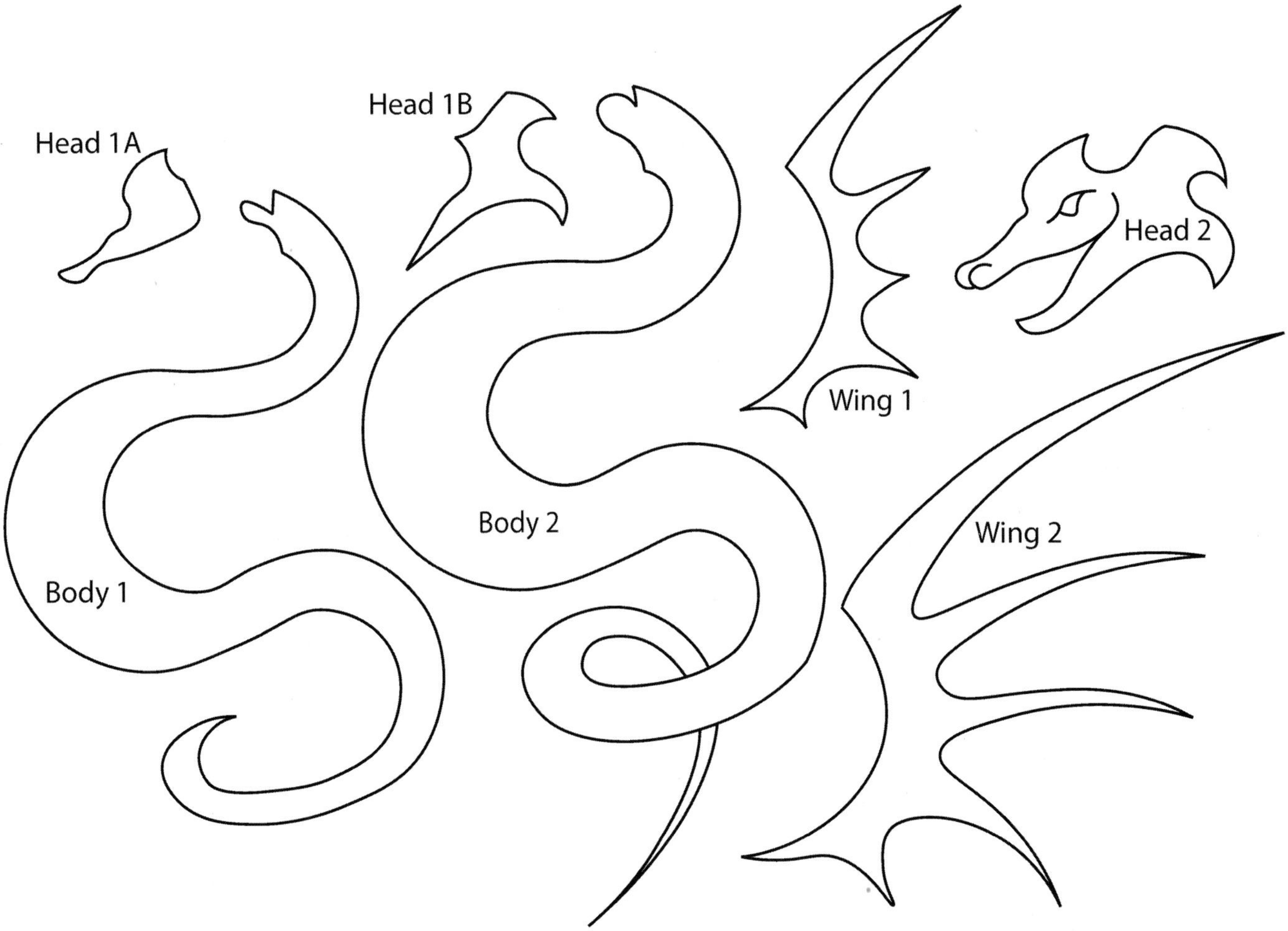

Felt templates.

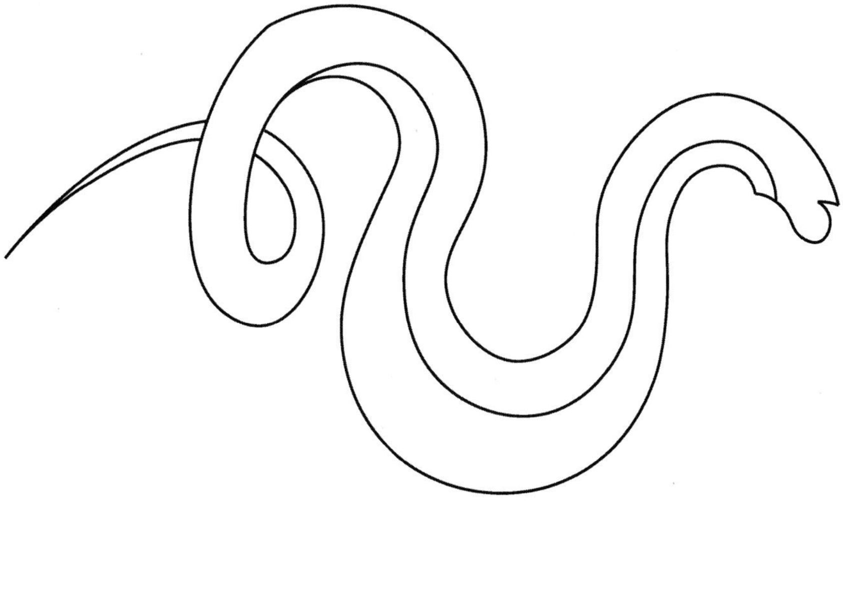

Kid Leather template.

CHAPTER 10

FINISHING A PROJECT

Most embroidery projects need to be finished in some way, whether that be in preparation for framing, wearing or displaying.

There are many ways to finish a project, and this chapter covers just a few to give you some ideas. Goldwork is particularly suited to making jewellery, so you will see how to create a simple brooch.

Large pieces or those for display on a wall will benefit from mounting, whether they are then framed or not. For really large pieces, have a hardware store cut a piece of hardboard for stability, and then add a layer of card as a protective barrier.

You may like to go on to explore goldwork on clothing, bags or boxes, three-dimensional items, or pretty much anything else you fancy – this is just the beginning.

FINISHING IN A HOOP

A hoop, whether it is the one you stitched the piece of embroidery in, or a new one, can be a charming way to display your work, hinting at the craft itself. You can choose to back the work with a matching or contrasting fabric, and even wrap the hoop with a pretty ribbon or bias binding for contrast.

1 First, draw round the inner hoop on to a piece of card (this could be any clean card from box card to mount board), and cut out the circle. This will support the backing.

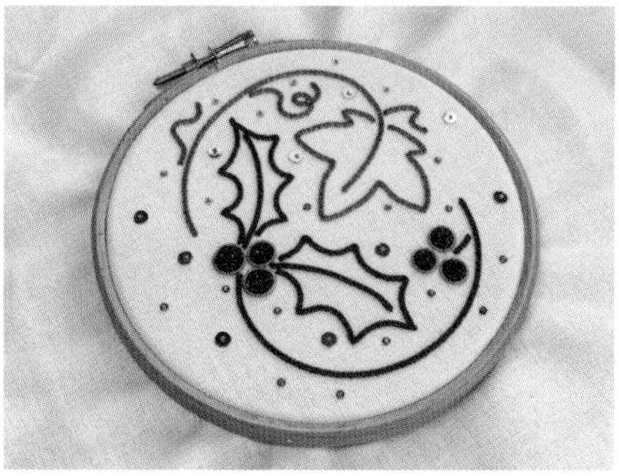

2 Position the embroidery how you want to view it, and tighten it in the hoop so that the fabric is straight. Make sure that the hoop itself is tight using a screwdriver.

3 Cut the fabric (both layers if there are two) with about 5cm (2in) excess all round the hoop.

4 Make a ring of tissue paper or bubble wrap to support the frame and prevent the embroidery from being squashed when you turn it over. Place the embroidery face down on the tissue ring.

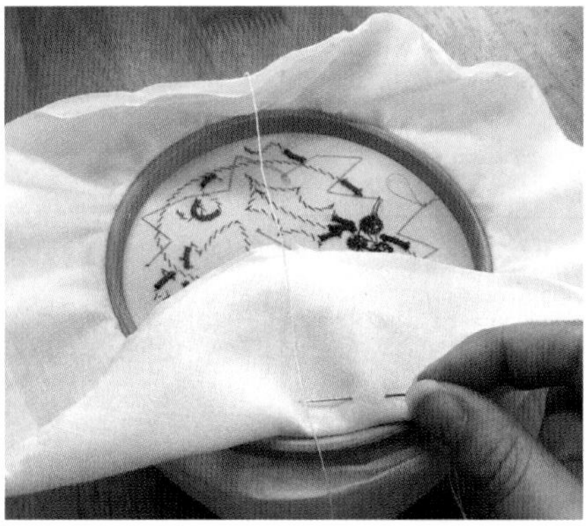

5 Fold the fabric in towards the centre on opposite sides. Take a long piece of extra-strong thread in a large crewel needle (size 5–7) and cast on to the fabric about 10mm ($^{5}/_{8}$in) from the edge, then carry the thread all the way to the opposite edge. Make a stitch about 10mm ($^{5}/_{8}$in) long. Pull the thread very tight.

6 Carry the thread back to the opposite side, making another stitch about 10mm ($^{5}/_{8}$in) from the first, and repeat this all the way round until you come back to the start, pulling each stitch very tight. Finish and start as many times as necessary.

7 Cut a piece of fabric (matching or contrasting) to make the backing. Use the card circle as a template – cut with about 25mm (1in) excess all the way round. Take a long piece of extra-strong thread and tie a knot in the end. Make a running stitch (without casting on) all the way round about 10mm ($^{5}/_{8}$in) from the edge, with the stitches about 6mm ($^{1}/_{4}$in) long.

8 Position the card in the centre of the fabric, and use the two ends of the thread to gather the fabric tightly around the card. Tie a knot and trim the ends.

9 Position the covered card on to the back of the embroidery hoop and pin it in place – a few pins will be enough.

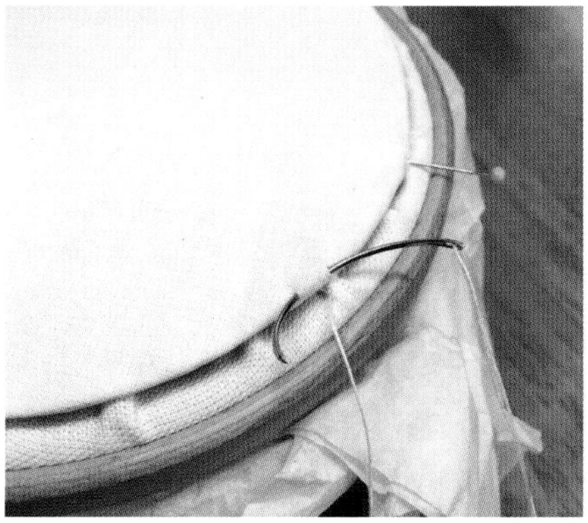

10 Take a long piece of extra-strong thread in a curved needle, and cast on just under the edge of the card. Make a 6mm (1/4in) stitch in the fabric covering the card – pass the needle through where the fabric folds round the card, starting from just behind where the thread emerged from casting on

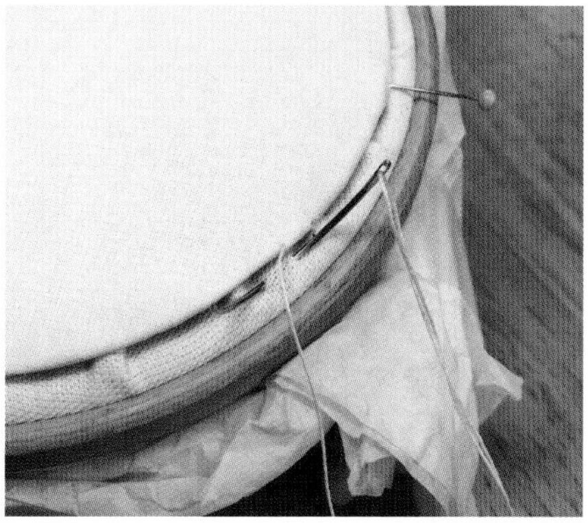

11 Make another stitch, this time in the embroidered fabric. Take the needle in just behind where it emerged from the card fabric. When you pull this stitch tight, the first one should disappear. This stitch is known as slip stitch (sometimes ladder stitch in dressmaking).

12 Continue to slip stitch around the card circle, removing pins as necessary and pulling tight so that the stitches are hidden. Stitching in this way helps to keep the fabric on the front taut and looking presentable.

A project finished in a hoop. It could now be displayed within a frame, or suspended on a piece of ribbon.

MOUNTING ON BOARD

Mounting on board is the traditional way to finish an embroidery project ready for framing. It is also the very best way to stretch and protect your work.

If you want your embroidery to last a lifetime (or much longer) you will want to use acid-free mount board, conservation-friendly glue and pre-washed fabrics so that no unwanted chemicals have contact with your embroidery. Ordinary card, PVA and fabric will also do the job perfectly well. 5–6mm (¼in) mount board is ideal if you can get it, otherwise use standard 2–3mm board doubled up.

Always use glass-headed pins for this process to avoid unnecessary pain in your fingertips. Remember to use a cutting mat while cutting the board.

1 First determine the size that the mount board needs to be. Use four sheets of paper or L shapes cut from card to visualize the finished work. When you are happy, measure the length and width of the piece. Bear in mind that a framer needs an extra rebate of about 10mm (⅝in), so add that if need be. Most designs benefit from at least 2.5cm (1in) space round the design, sometimes much more. Mark the halfway point of each side on the fabric with a pin.

2 Draw the shape on to mount board with a propelling pencil. Make sure that all marks you make are light. Begin by drawing one pencil line a bit longer than one of the sides. Mark the correct measurement along this line. Use a set square to mark a right angle at one end, and then the ruler to measure and mark the side. Repeat this until you are back at the beginning, where the side should meet up with the first mark. Be very careful about this step: take your time.

3 Carefully cut the board with a sharp knife or scalpel against a steel ruler. If you are right-handed, keep the knife to the right of the ruler for the best cut, and vice versa. Hold the ruler steady and keep it in place until you are completely sure the board is cut through. Position the knife just ahead of the line and gently slide it along the ruler, keeping it straight, not angled under or away from the ruler. Do this as many times as necessary to cut through, rather than pressing hard.

4 Cut a second board the same, and glue the two together. Cut a piece of calico larger than the board with about 10cm (4in) excess all the way round. The grain of the fabric should be straight with the edges of the board. Place the mount board on to the calico, with the excess even on all sides. Apply a line of glue about 2.5cm (1in) from the edge along one side of the board (start with a long side if working on a rectangle).

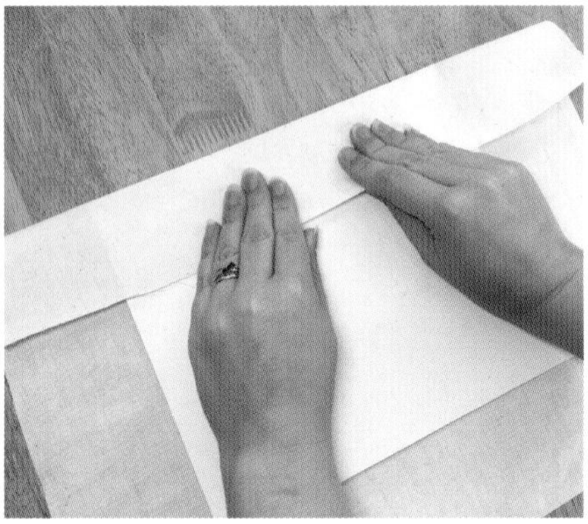

5 Fold the calico on to the board and press it firmly into the glue.

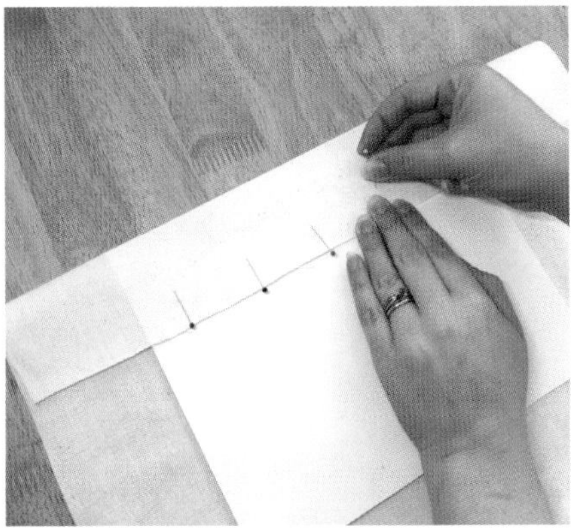

6 Use a few pins to keep the calico in place while the glue dries. Insert the pin pointing towards the centre of the board, then flip it to slightly stretch the calico and push it into the board a little bit. Repeat this on the opposite side of the board, pulling it as tight as possible and using more pins to secure it. Wait for the glue to dry before proceeding.

7 Remove the pins. Trim the corners of the calico – starting where it sits on the board, cut outwards to about 6mm ($^1/_4$in) above the corner. Then cut the remaining flap so that it looks like an envelope.

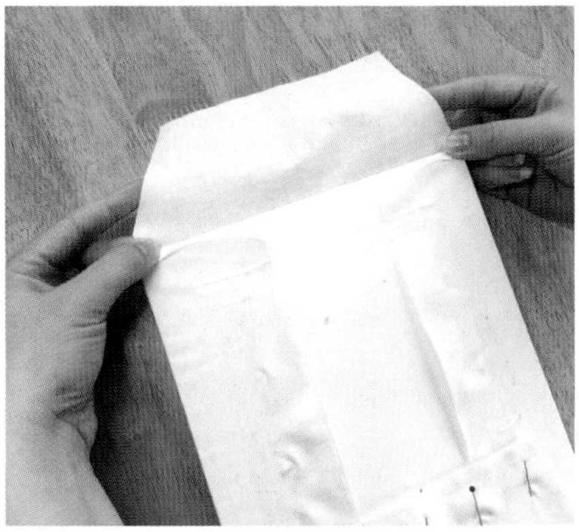

8 Apply a line of glue about 2.5cm (1in) from the edge along one of the remaining edges of the board. With your thumbs, tuck in the corners of the calico flap. Then using your fingers, pull the rest of the flap over and press it into the glue – this should result in a neat (and not bulky) corner. Use pins to hold the calico in place, and repeat with the opposite end. Mark the centre of each side with a pin or pencil line.

9 Cut a piece of cotton wadding just a little larger than the board (it will be trimmed later so doesn't have to look beautiful). Place this on top of the calico. From this point on, work on top of a sheet of tissue paper to make sure the surface is completely clean.

10 Remove the embroidery from the frame and position it on the board, on top of the wadding, matching the pins in the sides to the pins or pencil lines on the board. Push pins into the edge of the board until they hold firmly. Add extra pins along each side about every 5cm (2in), keeping the grain of the fabric straight along the edge of the board. Don't worry about pulling very tight at this point – straight is far more important.

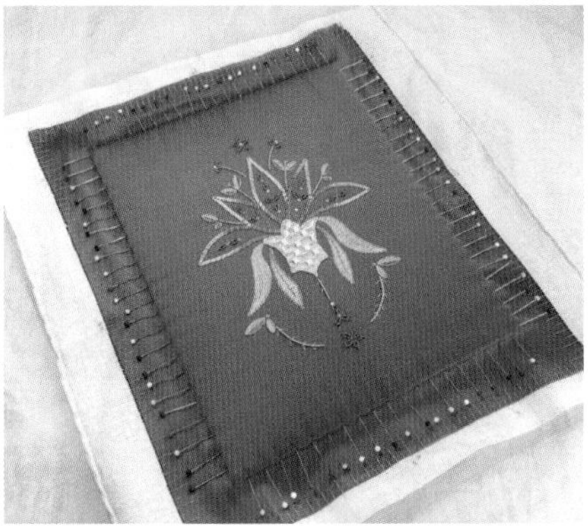

11 Check that the design looks how you intended on the board, and make adjustments if necessary. Once you are happy, start in the middle of one side and work your way round the board, gradually pulling a little tighter and adding pins until the fabric is tight and straight, and has no ripples or bubbles in the centre. By this point the pins should be no more than 10mm ($^5/_8$in) apart, and preferably a little closer.

12 Turn the embroidery so that it is face down, protected with a bubble-wrap frame so that the embroidery cannot be crushed. Very carefully trim away the excess wadding so that it sits flush with the board. If the fabric is excessively large, trim it down to 10–20cm (4–8in) to make it more manageable (it will be trimmed further at a later stage).

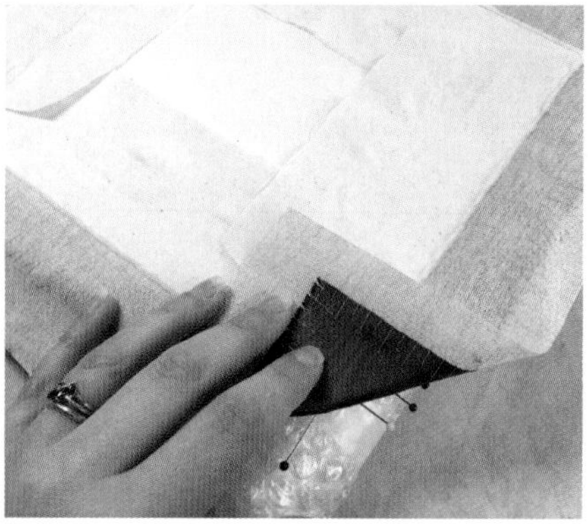

13 Fold one corner of the fabric towards the middle, so that the grain lines of the fabric run straight with the edges of the board.

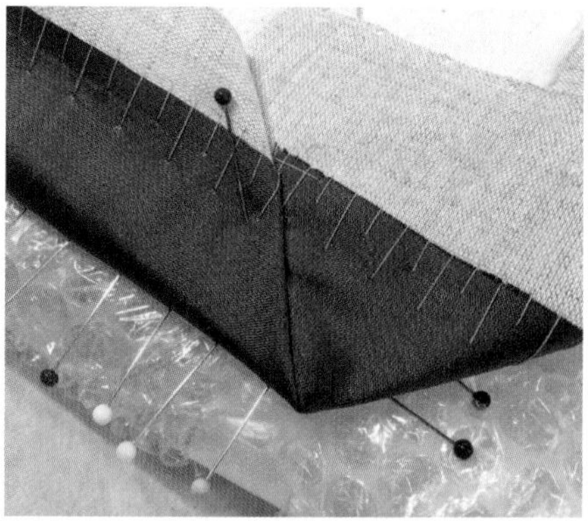

14 Fold in one side of the fabric so that the edge of the fold is at 45 degrees to the edge of the board and goes right into the corner. Use a mellor to help get a sharp point by sliding it underneath to push the corner out. Use a pin facing the corner to hold the fold in place.

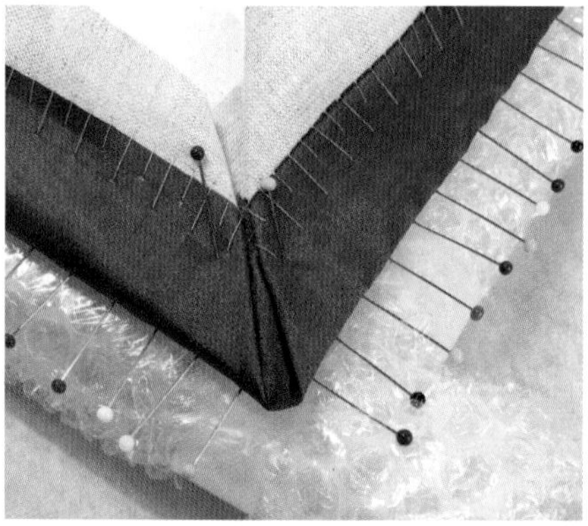

15 Do the same with the other side, ensuring that the fold goes right into the corner. There will be a small gap that will be pulled together with stitching, but it should already look quite neat. Repeat this for each corner.

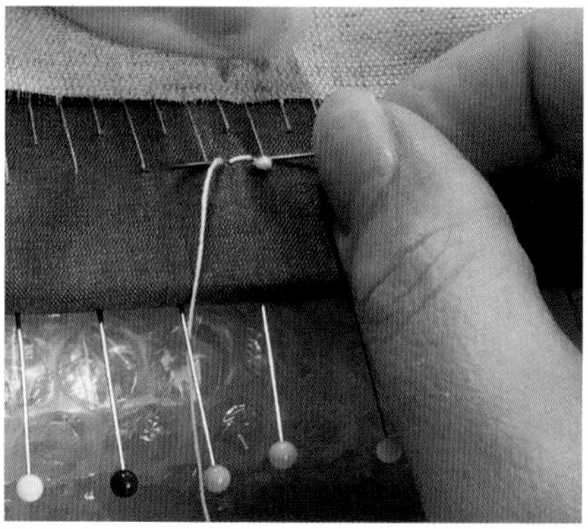

16 Beginning in the middle of a long side, work a herringbone stitch to fasten the fabric to the glued calico on the board. Pull the fabric very tight around the board all the while that you are stitching it in place. First cast on a long piece of extra strong thread in a curved needle, by making a couple of overcast stitches through all the layers of fabric and calico. These stitches should sit about 2cm ($3/4$in) from the edge of the board.

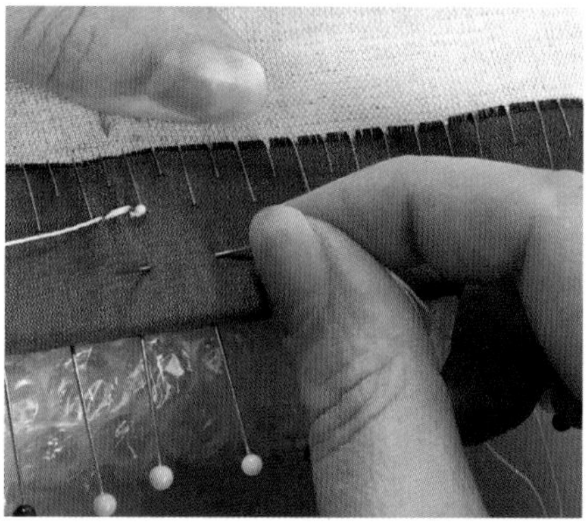

17 Next, make a stitch a little to the right, about 10mm ($5/8$in) from the edge, scooping through all the layers of fabric with the needle running right to left. Pull the stitch tight.

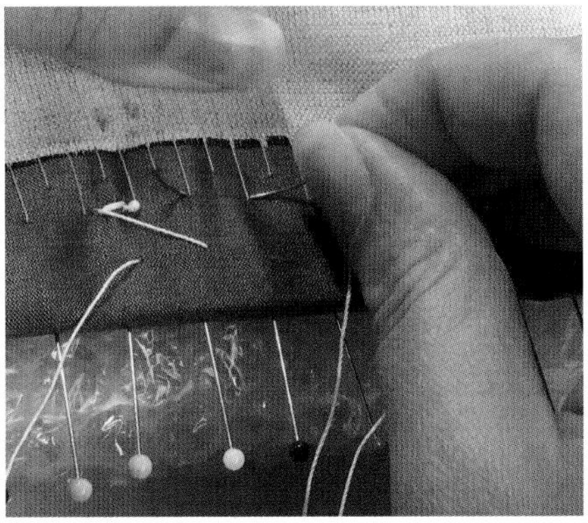

18 Make another stitch in line with the cast-on stitches 2cm ($^3/_4$in) from the edge, again with the needle running right to left. The end of this stitch should sit so that it lines up with the beginning of the previous one, or overlaps. Pull the stitch tight.

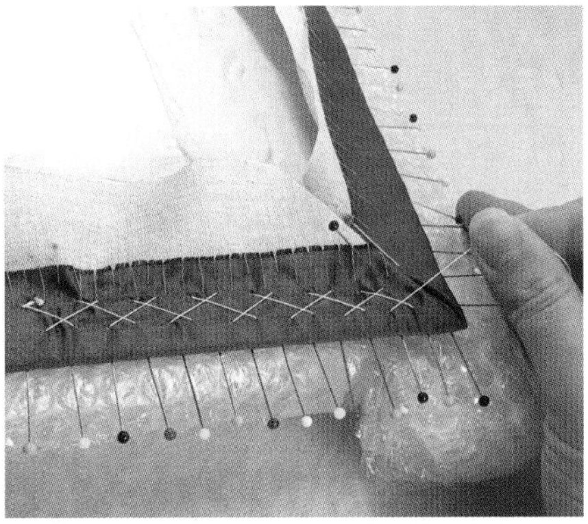

19 Repeat the herringbone stitch all the way to the corner, pulling each one tight. When you reach the corner, use a mellor to work your way along from the start, pulling the stitches even tighter until they are as tight as they will go. This may cause small wrinkles and ridges in the fabric, but as long as the front is still tight and straight this is nothing to worry about.

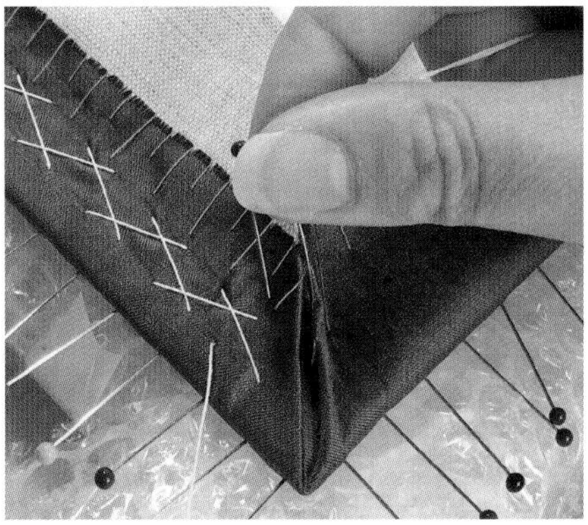

20 To mitre the corner, first take a stitch up towards the middle of the board by about 2cm ($^3/_4$in), making a small slip stitch through the opposite fold, about 4mm ($^1/_8$in) in length.

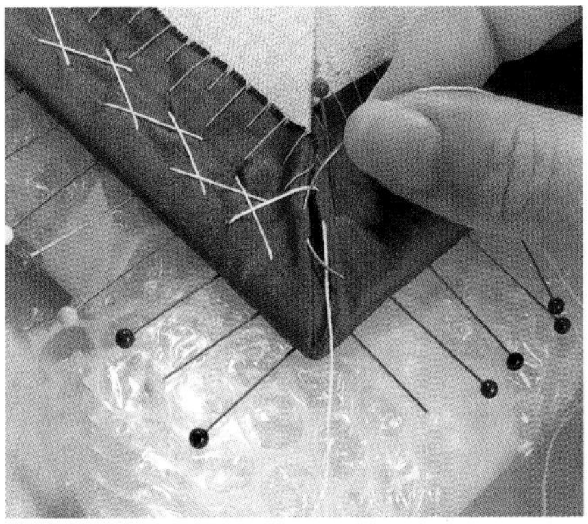

21 Make another slip stitch in the other fold, starting it just a fraction behind the end of the first stitch.

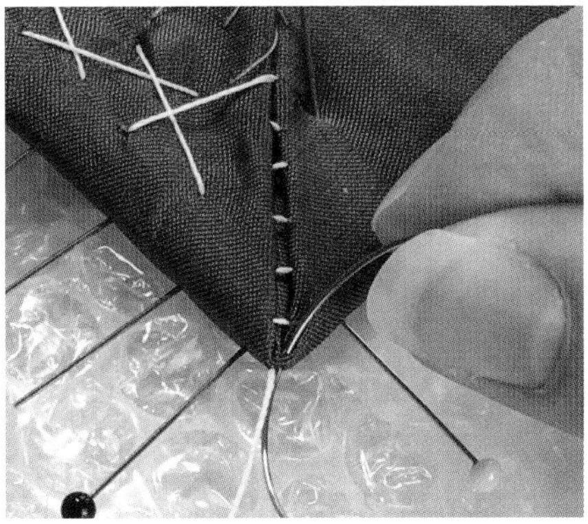

22 Slip stitch the two folds together down to the corner, keeping the stitches the same length. Keep going right into the very point of the folds, and pull tight so that the folds come together neatly.

23 Insert the tip of the needle back into the fabric right at the corner, and scoop through the layers of fabric to come out about 2cm ($^3/_4$in) from the corner. Pull very tight to finish the corner neatly.

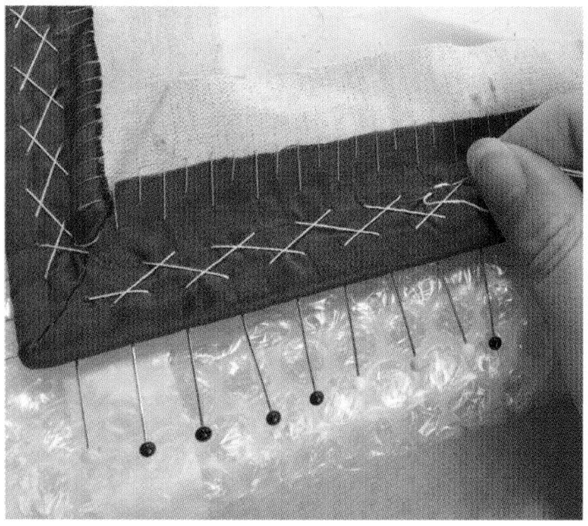

24 Begin to stitch the next side, remembering to pull the fabric very tight round the board while you stitch. When you need to finish a thread, pull the stitches very tight before you do so.

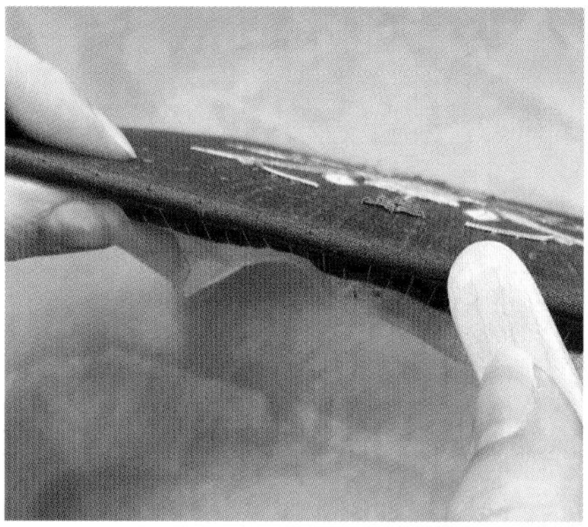

25 Repeat this process for the remaining sides and corners until the fabric is fully attached. Then remove the pins from round the edge, and rub out any pin marks with a mellor.

26 Trim away excess fabric with sharp scissors. It is wise to leave a reasonable amount in case the piece needs remounting at a later date – about 10cm (4in) is ideal. The corners are often bulky – you can trim away a little more to allow it to lie flatter.

27 Cut a piece of backing fabric larger than the board by 5–10cm (2–4in) all round. The fabric should not have any stretch, and should be densely woven – plain woven cotton or linen work very well, and strong cotton sateen is also a good choice. The grain of the fabric should be straight with the edges of the board.

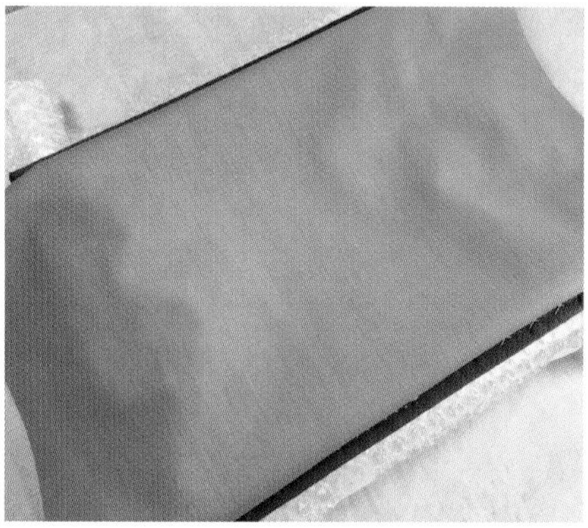

28 Lay the fabric on to the back of the embroidery and soft-fold (that is, do not pinch, so as not to crease) the long edges underneath. The fold should sit 3–6mm ($^1/_8$–$^1/_4$in) from the edge of the board.

29 Halfway along one side, use a pin to secure the backing fabric to the embroidery. First, place the pin facing out from the centre of the board, and then flip it so that it stretches the fabric slightly.

30 Do the same on the opposite side. The fabric between the two pins should feel quite tight.

31 Place another pin between the middle and the corner with the same method so that the fabric is stretched. For larger pieces, place a pin roughly every 7cm (3in). Do not pin any closer than 5cm (2in) to the corner yet.

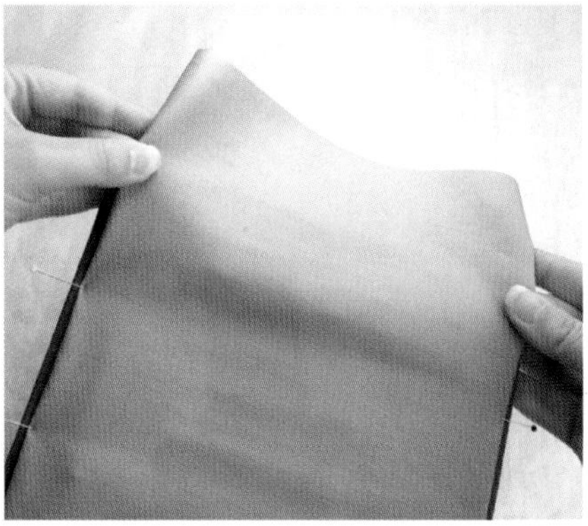

32 Use your fingers to slightly roll in the edges at the corners, and then tuck the fabric flap underneath.

33 Soft-fold it so that the fold sits the same distance from the edge as the sides. Pin from the centre out with the same method so that the fabric is stretched. Do the same with the other end. Don't pin the corner yet.

34 Finally, pin all the corners, pulling in both directions at once so that the corner sits at a right angle the same distance from both edges – it should feel quite tight and be a little tricky to pull, but if it is really tough you may need to untuck the fabric a little.

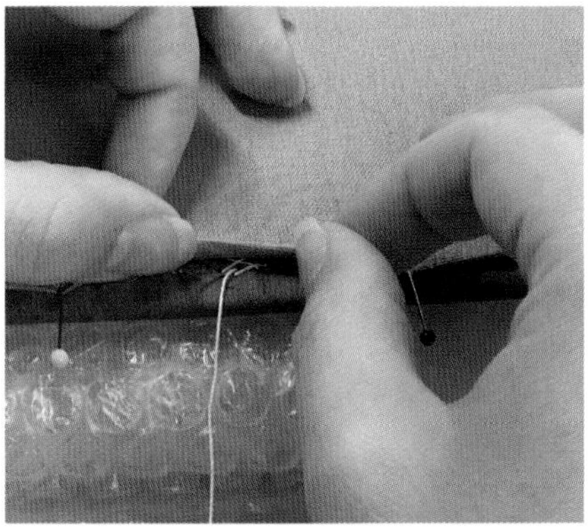

35 To secure the backing fabric use a slip stitch all round the edge. If the embroidery is small, one long piece of extra-strong thread will suffice. Thread this into a curved needle, and cast on with an overcast stitch into the embroidered fabric underneath the edge of the backing fabric. Partway along one of the long sides is a good place to start.

36 Pass the needle through the fabric once more so that it comes out level with the edge of the backing fabric, and then make the first slip stitch into the backing fabric. Take the needle through the folded edge, starting a fraction back from where the thread emerged. Slip the needle behind the fold and bring it out 3–6mm (1/8–1/4in) along.

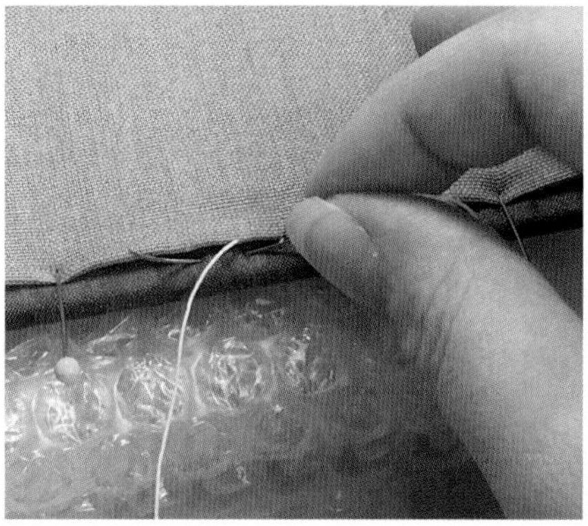

37 Make the second slip stitch into the embroidered fabric. Take the needle into the fabric a fraction back from where the previous stitch emerged, and scoop through the layers, bringing it up 3–6mm (1/8–1/4in) along. Pull very tight as you bring this stitch through – the previous one should close up and disappear.

38 Repeat this towards the first corner. When you reach the corner, make the final stitch in the backing fabric (adjust the previous few stitches in length if necessary to achieve this).

39 Before going round the corner, make sure that the stitches are all pulled up tight enough to disappear. Then make the first stitch on the next side into the embroidered fabric and pull tight again to make the corner look neat and tidy.

40 Continue round the board, making sure that you pull all the stitches tight along the way. This step isn't just about looking lovely, it secures the embroidery should the glue ever fail.

Once complete, remember to keep the embroidery protected until it is framed or displayed, especially if you have used the more delicate techniques.

FINISHING AS JEWELLERY

Goldwork obviously lends itself to jewellery – its glamour and its three-dimensional quality are perfect to be worn.

Making a piece of goldwork into a wearable form is usually quite simple – even if the more delicate techniques are used.

The most important thing is to make sure that the piece is supported with a strong backing. The less dense the stitching, the more supportive the backing that will be required.

Then you need to create an attractive backing and attach the jewellery finding of your choice (whether brooch pin, earring, pendant).

1 Begin by cutting out the embroidery with a small excess of 6mm (1/4in). If there are tight curves or corners on the edge, clip into these areas with sharp scissors. If the stitching is on two layers of fabric, cut away the backing fabric as close as you can to the embroidery. Turn it over and spread a thin layer of glue on to the back of the embroidery using a soft paintbrush (preferably the glue should be conservation friendly, but PVA will do).

2 Cut a piece of very firm interfacing a tiny bit smaller than the embroidered shape. Place this on to the still-wet glue and press into place (bearing in mind any delicate stitchwork on the front). If there are bulky areas on the back (from plunged threads, for example), trim away the interfacing in those areas to even it out. If it is very thick, apply another layer of glue and interfacing, again trimming the interfacing as needed.

3 Spread a little glue round the edge of the interfacing, and fold the fabric excess on to the interfacing, pulling firmly so that it can no longer be seen from the front. Allow the glue to dry before proceeding – you may have to hold it while this happens, as the fabric resists being forced out of its natural shape.

4 Apply a felt backing to tidy up the back and give a nice soft feel. The best way to make sure it covers all possible lumps and bumps is to spread a layer of glue on to the back of the interfacing and press it on to a larger piece of felt. Then trim away the excess felt carefully with a sharp pair of scissors.

5 Finally apply the jewellery finding of your choice. Make sure that you consider how it will sit/hang once complete. For example, a brooch pin typically works best if placed near the top. Stitching is the most secure way to apply the finding, although you can use strong glue. Ideally, use a curved needle to overcast the finding on to the felt with a matching thread.

Acknowledgements

I would like to thank all those who have made this book possible. Firstly, my husband Stephen, who has had to put up with a very busy wife in our first years of marriage and is a source of support, love and comfort in the best and worst of times. While I have been writing this book, we have also welcomed our son Harrison, whose smiles never fail to inspire me when I run out of ideas.

My heartfelt thanks go to Helen Richman, to whom I go with all my silly questions, and who is always ready to give me a pep talk. Helen has been on this road alongside me since our Royal School of Needlework apprenticeship interviews, and without her this book could not have happened; I would never have completed my apprenticeship at the Royal School of Needlework and gained the skills I am now able to share.

Thank you to all my friends and colleagues at the Royal School of Needlework for their continuing support, and to Susan Kay-Williams for her kind permission to include photographs of their beautiful embroideries. Also to my marvellous students, who inspire me with their creativity and passion in every class. Most especially to those of you who have allowed me to showcase your work in this book.

Thank you to Becky Quine, once a student and now fellow tutor: my sincere thanks for the loan of your lovely work, which is so different to mine in style that it shows a whole other way of using gold.

My thanks to Jo Heyde for allowing me to showcase your stunning 'Death by Chocolate' skull inspired by the Mexican Day of the Dead.

Enormous gratitude to my mum and dad for encouraging me to pursue this weird and wonderful career, and attending goodness knows how many stitching events with me over the years, not to mention their financial support as I got my business off the ground.

And finally, thanks to my loving grandparents. Especially to my granny, who first taught me embroidery when I can barely remember, and who sadly passed away while I was writing this book.

ABOUT THE AUTHOR

Lizzy Pye (neé Lansberry) is a specialist hand embroiderer based in East Hampshire. She is the proprietor of Laurelin, a specialist embroidery company providing tools and materials for the fine needlework in which Lizzy specializes, including goldwork supplies.

Lizzy started needlework early, learning basic embroidery stitches, knitting and machine sewing with her mother and grandmother from the age of three. She embarked on embroidery as a career when she joined the Royal School of Needlework apprenticeship. Lizzy has taught regularly with the RSN ever since alongside her own business.

Suppliers

DeVere Yarns
www.devereyarns.co.uk
Beautiful silk and wool threads.

GJ Beads
www.gjbeads.co.uk
A wide range of beads and related items.

John James Needles
www.jjneedles.com
Suppliers of high quality needles.

Macculloch and Wallis Ltd
www.macculloch-wallis.co.uk
Suppliers of high quality fabrics, including silk velvet and linen blends.

Laurelin Embroidery
www.laurelin.co.uk
The author's online store – kits, goldwork supplies, specialist and more general needlework tools.

Benton and Johnson
www.toyekenningandspencer.co.uk/shop/benton-johnson.html
The author's preferred manufacturer of goldwork threads and wires; supplied in bulk quantities.

The Silk Route
www.thesilkroute.co.uk
Suppliers of silk fabrics such as dupion and silk tissue.

The Wool Felt Company
www.woolfeltcompany.co.uk
Suppliers of pure wool and blended felt fabrics.

Further Reading

A–Z of Goldwork with Silk Embroidery (Search Press Classics, Search Press, 2015).

Dawson, Barbara *Metal Thread Embroidery* (Batsford, 1968, 1976).

Dier, Margaret *Thread Painting and Silk Shading Embroidery, Techniques and Projects* (The Crowood Press Ltd, 2018).

Everett, Hazel *Goldwork: Techniques, Projects and Pure Inspiration* (Search Press, 2011).

Franklin, Tracy A. *New Ideas in Goldwork* (Batsford, 2008).

Lemon, Jane *Metal Thread Embroidery* (Batsford, 1987, 2002, 2004).

Long, Sophie *Ribbonwork Embroidery, Techniques and Projects* (The Crowood Press Ltd, 2017).

Nicholas, Jane *Stumpwork and Goldwork Embroidery, Inspired by Turkish, Syrian and Persian Tiles* (Milner, 2010).

Nicholas, Jane *The Stumpwork, Goldwork and Surface Embroidery Beetle Collection* (Milner, 2004).

Richman, Helen *Stumpwork Embroidery, Techniques and Projects* (The Crowood Press Ltd, 2017).

Quine, Rebecca *Crewelwork, Techniques and Projects* (The Crowood Press Ltd, 2020).

Index

Related Titles from Crowood

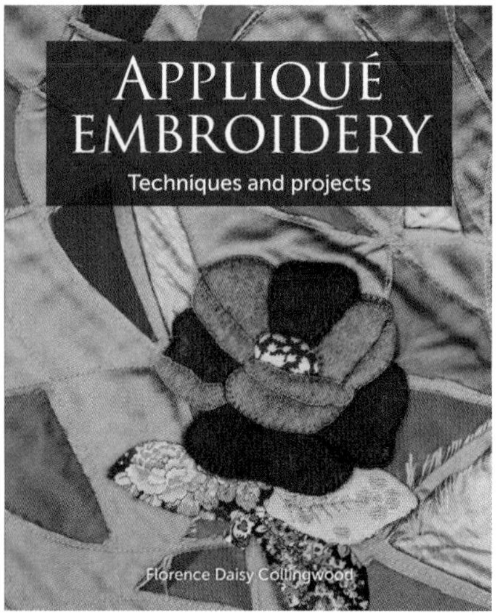

9 781 78500 539 8

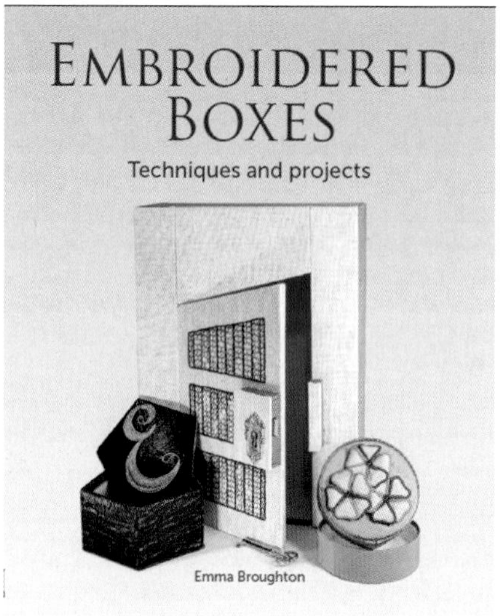

978 1 78500 563 3

978 0 90358 534 7

978 1 78500 252 6

978 1 78500 294 6

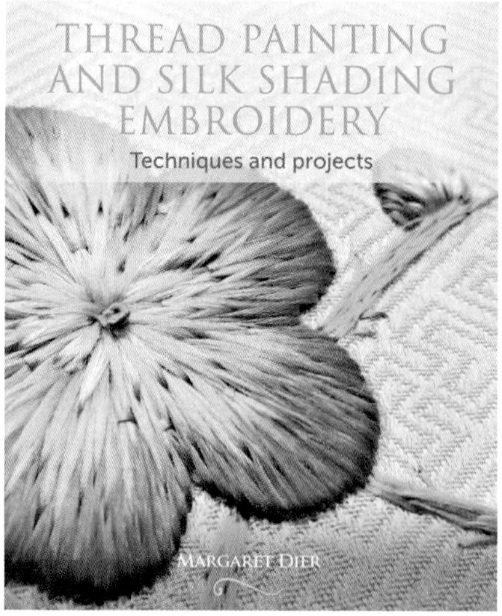

978 1 78500 477 3